The Angler's Guide
to MONTANA

The Angler's Guide
to **MONTANA**

by
Michael S. Sample

FALCON™ Falcon Press® Publishing Co., Inc. Helena, Montana

Library of Congress Catalog Card Number: 91-077722
ISBN: 1-56044-147-X

Printed in the United States of America

Falcon Press Publishing Co., Inc.
P.O. Box 1718, Helena, MT 59624

Cover Photo: Michael S. Sample

First Printing—June 1984
Second Printing—June 1986
Third Printing—July 1989
Fourth Printing—May 1992
Fifth Printing—July 1994

♻ *PRINTED ON RECYCLED PAPER*

This book is dedicated to the fisheries biologists of the Montana Department of Fish, Wildlife and Parks and the U.S. Fish and Wildlife Service who were so helpful and who work so hard on behalf of our fisheries.

ACKNOWLEDGMENTS

A book of this scope requires large measures of time, work, and help. One of the joys of researching and writing this book has been working with some very helpful people. My thanks for their efforts are noted here.

Most importantly, three people contributed materially by writing sections of the book for me. In so doing, they saved me considerable time and added their valuable insights on particular waters. Karen Zackheim wrote the Beaverhead, Jefferson, and Rock Creek chapters as well as substantial portions of the Glacier and Yellowstone national parks sections. Hugh Zackheim penned the Gallatin and Madison river chapters. Wilbur Rehmann did all the writing on the lake section, and Will Harmon created the section of alpine lake fisheries.

Valuable information came from personnel of the Montana Department of Fish, Wildlife and Parks. Pat Graham, Don Peters, Jim Vashro, Jerry Wells, and Ron Marcoux not only helped tremendously in the research stages, but also kindly reviewed written chapters and gave helpful suggestions. Bruce Rehwinkel, Al Wipperman, Bob Domrose, Al Elser, Joe Huston, Dick Vincent, Dennis Workman, Phil Stewart, Jim Darling, Steve Leathe, Dick Oswald, Ron Spoon, Bill Pryor, Laney Hanzel, Wade Fredenburg, Steve McMullin, Larry Davis, and Steve Swedberg also have my gratitude for their substantial contributions.

I am deeply indebted to Leo Marnell, Ron Jones, and Bob Gresswell, biologists with the U.S. Fish and Wildlife Service, without whom the park sections would be considerably less authoritative.

Fishing guides and purveyors of fishing tackle furnished much of the advice contained in this book. Ray Hurley, Richard Parks, John Bailey, Bud and Pat Lilly, Al Troth, and Frank Johnson bestowed large amounts of time and attention toward making this book more helpful. Fred Tedesco, Mike Brady, Fred Terwilliger, Phil Wright, Curt Collins, Rich Stevenson, Don Alley, George Anderson, Scott Waldie, Tony Schoonen, Fran Johnson, Dave Kumlien, George Grant, Gary Evans, Becky Garland, Hap Jensen, Mike Craig, Ed Curnow, Bob Jacklin, and Mike Mouat were other valuable contributors I would like to thank.

I continue to miss the peaceful, thoughtful presence of Dan Bailey, who kindly shared some of his wisdom with me before his untimely death.

I also continue to be inspired by the memories I hold of the late Joe Halterman, whose courage, intelligence, and drive for excellence have benefitted Montana fisheries for generations.

Other people who contributed in one way or another include Hank Fischer, Bill Haviland, Vince Ames, Ridley Taylor, Lou and Bud Morris, Bob Schumacher, Dan Lamont, Greg Zem, Rev. Charlie Gorman, Mark Henckel, Paul Schullery, Paul Roos, Stu Swenson, Jim O'Loughlin, Bob Martinka, and John Varley. A big thank you goes to George Holton of the Montana Department of Fish, Wildlife and Parks, who gave Wilbur Rehmann much help with the lakes information. Thanks also to Norm Peterson and Larry Peterman for their assistance. I am especially grateful to Bill Schneider, Sanna Porte, Will Harmon, and Helen Ibach for editing, proofreading, typing, and helpful advice on content and presentation.

Lastly and most especially, I wish to express my deep appreciation to my parents and my wife for their long-standing support.—*Michael S. Sample*

There's no limit on beautiful scenery and peace of mind on this river. Darrin Schreder photo.

CONTENTS

MONTANA'S MAJOR RIVER SYSTEMS

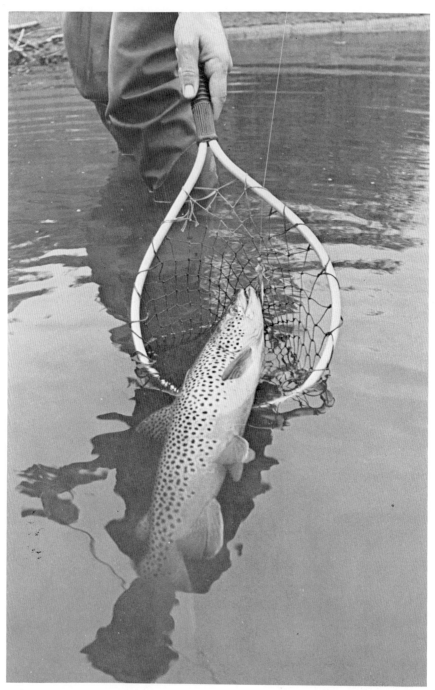

Fishing in general—and trout fishing in particular—have helped make Montana famous. This fat brown trout is merely one sample of Montana's fabulous fisheries. Frank Martin photo.

INTRODUCTION

Why write a fishing guide? The answers to that question tie in closely with the answers to another question—why fish? As with any sport, the purpose of fishing can be reduced to ludicrous simplicity. The goal, at least apparently, is to fool a pea-brained aquatic animal into biting a hook, whereupon the angler cranks the creature in with the help of line, reel, and rod. A definition of this sort is akin to describing the Statue of Liberty as a hunk of copper in a New York City harbor.

In truth, fishing may have as many meanings and purposes as it has participants. As beauty is in the eye of the beholder, so is fishing in the mind, heart, and soul of the angler. An abbreviated list of commonly pronounced reasons for fishing might include: fun, exercise, escape from the pressures of work, escape from the ugliness of city life, the beauty of fish domains, solitude and/or comradeship, relaxation, the chance to do something wholesome with one's family, the chance to exercise one's creativity, the joy of developing a skill, feeling at one with nature, obtaining food, inspiration, refreshment, celebration of seasons, and the challenge of catching fish.

Catching fish is not the only purpose of fishing, but it does contribute often to the experience. Yet it is often observed that a small percentage of anglers catch most of the fish while the large majority catch few or none at all. Fishing guide Ray Hurley once observed, "Fishing must be a wonderful hobby, because so many people have so much fun doing it and yet are so terrible doing it."

There is no such thing as a born angler; people do not come into this world with or without fishing genes. Instead, fishing is a learned skill. Anyone with a modest amount of physical ability and motivation can become a proficient angler. A guidebook such as this can be a valuable aid in the learning process.

Thus, to answer the opening question, *The Angler's Guide to Montana* was written and published to meet a need for information and education. This book will help anglers do better what they already enjoy!

Some guidebooks offer the reader the knowledge of one expert; this book cites more than sixty pros. And that is important with a subject as vast as Montana fishing. Not only is there a tremendous amount to know, but also a diversity of opinions helps the angler know there often is more than one answer to questions.

Rather than covering every mountain lake and stream, this book concentrates on Montana's larger fisheries. The bulk of fishing in Montana occurs on the bigger rivers, lakes, and reservoirs, most of which are readily accessible. This edition of *The Angler's Guide to Montana* also contains a new section describing the major alpine lake basins and their fisheries. Many of these lakes are remote wilderness tarns, reached only on foot or horseback.

Sooner or later, an angler who really cares about the quality of fishing becomes an advocate. Going to bat for a favorite fishery might mean testifying at a Fish, Wildlife and Parks meeting or keeping a fisherman's log or joining an organization such as Trout Unlimited. TU has shed its elitist image in recent years and has begun actively working on behalf of all anglers. The Montana Wildlife Federation and the local Rod and Gun clubs have also actively benefitted Montana fishing. The professional fishery managers can't do their job alone—they need public input and support. They also need better funding, which can only come when the fishing public pressures state legislators to allocate more money for research, acquisition of public fishing access, and adequate salaries.

Clearly, we in Montana are blessed with some of the best trout fishing in the nation. This is undoubtedly the result of many factors, but certainly one of the biggest is the outstanding habitat—high water quality. Anglers often worry about such factors as fishing pressure, trash fish, regulations, or limits. But in the end, without good habitat, these questions are moot. Protect the habitat, and good fishing will follow.

Rumor has it that when concerned out-of-state anglers call a certain Montana tackle shop to ask how the fishing is, the sales clerks always respond with enthusiastic reports, even when the liars haven't been catching anything. While this may seem an unfair policy, it has its point. As an old saying goes, "Fishin' is always great-it's the catchin' that varies." Here's hoping you have great filshing and tight lines.—*Mike Sample*

Casting on the Yellowstone.

BEAVERHEAD RIVER

The Beaverhead River is among Montana's premiere big-fish fisheries, supporting a phenomenal population of large trout in its upper reaches. Each year, the Beaverhead rewards anglers with scores of browns and rainbow over three pounds and a few weighing over ten pounds.

But don't count on catching trophy trout on every trip. It takes an experienced angler to be consistently successful on this river. The Beaverhead is without question one of the most difficult rivers in Montana to master.

Beginning twenty miles south of Dillon at the outlet of Clark Canyon Reservoir, the Beaverhead River meanders for about fifty air miles to its junction with the Big Hole River north of Twin Bridges. The upper river, the fifteen-mile stretch between Barretts Diversion and Clark Canyon Dam, winds through a narrow valley with picturesque rock outcrops. The lower river runs through a large broad valley ringed by a series of small mountain ranges.

The reason for the Beaverhead's excellent fishery is, in a word, habitat. The Beaverhead differs from the braided-channel, riffle-pool-run pattern of most larger western rivers; instead, the river meanders extensively in a single, smooth-surface channel. The swift current, undercut banks, and thick overhanging willows along the Beaverhead's entire length provide protective overhead cover and the good holding water in which trout thrive.

Typical of most valley rivers draining alkaline western soils, the Beaverhead's water is extremely rich in nutrients. Water flowing from the bottom of Clark Canyon Dam provides nearly constant water temperatures on the upper Beaverhead. This clear, cold water combined with the rich nutrient levels and excellent habitat creates perfect growing conditions for trout and the insects on which they feed. The river supports a variety of insect life, including caddis flies, crane flies, mayflies, midges, and a few small stoneflies.

The combination of habitat conditions on the Beaverhead translates into an abundance of fast-growing trout. According to Jerry Wells, a fisheries biologist and now division administrator with the Montana Department of Fish, Wildlife and Parks (FWP), "Growth rates are tremendous on the upper river, some of the best in the state." The more abundant brown trout average 2.5 to 3.5 pounds at four years of age and older. Rainbow in that age bracket average four to six pounds, gaining nearly a pound a year.

The upper Beaverhead also supports one of the best trout populations in Montana. Few rivers can match the 2,000 trout per mile of this remarkable stretch of river. This amounts to nearly 3,500 pounds of fish for every mile of river. Put another way, if you float the river at a normal speed, you will pass by a trout eighteen inches or longer every ten seconds.

Sounds good? Now consider the bad news. The habitat that makes such outstanding trout populations has its drawbacks for the fisherman. Fishing is exceedingly difficult because the river is so narrow and thick with willows. Steep drop-offs along the banks and a swift current make wading difficult on much of the river. The brushy banks limit access for the bank fisherman, making it difficult to get to a lot of fish.

Floating solves some of the problems but creates others. It allows the fisherman a better casting angle and room for backcasting. Floating also provides access to otherwise inaccessible waters. But the willows still present a problem to the floater trying to cast a fly tight to the bank. The Beaverhead willows claim many flies and lures. Some guides reportedly augment their supplies by retrieving flies and lures from the bushes.

The Beaverhead is also a tricky river in which to maneuver in a boat. The meandering, swift current puts a premium on oarsmanship. It's easy to be swept into the bank, and at Hildreth's Bridge, two miles below Clark Canyon Dam, it's necessary to stop the boat and slowly guide it under the bridge. High profile drift boats don't belong on this stretch of river. Inexperienced floaters would be wise to hire a guide the first time they attempt the Beaverhead.

Outfitters and guides from Dillon and Twin Bridges float various sections of the upper Beaverhead extensively. In fact, one of the biggest complaints about the river concerns the excessive number of boats on the upper reaches. Steve McMullin, FWP's fisheries biologist, says, "This is only an aesthetic problem, not a biological problem. The trout population hasn't been hurt by the pressure yet." Many fishermen release their fish on the upper Beaverhead, and this may prove to be an important factor in maintaining such good populations in the face of the heavy fishing pressure.

Over the past few years, biologists have become concerned about a decline in yearling rainbow trout populations on the upper Beaverhead. McMullin notes, "There is no readily apparent answer or solution to this sudden decline, but it is a high priority research item." Extensive creel surveys proposed for the river may provide some needed information. In the meantime, McMullin encourages anglers to release rainbow and keep only the more abundant ten- to fourteen-inch browns as a precautionary measure to help protect the rainbow fishery on the Beaverhead. For now, there is a daily limit of one rainbow.

The lower Beaverhead receives very light fishing pressure compared to the upper river, earning it a rating as an untapped fishery resource. In fact, the lower Beaverhead has a much greater reputation as duck and goose hunting water than as a fishery. But there is good trout habitat throughout the length of the river. The thick willow banks and meandering flows persist on the lower river, although the current is slower than on the upper reaches.

The few fisherman that do use the lower river find much of it virtually wild and untouched by human activity. There is an abundance of wildlife along the river including owls, great blue herons, a variety of waterfowl, and white-tailed deer. The wild surroundings contribute to the angling experience on the lower river. If solitude is what you want, the lower Beaverhead is the place for you.

Rainbow disappear downstream from Dillon. Brown trout are the predominant species, averaging twelve to fourteen inches. An occasional lunker exceeding five pounds is taken from these waters. Anglers generally do well on the lower Beaverhead, even though the trout populations are not as spectacular as those of the upper river.

The exceptional habitat found on the upper Beaverhead progressively declines below Barretts Dam. The beneficial effects of constant water conditions on insect and trout populations are lost rapidly. The waters of the lower river drop to near freezing in winter and can overheat in summer. Irrigation withdrawals below Dillon reduce flows and current, compounding the summer

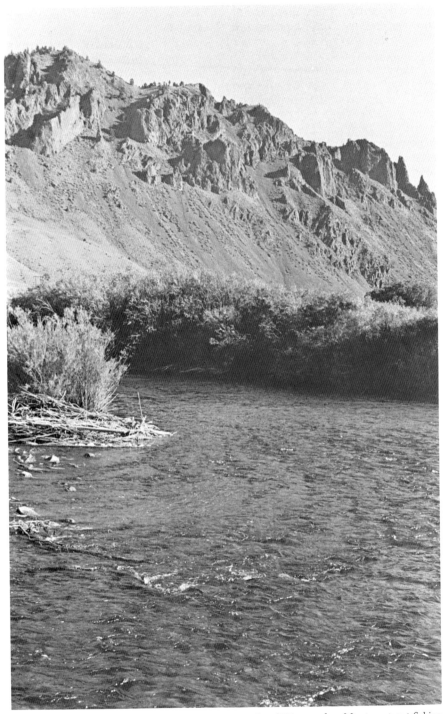

Outstanding aquatic habitat such as the upper Beaverhead River makes Montana trout fishing the envy of the nation. Michael Sample photo.

warming effect. The lower river has only about half as much good willow bank cover. Together, these conditions mean a smaller trout population because growing conditions are less than ideal.

The lower Beaverhead has another problem that has probably affected trout populations adversely. Water turbidity has become a major concern for anglers and fisheries biologists over the past few years. Spring runoff is only a short-term contributor. Erosive banks and return irrigation flows contribute silt to the river throughout the year but especially in the summer. The result is usually murky water, with visibility less than six inches not uncommon. Rarely is visibility better than a few feet. Long-time residents of Twin Bridges still remember when the Beaverhead's water was clear as it ran through the town. Fortunately, FWP has plans to study the problem and try to alleviate the condition—welcome news for fishermen.

In summertime, the Beaverhead is a phenomenal fishery but very difficult to fish. Because of serious landowner-floater problems, anglers should be ultra-careful not to aggravate the situation. If anglers abuse their privileges, fishing certain sections may become impossible.

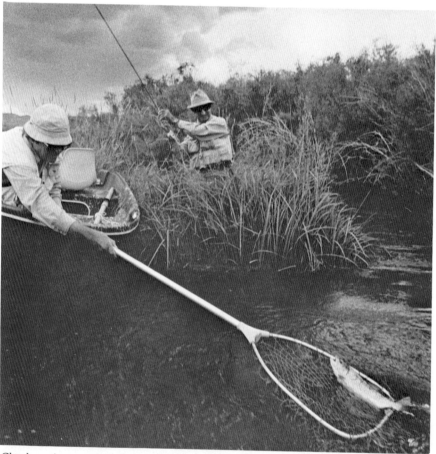

Cloudy, rainy weather during summer months often improves fishing success on the Beaverhead. Al Troth photo.

Fishing Strategies.

With its excellent trout populations and large numbers of big fish, the Beaverhead River can provide exciting fishing for the determined angler. But the fish are wily and have all the advantages a river can offer—good bank cover, swift current, and an abundance of readily available food. With all the odds in favor of the trout, it takes skill and patience to outsmart them.

Fishing the Beaverhead requires techniques suited to its tough conditions. The foremost consideration is getting the fly to where the fish are. This means casting under willows and tight into the banks. It pays to be a gutsy caster on this river, but it can be expensive.

Almost ninety percent of the fishing is done with big, weighted flies. Girdle bugs, named for their rubber legs originally made from old girdles, are black-bodied, plain-looking flies. Some anglers contend that they resemble juicy crane fly larva, but the trout's perspective is unclear. In any case, they work. A local favorite, the Zonker, is a silver-bodied fly with a rabbit hair strip down the back. Other good flies include black or olive Matukas and Maribou streamers.

According to Al Troth, nationally renowned fly tier and resident expert on the Beaverhead, "Fast, accurate but short casts are very, very important on the Beaverhead, because you have so little time to adjust your line when floating." With the boat moving quickly down a narrow, meandering river, the angler is rarely in perfect casting position and must learn to read the water rapidly. Troth also believes a good backhand cast is important in order to take advantage of both banks. Presentation of the fly is critical on the Beaverhead. Troth suggests that anglers "make the fly swim as slowly and deeply as possible" to be successful.

Generally, the idea is to imitate the action of sculpins and other small fish. Lures can be effective at this and do work well on the Beaverhead within the limitations of such a narrow river. The Panther Martin and Rapala are reported to be especially good. Flies on spinning gear is a particularly effective technique.

Although purists might scoff at the idea, one key to success on the Beaverhead is a heavy leader. Fifteen-pound test is about standard and affords several benefits. First, because you are casting into willows, which you will catch as often as not, you are more likely to retrieve your fly using a heavy leader. This means you will have more time to fish instead of tying on a new leader and fly. Consequently, you increase your chances of catching a fish. Should you hook a big one, that heavy leader will give you a better chance of landing it. Nevertheless, take along plenty of extra flies, lures, and leader material, because you're bound to lose your share.

Float-fishing is the best method of fishing the Beaverhead because it provides access to so much otherwise inaccessible water. The thick willow banks and deep, swift water make wading difficult in all but a few spots. The banks are mostly private land, further limiting good access to the river.

Bait fishing is predominately done from shore due to the need for slower water and more time to drift the bait in deep water. Limited bank access means few opportunities to find good fishing spots. Sculpins, night crawlers, and salmon eggs are the most popular baits.

Although the Beaverhead is not noted as a dry fly stream, there is some good action on top. Caddis flies provide the bulk of the surface fishing throughout the summer. Size 12 to 14 imitations will do the trick. Early

BEAVERHEAD RIVER

summer mornings witness a good hatch of size 14 to 18 mayflies. A few small stoneflies, size 10 to 12, hatch in the riffles around midday in July and August. Small nymphs are worth a try before and during a hatch in the widely spaced riffles along the Beaverhead.

The crane fly provides a unique hatch on the Beaverhead. Crane flies live in riffles in clean gravels. Crane fly larva are like juicy, pastel caterpillars. Hatching in late August and September, the adults resemble giant mosquitoes. Over an inch long with giant wings, they dance high on the water's surface. Fish rise explosively to feed on these giant flies, even climbing the bushes to grab one. For best results, skate a well-hackled, slender-bodied, high-floating imitation on the water's surface. Fish will often take the fly on their way down, so don't be too quick to set the hook or you may pull the fly out from under the fish.

Salmon flies are not among the trout's fare on the Beaverhead. Unlike most southwestern Montana rivers, the Beaverhead does not have the rocky substrate necessary to support this notable insect. The river bottom is too silty and lacks the high spring runoffs that normally cleanse river bottoms.

Fishing on the Beaverhead heats up with the water. Because the Beaverhead taps the cold waters from the depths of Clark Canyon, it takes warm summer air to heat the water sufficiently for fish to get active. This often takes until July. Fishing stays good into the fall.

The best time of day to catch fish is when they're feeding in the mornings and evenings. As with most rivers, fish don't seem to be very active on sunny afternoons. But midday on a cloudy day can prove highly productive.

A problem that occasionally interferes with fishing on the upper Beaverhead is the irregular fluctuations in water flow from the dam in response to irrigation needs. While river flows rarely fall below minimum levels necessary for the fishery, due to excellent cooperation with the East Bench Irrigation District, sudden rises in flow can make the trout inaccessible to anglers. The current becomes too fast and deep to get a fly or lure to the fish. When water levels suddenly drop, the trout get spooked and rarely hit a fly or lure.

Fishing the lower Beaverhead generally requires the same skills and techniques as the upper river. However, because the character of the river changes below Barretts Dam, there are some differences worth noting.

The stretch from Barretts to Dillon provides the best conditions for bank fishermen. Reduced river flows and slower currents make wading possible in this stretch. The river flows through hay meadows with fewer willow banks, making bank access easier. Fishing is very good for good-sized browns and rainbow. Ask permission for access to private lands along here.

Float-fishing provides the best opportunity to explore the Beaverhead River downstream from Dillon. However, because the current is fairly slow unless the water is high, travel can be very slow. This end of the river is strictly brown trout fishing, so work the banks hard.

On the lower river, water conditions often dictate angler success. Water turbidity presents the biggest problem because visibility gets so poor. Fish can't see the fly or lure unless it lands right in front of them. Dry fly fishing is only good when the water is relatively clear, with visibility at least a foot or better. When turbidity is high on the lower river, don't even bother fishing it. Head for the river above Dillon, where conditions are always much better.

When visibility is good, fishing can be excellent on the lower Beaverhead for one- to two-pound browns. There are bigger browns here, too, but they are tough to catch.

Weighted streamers, girdle bugs, and lures cast tight to the willow banks are the best methods for success. A few hatches provide occasional good dry fly fishing. Caddis hatch in the evenings all summer long, and crane flies hatch in the late summer, although in fewer numbers than on most upper sections. Late in the summer grasshopper imitations work well, especially in areas with grassy banks.

Bait fishing opportunities are better on the lower Beaverhead than the upper river. Slow current and occasional deep holes provide excellent conditions for drifting sculpins, nightcrawlers, and grasshoppers.

Water temperatures on the lower Beaverhead rise substantially during the summer due to lower flows and slow current. As a result, fishing quality declines during August. Trout get sluggish in the warm water and aren't very active during the day. When the days are warm, it's best to be out fishing in the early mornings or evenings when the water is a little cooler.

Tributaries

Red Rock River, the Beaverhead's major tributary, has its headwaters in the Red Rock Lakes National Wildlife Refuge. Running through swamplands and a series of picturesque lakes, these waters provide one of the last trophy grayling fisheries in the state. Unfortunately, the upper lake is silting in, threatening the survival of this remnant native population.

There are some cutthroat in the Centennial Valley portion of the Red Rock,

The Beaverhead has a reputation for trophy-sized trout, but it can be hard to fish. Michael Sample photo.

but fishing is not very good. The river has been altered and the banks overgrazed, causing a severe silting problem. Trout populations are depressed.

Below Lima Dam the river has little water most of the year, and fishing is poor. Despite some good hatches, whitefish seem to be the dominant fish in these waters.

As it picks up spring waters along its length, the last fifteen miles of Red Rock is an excellent fishery. Rainbow and brown trout are abundant, with browns reaching two pounds plus. The fall brings good spawning runs of very large browns out of Clark Canyon Reservoir.

This reach of river is not hard to fish. The river meanders through a cottonwood bottom and has lots of deep holes and good bank cover. The water is never crystal clear, but it has good visibility. Small mayflies and caddis provide most of the surface action in mid-summer. Wet flies and streamers achieve the best success, however.

The Red Rock River receives little fishing pressure because it is surrounded by private land. The ranches are huge in this area, so getting permission to fish from one landowner will provide access to a lot of river and a full day of fishing.

Grasshopper Creek, another tributary, is still suffering from the effects of gold dredging in the early 1900s. The first big gold strike in Montana was in Grasshopper Creek near Bannack, Montana's first territorial capital. Violations of heavy metal water quality laws have been fairly well cleaned up. If current conditions can be maintained, stream quality and its fishery should gradually improve. FWP is monitoring the stream and is already seeing some improvement.

Trout populations are depressed below Bannack, but the stream still supports ten- to fifteen-inch brown trout in small numbers.

Fishing gets much better above Bannack. There is excellent trout water in this stretch, and it receives only light pressure. But because the surrounding land is all private, access is difficult.

The upper reaches of Grasshopper Creek have a good population of tiny brook trout. Access is provided through Forest Service land.

Poindexter Slough, just south of Dillon and running roughly parallel to the Beaverhead, is a spring-fed creek that supports a good population of twelve- to fifteen-inch rainbow and brown trout. Poindexter can provide some excellent fly fishing for the experienced angler, but it's not easy fishing. Weed beds, willow banks, and extremely wary trout limit one's success here, and an overabundance of large mosquitoes during the summer severely dampen the pleasures of fishing.

The roughly twenty-five miles of Ruby River below Ruby Dam resemble a small-scale version of the Beaverhead River. It provides the same prospects and problems that characterize the lower Beaverhead. Thick willow banks make casting difficult. Fluctuating water levels and eroding banks make the water muddy until mid-summer. In wet years, such as 1982, large water releases from the reservoir in fall turn the river muddy again in September. But most years, the lower Ruby offers good fishing for one- to three-pound browns in the early spring and again in the fall when the water is clear and low. Despite its good fishing, this river receives little pressure and provides solitude for the angler.

The Ruby drains into the Beaverhead three miles upstream from Twin Bridges. The lower reaches are bounded by private land, so permission is required to fish. Fee fishing has been instituted on some ranches.

Above Ruby Reservoir there is good fishing for ten- to fourteen-inch rainbow trout. It's a small river at this end, and access is difficult until you get up into the Beaverhead National Forest lands. The upper Ruby is a good stream for beginners. Ruby Reservoir is not noted for its fishing, though it is stocked with rainbow and cutthroat trout.

Access

Almost the entire length of the Beaverhead runs through private land. A number of bridges and public access sites provide access along the river, although there are still extensive stretches of relatively inaccessible river downstream from Dillon. You'll need permission from landowners to get into many remote areas.

The farthest upstream access point is at the river's source at the base of Clark Canyon Dam. There is a public access and campground site here that is very popular during the summer. Another access point, as yet unnamed, is being developed by FWP just downstream from the first interstate bridge over the Beaverhead. About two miles downstream, just off Interstate 15 from the Daley's exit on the frontage road, is the High Bridge access. This spot is one of the most popular sites for launching float trips. Henneberry Bridge, also reached from the frontage road, has been rebuilt after a wash out, and FWP is developing a fishing access site (FAS) here for boaters. Pipe Organ, named after a unique rock formation along the river, provides the final access from the frontage road before the river crosses under I-15 again. This is a good take-out spot for floaters.

East of the highway downstream from Pipe Organ, FWP maintains Grasshopper FAS across from the mouth of Grasshopper Creek. Use the Grasshopper Loop exit from I-15. The Bureau of Reclamation maintains a good fishing access site at Barretts Diversion Dam. There is also a picnic area and

Fishing from a boat gives anglers a better casting angle to the trout hiding under the willows.
Al Troth photo.

small campground here. Boats must be taken out of the water here and walked around the diversion. Towards Dillon, FWP has another fishing access site at Poindexter Slough. It's an easy walk to the Beaverhead from here. Many local floaters enjoy the "Tash-to-trash" section of the Beaverhead, putting in at the Tash Ranch Bridge downstream from Poindexter Slough and running down to the road to the city dump west of Dillon. Floaters also use the dump road as a put-in to continue downstream of Dillon. At the north end of Dillon, Highway 91 crosses the river via Selway Bridge, where there is limited access to the river.

Downstream from Dillon access is more limited and float times tend to be longer. Low water can further prolong an outing on this reach of river. The Beaverhead Rock, just off Highway 41 about halfway between Dillon and Twin Bridges, is owned by FWP and provides the last public access until the highway bridge in Twin Bridges. Two bridges, about seven miles in either direction from the Beaverhead Rock, cross the river, but you should ask landowner permission for access.

Available access sites are generally adequate for float fishermen willing to put in a long day on the river. Bank fishermen, however, must seek permission from landowners along much of the river's length, particularly to gain access to more remote reaches. FWP is currently interested in acquiring new access sites between Dillon and Beaverhead Rock to help remedy this situation. Please ask permission where necessary and be considerate of the private landowners' property and rights.

BIG HOLE RIVER

"If you were going to make trout streams, the Big Hole is what you would use for the model."

So says George Grant, a veteran fisherman of the Big Hole for more than fifty years. He may be prejudiced, but thousands of anglers share his opinion.

The free-flowing, "blue-ribbon" Big Hole River flows 150 miles through one of Montana's most scenic valleys to join with the Beaverhead River. Along the way, the rich, diverse waters foster bountiful aquatic life, including river otters, grayling, salmon flies, and trophy trout.

Two controversies cloud an otherwise bright picture of Grant's ideal trout stream. First, in dry years, irrigation diversions almost completely drain the lower river, resulting in substantial fish mortality. Second, heavy fishing pressure, especially during the salmon fly hatch, may be reducing the population of big rainbow. Possible solutions to both problems are now under consideration.

Prior to 1910, when high water washed in rainbow stock from a private pond, the Big Hole contained native cutthroat, eastern brook, and grayling. In the succeeding twenty years, rainbow up to nineteen pounds rewarded anglers.

Brown trout were planted in the lower Big Hole in the 1930s. The remnants of a dam at Divide blocked the browns, locally known as Loch Levens, from ascending into the upper river until another high runoff removed the barrier in 1966. Today, browns are common upstream to Fishtrap Creek and a few individuals roam as far as Wisdom. Divide no longer marks a dramatic division of two separate fisheries.

Brookies, cutthroat, and grayling still survive in the upper reaches of the Big Hole. An eagle soaring high over the upper watercourse would see innumerable creeks from the Bitterroot and Pioneer mountains mingle in the immense upper valley, or "Big Hole," as it was known to trappers and Nez Perce Indians.

Phil Wright, a long-time fly fishing guide who operated out of Wise River, thinks the alkaline chemical balance in the upper basin benefits the rich aquatic life of the river. He backs up his argument by pointing out that Kentucky thoroughbred owners once shipped hay from the Big Hole because of its high nutritional value.

Grayling in the upper Big Hole represent one of the last important river-dwelling populations in the lower forty-eight states. This brightly colored fish, with its generous dorsal fin, does not compete well against some introduced species. Once found throughout the Big Hole, the grayling now hold out principally in the stretch from Jackson to Wisdom and in some tributaries. Fishing for grayling is catch-and-release only throughout the Big Hole.

The native cutthroat did not compete well either and now make up an insignificant percentage of the fish population. Brookies, on the other hand, thrive above Ralston, with "lots of fair-sized fish in tributary streams—up to 500 brookies per 1,000 feet of stream," says Dick Oswald, fisheries biologist for the Montana Department of Fish, Wildlife and Parks (FWP). Oswald says the brookies could stand more harvesting and that they provide a relatively easy catch.

From Ralston downstream for several miles, the rainbow rule. Jerry Wells, an FWP fisheries biologist and administrator, has shocked a few big rainbow up to eight pounds, but fears they won't be found there much longer because they are "very vulnerable" out in the riffles. The banks in this section have been heavily grazed for decades and offer little cover.

The Big Hole—definitely one of the most beautiful, undammned rivers left. Al Troth photo.

The meandering, relatively flat water of the upper river picks up speed and changes character near the settlement of Wise River. Boulders now punctuate the cobble streambed as the river enters a series of canyons. The canyons mark a transition zone: the number of browns increases in these waters, while the number of rainbow drops progressively. Rainbow are still the dominant fish all the way to Melrose, however. Demonstrating the drop in altitude here, cottonwoods increasingly provide streambank cover along with the willows from this point on.

From Melrose to the mouth of the Big Hole, the river returns to a meandering pattern, throwing its current first one way against the thick brushy bank, then sweeping to the other side. Long riffles and pools characterize this last thirty miles of the river. The Big Hole frequently braids into two channels here. The jungle of growth on the banks grants superb cover for the dominant brown trout.

On an August evening in 1935, Butte fisherman Charlie Cook floated a number 8 Dr. Mummy fly beneath the overhanging willows near Melrose. He knew this water harbored some large trout and therefore "was on edge and alert when I felt a heavy strike." Cook fought the fish up and down a long pool and successfully turned the fish's runs without losing the last few loops of line on his reel. His arm was tiring at the wrist, but with the help of his companion, the fish was finally netted. Fourteen hours later, the "beautiful specimen of the Loch Leven variety" still weighed 11.25 pounds.

Cook's account appeared in *Field and Stream*, which awarded him first place in a national contest. As George Grant says in his book, *Big Hole River Memories*, the fish was "undoubtedly one of the largest brown trout ever taken from the Big Hole on an artificial fly."

Wells reports that he still finds a rare brown of that size when electrofishing from Divide to the mouth. The chances of catching a three-pound brown, though, are fairly good. Of over two thousand fish examined in a creel census, the average size was an impressive fourteen inches. Oswald adds that above Divide there are still respectable numbers of browns in the five-pound range and up, including a fifteen-pounder. He also notes reports of a sixteen-pound brown below Glen and a goliath 20.5-pounder pulled from the river below Melrose.

Nevertheless, long-time anglers and river guides worry about the Big Hole's big fish. Tony Schoonen, a guide for many years on the Big Hole, says, "Certainly, there are lots of fish, but not as much size to them." Grant, who may have fished flies in the Big Hole more days than anyone, reports, "From my own experience, the average size of the trout is diminishing. The fishing of the 1930s, 1940s, and 1950s was far superior to what it is today."

Wright describes hatchery fish as "three-year fish," because they grow rapidly the first three years, then slow down sharply as they achieve sexual maturity. Hatcheries discourage other genetic strains of fish, some of which mature late, perhaps not for five or six years. Some of these strains eventually grow to great size because they convert food to growth instead of reproductive energy. Wright's reasoning follows that killing the lunkers will soon deprive the fish population of the best genetic strains, leaving only fish of smaller size. "You can't kill the goose that lays the golden egg," he warns.

Wright, Grant, and Schoonen need only point to the Madison River and Rock Creek as examples. The mortality of large fish was so high in those two fisheries that the average size of trout caught declined sharply until the crisis

BIG HOLE RIVER

was recognized and FWP instituted regulations reversing the trend.

At least for the brown trout, no crisis now exists on the Big Hole, in the opinion of Wells and Oswald. Oswald stands by his records showing the continued presence of decent numbers of lunker browns, as noted above. He also cites a number of factors that would account for any apparent decline in the population of larger fish: fishing pressure has increased; stream flow has decreased on average in recent years, a situation made worse now that many ranchers continue irrigating into October; and the number of browns per mile has gone up. Fish biologists are fond of pointing out that as fish density increases, size tends to decrease because a stream can support only a given amount of biomass. Oswald notes that FWP ceased stocking the Big Hole in 1974, allowing the wild strains to better compete for food and space, but that these same fish tend to grow more slowly than hatchery strains.

On the plus side, the annual mortality of older browns currently runs forty to fifty percent, which is much less than it is on the Madison. "It's the rainbow that are getting annihilated," Wells reports.

"We don't want to wait for a crisis to happen," appeal some anglers and guides. And they don't want to lose the rainbow. One fisherman at a Trout Unlimited meeting in Butte added, "I don't know what those rainbow were made of, but they were really something." Another pointed out that twelve-inch trout abound in numerous rivers, but only a few rivers can support trophy fish.

The outgrowth of this debate is that some of the Big Hole is managed for larger trout. Under trophy fishery management, anglers can keep the better-tasting, smaller fish, but should carefully return most larger fish.

Will anglers be willing to bring home a photograph instead of a bragging-sized fish? Perhaps the question should be this: when a fish attains such a great size, why not save it to reproduce and to thrill several anglers instead of just one?

On another front, the Big Hole drainage, lush though it usually is, periodically suffers drought just as much of the rest of Montana does. During dry years, ranchers whose livelihoods depend on the Big Hole to irrigate their hay fields and pastures drain much of the river's water. The toughest time usually comes about mid-August. "They nearly dried it up two or three years that I've seen," says Schoonen.

Wells, in his study of the Big Hole between Melrose and Divide, found that the controlling factor for the fish population was the level of flow. "Without sufficient flow, we found fewer numbers of fish. They're simply gone from the population."

And where they go is not entirely clear. Wells wonders whether anglers don't take a greater number of fish because their hiding places are so exposed in low water. Add to this the stresses of less living space and the low oxygen content in warm water. The result is higher mortality. "It takes a long time to come back from a low water year," testifies Schoonen. "We need to have water adjudicated for trout."

A possible solution is to have one or several off-stream reservoirs to hold some of the spring runoff until it's needed later in the summer. But ideal sites are difficult to find, and who would fund such a project?

Another solution lies in allocating some water for use in the stream to benefit the fishery. FWP is currently pursuing several methods of maintaining such "instream flow" on Montana's rivers, either through obtaining a legal water

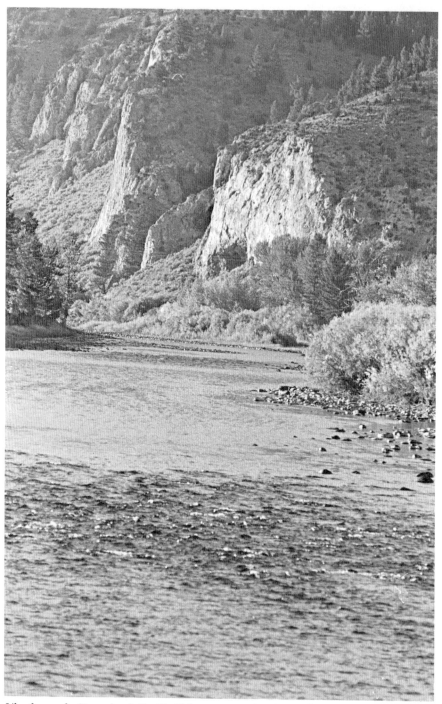

Like the nearby Beaverhead, the Big Hole attracts anglers in search of trophy trout, especially during the late-June, early summer salmon fly hatch. Michael Sample photo.

right, or by leasing water from other, willing, water users.

Streambank stability is another concern associated with irrigation diversions. Schoonen maintains that he finds the big trout where the streambanks have been stable for long periods of time. Conversely, stretches where the streambed has been gouged and the river's current changed by wing dams have been shown repeatedly by studies to be poor water for trout.

"I hate to say it, but bulldozers are the worst thing that ever happened to the Big Hole," says Fran Johnson, whose fishing shop has served anglers in the Butte area for many years. Ranchers used the dozers to divert water from the river for irrigation.

"But," points out Wells, "there has been incredible improvement compared to the way things were even five years ago, when guys just took their cats out in the stream and tore it apart." The Streambed Preservation Act requires a permit before anyone can physically alter the bed or banks of a stream, and this has encouraged more responsible action. Under the auspices of the River Restoration Act and the Big Hole River Foundation, FWP has also pursued funding for special projects to replace the bull-dozed diversions with more efficient—and less disruptive—channel alterations on the Big Hole.

In the conversation of anglers, one other problem surfaces: is the Big Hole being loved to death? Except at peak runoff, the Big Hole is a small river, yet it receives tremendous fishing pressure. For 1975, FWP estimates approximately 66,000 fisherman days spent on the Big Hole.

Grant thinks that the Big Hole just can't handle these numbers, especially with the Madison regulated now. So many boats and anglers have taken some of the fun out of fishing the river, Schoonen admits. "A lot of the old-timers have given up on it."

The greatest influx of anglers coincides with the famous salmon fly hatch. Wells remembers when seventy boats passed one point on the river in one day. In such a flotilla, a social problem develops. Johnson thinks, or at least hopes, that problems will be self-regulating; many boats will keep the fish from biting; fewer bites will keep the number of floaters down.

Anglers take about thirty percent of the year's catch during the three-week salmon fly hatch in June. For anglers preferring more solitude, the river is almost deserted prior to the hatch, a favorite time for Wells who notes that the trout are really active then. Some of the crowd departs right after the hatch, but perhaps the best time for prime fishing with little company is mid-September to mid-October. A bonus of autumn is the golden beauty along this blue-ribbon stream.

Fishing Strategies.

Throughout most of the Big Hole, in late summer, an angler can stand in the middle of the river and reach either bank with proficient casting. Anglers like this size of river. The river is not so large that it intimidates, yet it's large enough to support trophy fish.

But don't stand in midstream during the spring runoff, at least not without concrete shoes and steel girders to keep from being swept down into the Jefferson River. The Big Hole swells in May and stays that way until mid-July. Especially in the lower reaches, the river is up into the willow thickets, making it almost impossible to fish extensively from the banks. Most anglers float in inflatable boats.

Happily, the Big Hole rarely gets so muddy that it is unfishable. The water, the color of strong tea, allows visibility of a foot or two. In such conditions, anglers should work bait in the eddies and along the banks. Johnson suggests nightcrawlers, hellgrammites and "bullheads" (mottled sculpins). Grant doesn't fish with bait, but if he did, salmon fly nymphs would be his choice. All of these work throughout the season, not only during runoff.

The Big Hole does not lend itself to lure fishing. A few anglers skilled in the use of hardware do reasonably well, but guides such as Schoonen generally steer spin fishermen to the Jefferson, where their chances will be better. For those who still want to try lures, Thomas Cyclones, hammered brass, Mepps, and Rapalas are good bets.

The Big Hole is one of the few Montana rivers where fly fishermen comprise the majority of anglers. Because the river is small and rarely reaches depths of six feet, the water is naturally more suited to fly fishing. Fly rods sprout like weeds during the salmon fly hatch. Depending on the weather, the two-inch bugs commence crawling out of the river and up the banks and willows in the Twin Bridges area about June 10. In a normal year, the hatch progresses upriver several miles each day and peters out near Ralston about the first of July. However, as Schoonen points out, the game does not always go according to plan. Hard frosts may snuff out the hatch completely. Or a hot spell may bring out the hatch the length of the river in just four or five days, instead of three weeks.

"The salmon fly hatch is one of the world's greatest crap shoots," says Wright. "When you hit it right, it's tremendously exciting. But it can be a complete bust." Wright thinks the hatch is vastly overrated, but it is a dramatic event. "The water is high, and you're just bombing down the river," he says.

"Your chances of catching any salmon fly hatch just right aren't very good," Wells explains, "unless you're there ten days. But even then, you might hit

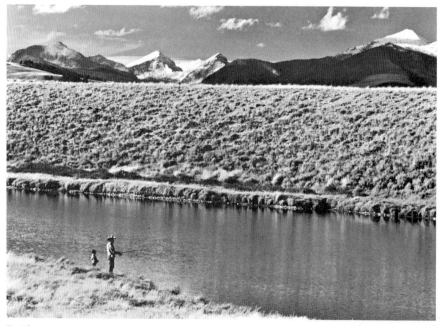

Besides scenery and trophy trout, the Big Hole offers good family fun. Michael Sample photo.

it hot for only twenty minutes." Wells recommends fishing just before the hatch.

Undeniably, most large trout are caught during the hatch. As Grant explains it, the big fish follow the nymphs to the river's edges and then wait near the surface for the clumsy insects to fall in from the willows. When the conditions are right, anglers using sofa pillows, fluttering stoneflies, and squirreltails find exciting surface action.

The salmon fly hatch is not, of course, the only hatch of consequence. Smaller stoneflies (several species) hatch through mid-summer. And caddis in tremendous clouds hatch throughout the summer. Grant explains that the Big Hole does not have many mayflies because larva are eaten by the stonefly nymphs.

The choice of which flies to buy and use often troubles neophyte fly anglers. However, Wright advises that "the perfect fly presented imperfectly will not catch fish, while an imperfect fly presented perfectly will often take fish." He also believes matching the hatch works occasionally, but generally the angler is after more of an impressionistic effect, especially when water is high and fast.

A well-stocked fly angler, in Wright's mind, would have elk hair caddis, Henryvilles, a hopper imitation, Matuka sculpins, Royal Wulffs, and some sort of big Maribou streamer. For the salmon fly hatch, he likes both a high floater and a low floater imitation plus, for the nymph, something "big, black, and ugly," such as the Bitch Creek fly.

Schoonen takes a somewhat different tack. He finds Royal Wulffs and Joe's Hoppers useful, but doesn't think much of matching the hatch. If the trout are feeding, Schoonen reasons, they rarely pass up a hellgrammite or minnow imitation. He cautions not to use too big a fly, though.

Boulder-studded runs like this one on the Big Hole have excellent pocket water where trout like to hang out. Al Troth photo.

Grant recommends the water above Wise River to the angler who wants to fish exclusively dry. On the lower river, most fishermen who take big trout are nymph fishermen. The typical riffle-pool combination has an open side with a rocky beach; the other side will be overgrown with willows and slightly undercut. Grant stands on the open side casting across or quartering upstream. The idea, he advises, is to keep the nymph drifting without imparting motion to it for as long as you can along the undercut area. Trout may hit it either when it shows up in their window or as it arcs across the stream on the drag.

In the more broken water of the canyon section, the trout's food factories are in the riffles. The pools serve generally just as resting areas. When the trout are feeding, they move up into the fast, foamy water. "Look for the dead spots. Watch the bubbles and see where they slow down," advises Wright. "One needs to develop the sense of current speed, of where a trout can hold."

What time of day is best? Ask four experts, and you'll end up fishing from daybreak to sundown. Johnson prefers summer fishing in the morning and evening. When the real hot spells come, the angler should be on the stream at first light. Schoonen maintains that the most consistent time is about 10:00 in the morning to 2:00 in the afternoon—"God's time, not the funny time," he says, in reference to daylight saving time. Wells likes the "gentleman's hours" from 8:00 to 10:00 in the morning. And Grant thinks the angler who is really serious about catching fish starts at daybreak, but he considers mid-day to be better suited for leisurely enjoying the river than for fishing.

Grant also feels certain that there are days when the finest fisherman in the world couldn't catch a fish on the Big Hole. "That darn Big Hole," Schoonen agrees, "when it shuts off, you can't catch them on flies or lures anywhere on that river." He feels a full moon and an east wind make a very tough combination for the fishing. "That east wind just kills the fishing nine times out of ten."

Tributaries

The Big Hole has countless small creeks flowing into it in the upper basin, but only a handful below the mouth of the Wise River. Fishing at the mouths of these little tributaries is often productive, and some of the larger creeks provide terrific fishing for unsophisticated, pan-sized trout miles from the main river. For young anglers with short attention spans, these creeks might be just the ticket.

Prior to 1927, the Wise River enjoyed a reputation as a fine fishing stream, but in that year the Pattengail Reservoir had a disastrous washout. The streambed has not yet recovered from the gouging of that flood. Dewatering due to irrigation withdrawals doesn't help it much, either.

Still, a side trip up the Wise River makes a scenic and cool retreat from the mid-summer heat, and the fishing can be lively for rainbow and brookies.

Access

Considering that the Big Hole flows through private land almost its entire length, the river is astonishingly accessible.

To gain access to the confusing myriad of springlets, brooks, forks, and branches of the Big Hole between Jackson and Wisdom (and above), explore the ranch roads off the highway and inquire locally. Families with youngsters will love the fast action the throngs of brookies provide here even when the rest of the river is skunking the pros. Be sure to ask permission before fishing from this private land.

The deep holes of the Big Hole produce trout in the 10-20 pound range—for anglers good enough to catch them. Al Troth photo.

Downstream from Wisdom, the river brushes Highway 43, granting the first point of casual access to the main river. The road then moves away for a couple of miles before coming back at a bridge that provides a commanding view of two big bends of gentle water. Some of the land on either side of the bridge is public, even though it is fenced.

Three developed accesses follow, each with an appreciable amount of river frontage. Fishtrap Creek, Sawlog, and Sportsmen's Park all receive heavy use. Downstream from Deep Creek and the highway from Anaconda, Highway 43 again crosses the river. A nearby dirt road gives access to the other side of the river for a couple of miles. Floaters use BLM's East Bank access about one mile upstream from Dickie Bridge as a launching point.

The next access (aside from one spot where the river briefly bends over to the highway shoulder) comes just after the little town of Wise River, when a gravel road off the highway quickly bridges the river on its way to Jerry Creek. BLM maintains an access site here, and there is also easy access from the highway for the next six or so miles downstream for wading or bank fishing. FWP has two new access sites—one at Dewey, about five miles downstream from Jerry Creek, and another just upstream from the Butte water intake dam.

Below the remnants of the old Divide Bridge and another BLM access, highway and river part company. The next access is off of U.S. 91 south of the town of Divide. A gravel road leads to Maiden Rock Bridge, which has an FWP boat launch. The bridge itself is private, but by walking either up or down the railroad tracks a short distance, the wading angler can reach some eminently fishable sections of river.

Another road (not to be confused with the road to Maiden Rock Bridge) leaves Melrose, immediately crosses the river, and winds up and down to the Maiden Rock Fishing Access. Bank fishermen will like this spot, especially upstream.

Thereafter follows a quick succession of three more bridges each with good access, the last at Glen, and some more casual access via the railroad tracks between Melrose and Glen. There is some walk-in access just downstream from Glen and the Notch Bottom access some five miles downstream. From Glen, one can travel a cantankerous old ranch road almost all the way to Twin Bridges. At times this road strays far from the river, but anglers who drive on will find a couple of places where the river brushes the roadside and Pennington Bridge with its FWP access site (boat launching can be difficult here). Just outside Twin Bridges, FWP has a fishing access site at the High Bridge.

As the access comes a little harder between Glen and Twin Bridges, fewer anglers venture to try this section of classic brown trout water. Those who do generally find the fishing worth the extra effort. Floating makes good sense through this section.

As numerous as all these developed and informal accesses are, still more numerous are the cooperative landowners who will grant anglers access if they ask permission. However, only respect and careful consideration for landowners and private property can keep it that way. For additional information on floating the Big Hole, pick up a copy of *Montana Afloat #8, the Big Hole River*.

BIGHORN RIVER

Prior to 1968, a trout anglers guide probably would not even mention the Bighorn River, but today, outdoor writers label it as possibly the best trophy trout fishery in the lower forty-eight states.

The building of Yellowtail Dam changed this silt-laden river into a clear, superb tailwater fishery. By flooding the seventy-one-mile canyon, the dam not only trapped the silt, but also created a giant heat sink which moderates the temperature extremes of Montana weather. Trout grow in temperatures between forty-four and sixty-six degrees Fahrenheit. The water in most trout streams comes between these two temperatures only about three months of the year, but in the Bighorn River where the water comes from 200 feet below the surface of Bighorn Lake, the growth period doubles from mid-June to mid-December.

The limestone watershed adds its rich minerals to the temperate water. Trout food, especially shrimp, minnows, and caddis, flourish in such salubrious conditions. And the clarity of the water allows sunlight to reach the bottom, giving rise to a profusion of moss and long, stringy weeds. In short, the conditions are terrific for browns and rainbow.

Numbers normally make for boring reading, but the Bighorn numbers are so impressive they cannot be ignored. Seven-inch rainbow plants would grow to fourteen inches in one year. Compare the Bighorn's average 2,911 trout over thirteen inches per mile with the Madison's 1,361 and the Big Hole's 912. Consider John Navasio's Bighorn record sixteen-pound, two-ounce rainbow. And note that the average fish captured measures better than fifteen inches long.

In all fairness, it should be pointed out that the upper ten miles of the

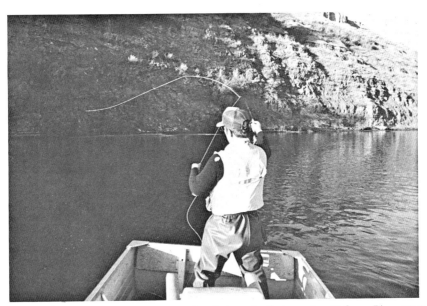

Casting downstream in slow water—good technique for fast-growing Bighorn River trout.
Michael Sample photo.

Beaverhead, itself a tailwater fishery, has even better statistics. But, as any one who has fished both rivers can testify, an angler has a much tougher time coaxing trout from under the willow jungle along the Beaverhead's banks than from the open riffles of the Bighorn. George Anderson, who runs the Livingston fly shop and guide service called Yellowstone Angler, writes that "...when the fishing is hot on the Bighorn, it is possible for a good fisherman to catch and release a dozen or more fish over three pounds and a few over four pounds in one day!" So protective is the cover along the Beaverhead that such a day would be almost impossible there.

Anglers pull slightly more rainbow than browns out of the Bighorn, but FWP electrofishing surveys show that in some stretches browns outnumber rainbow by a whopping nine to one ratio. Browns started dropping out of the tributaries and populating the main river as soon as the dam made the Bighorn suitable. Now, thanks to the regulated temperature of water flows in November and December, the browns' spawning success is nothing short of phenomenal. In 1984, Pat Marcuson, biologist for the Montana Department of Fish, Wildlife and Parks (FWP), wondered if too much of a good thing might not end up being bad news. "If we have two successive years of strong recruitment, we might have a Cambodia situation in the river, with lots of snakey browns chasing a limited amount of food."

Marcuson's words proved prophetic when, in 1986 and 1987, the brown trout population rocketed to a record high of 8,459 fish per mile. As more browns crowded into the river, mortality rates for the larger fish (four years and older) reached ninety-eight percent. The reason for this was clear. A riverine ecosystem will only produce so many pounds of trout food, which in turn will feed only so many inches of trout. Intense competition for food by smaller browns seriously hurt the condition and numbers of the large brown trout.

Ironically, it took a drought to rescue the big browns from their own kind.

BIGHORN RIVER

As flows in the Bighorn dwindled during the dry years of 1988 and 1989, water temperatures also decreased, and the number of brown trout per mile plummeted to 4,601—a reduction of nearly forty-six percent from the 1987 population. Despite this dramatic decline, the number of big browns (eighteen inches or longer) actually increased to about 400 fish per mile. Unfortunately, this boom and bust scenario may repeat when aquatic conditions once again favor brown trout reproduction.

The Bighorn's rainbow fishery was once supported almost entirely from state hatcheries. Anglers, and especially commercial guides, loved the hatchery fish because they could catch the showy trout more easily than the browns, and the 'bows put on weight faster than the browns, becoming what are known locally as "Bighorn swimming pigs," fish with small heads and big, deep bodies.

But the planted rainbow quickly became successful spawners, and the last hatchery fish were planted here in 1983. Today, the rainbow population is gaining on the browns, and these wild rainbow are a more durable, if slightly smaller, fish than their hand-fed ancestors. The average rainbow in the Bighorn measures a plump eighteen inches long.

One fish usually conspicuous in the cast of characters on other trout streams in Montana rarely shows up in the Bighorn—the whitefish. Perhaps the browns eat whitefish fry and the generally unpopular fish has never established a good foothold in the Bighorn. FWP speculates that nitrogen supersaturation from the operation of Yellowtail Dam may help suppress any whitefish recruitment. Nevertheless, anglers now report catching occasional whitefish where they were previously unreported.

The Bighorn runs at an average of 3,000 cubic feet per second, which makes it considerably larger than the Big Hole or the Madison. Except in a few of the wider riffles, anglers find they cannot wade across the river. Fluctuations in water levels for power purposes do not pose a threat to safety as they do on the Flathead or Kootenai. Because the streambed is made up of small rocks and gravel, anglers have good footing. In fact, the bottom seems almost cemented in place because of the lack of a spring runoff which would loosen up the aggregate.

The river heads from the afterbay to the Yellowstone in relatively straight fashion. Bill Haviland, who worked for the Park Service's Bighorn Canyon National Recreation Area, estimates about twenty islands braid the course of the first thirteen miles. The river has no whitewater to speak of, but moves at a moderate clip between its relatively stable banks. Here and there, cottonwoods have fallen in making a hazard for boaters. Also watch for the whirlpool about one mile downstream from Afterbay Dam and the short set of rapids near the Bighorn access site.

Haviland calls attention to another hazard. Because of the reservoir-caused time lag in the spring, the water remains very cold even in mid-June. On hot June days, Haviland wears a T-shirt, while adding long underwear under his trousers and waders to protect against chilling. "Hypothermia is a very real problem. We had four cases of it just this past spring," he says.

Between the afterbay and Hardin, the river flows through the Crow Indian Reservation. While the Crows have historically shown little interest in fishing, they have contested the right of non-Indians to float and fish the Bighorn. The state diplomatically closed the river until the Supreme Court ruled the water belonged to Montana and not exclusively to the tribe.

When the state reopened the river to fishing in 1981, there was some initial tension between Crows and non-Indians. While the bad feelings have since calmed down, anglers should be aware of the sensitivity of the situation. In particular, anglers must stay within the high water marks unless they have permission from the landowner. FWP defines the high water mark as "the continuous area where vegetation ceases."

With all the publicity of the Supreme Court case and enthusiastic reviews of the subsequent fishing, anglers have predictably flocked to the river, and angling pressure has become a problem. FWP figures show that use peaks in September and that weekends and holidays bring by far the largest crowds.

Angling pressure has certain predictable results. First, trout become more educated and selective. On the Bighorn, FWP studies show that only one of twenty fish caught on average will be kept. The returned fish reassume their feeding stations with an increased skepticism of feathered and metallic offerings. Haviland, Anderson, and guide Curt Collins all acknowledge that the fishing is more difficult now than immediately after the river was reopened.

Second, social problems develop. Anglers put their boats in and float down the river only to find their favorite holes already occupied. Anglers who have already staked out a spot get miffed at other anglers floating through their fishing water. On the Bighorn, FWP hopes to alleviate this sort of problem by purchasing additional access sites, such as the recently acquired Mallard's Landing. It would also help the situation if more anglers utilized the lower half of the river. This section holds somewhat fewer fish, but those fish see far fewer hooks than their upstream brethren.

Third, some anglers become concerned about how many fish are being taken out of the river. Those anglers push for more restrictive limits or "catch and release only." Other anglers who like trout on their tables protest. FWP biologists sit in the middle, listening to both sides and working to determine what would be best for the resource.

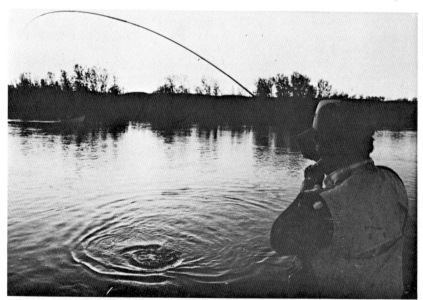

Evening fishing is often best for brown trout on the Bighorn. Michael Sample photo.

At a meeting held by FWP to air such differences of opinion, Don Tennant strongly supported a return to a more liberal limit, or no limit at all. He argued that a river can only support so many pounds of trout. Trying to "stockpile" extra fish by tightly limiting the creel limit only results in more but smaller fish. As a corollary, Tennant rejected regulations which discriminate against anglers who wish to use bait. Tennant suggests such regulations un-fairly treat older anglers and kids, who are most likely to depend on bait to catch their trout.

Anderson and several others countered that the limits should be imposed to protect the larger fish. "What we're seeing is a real reduction in trophy class fishing. It's a shame that such a great fishery is being pounded down." Anderson added that "the rainbow in the four- to six-pound category are really getting wiped out." As for Tennant's suggestion on bait, the fly and spin sponsors point out that a trout usually swallows bait deeply and will die whether or not the angler puts it back in the river or in the cooler.

In 1988, FWP reached a compromise between the two points of view by establishing a relaxed limit on browns, which seem able to hold their own under intense fishing pressure, while protecting rainbow, particularly larger ones. Current regulations split the Bighorn into three sections. In the upper-most twelve miles of river, from the steel cable below Afterbay Dam to Bighorn Fishing Access Site (FAS), there is a five trout limit, only one of which can measure over eighteen inches. Rainbows are catch-and-release only, and no bait-fishing or motor boats are allowed. From Bighorn FAS downstream to the Interstate-90 bridge at Hardin, bait-fishing and motors are permitted, and anglers may keep one rainbow. The five-trout limit, of which only one can be over eighteen inches, also applies to this reach of river. Downstream from Interstate 90, motors and bait-fishing are allowed, and the limit is ten trout with no restrictions on species or length.

Other than the difficulties with access and fishing pressure, anglers may have one other, less immediate, problem about which to worry. The Bighorn's proximity to Montana's coal fields may make it tempting to extract water for a slurry pipeline. While not currently a threat, this possibility would prove a nightmare for the fishery if it became a reality.

Until such a disaster befalls the Bighorn, anglers will continue to try for the trophy fish. Success does not come easily, but many anglers feel the fun is mostly in the chase and not the catch. Haviland remembers one haunting day with great enjoyment. On this particular day, he was having little success until he tied on a shrimp imitation and cast up in a riffle. "All of a sudden the line stopped and wouldn't budge. I was just starting to think I'd hooked a log when it took off. In one run, it took out my forty yards of line and seventy yards of backing. I ran after it, but it straightened the hook and got off."

Instead of getting depressed about losing a lunker, Haviland relishes the experience. His parting words: "Ain't fishin' great!"

Fishing Strategies

As with almost all trout streams and rivers, a small percentage of anglers catch most of the fish on the Bighorn. What do these successful anglers know or do that other anglers don't? A number of factors figure into the answer, but several experts suggest that adaptability makes the biggest difference.

Successful Bighorn anglers are willing to change their strategies, methods, and offerings if their first try of the day doesn't produce fish. If trout don't take dry flies, try a nymph down deep. If a brass spoon hasn't produced a strike in half an hour, put on a lure with a different color or action. Six great-looking riffles and not a strike? Try the banks and the deep pools.

Vince Ames fishes the Bighorn frequently. He would modestly argue that he is not an expert, but other anglers note that Ames catches many more than the average angler. Ames tries to arrive at the riverbank without preconceptions. "Be open-minded and keep loose" until observations show the angler what to try first. Is there any surface activity? If so, are the fish actually feeding on the surface (duns or spent flies?), or are they nymphing just below the surface film? If Ames sees no surface activity, he then decides either to fish a nymph deep or to try a streamer. If he decides on nymphs, he tries to figure out by observation whether to use a mayfly nymph, which swims, or a caddis larvae imitation, which should be presented on a dead drift.

Anderson asks the anglers he guides to "bring two outfits, one for fishing dry flies and nymphs on a floating #5-6 line, the other a more powerful rod for fishing streamers on a #7-9 line." For the latter, he recommends either a Hispeed Hi-D shooting head or a full length weight forward twenty- or thirty-foot Hi-D sink tip. And, he adds, "Be sure to have the reels loaded with at least seventy-five yards of backing."

Collins points out that from November to the first of May, the fly fisherman uses nymphs and streamers, while from May to November the angler can add dry flies to the arsenal.

For mayfly imitation, Collins likes patterns such as Adams, Blue Duns, and Blue Quills in size #14-18; Blue Wing Olives and light Cahills #16-20; and Mosquitoes, White Millers, and White Wulffs #14-16. For caddis, Collins rates the elk hair caddis as a "great fly" and adds a slate grey Henryville caddis to imitate the darker caddis. Collins adds some terrestrial patterns for hoppers, ants, and spiders. Anderson does not pin any hopes on hoppers; he has tried hopper imitations many times during the grasshopper season without good results.

In the nymph department, scud and shrimp patterns get high marks for effectiveness any time of the year. Some of the smaller stonefly nymphs fished on a dead drift will fool fish, but the Bighorn currently is not a stonefly stream. Collins likes small Hares Ear for imitating nymphs floating in the film. Anderson's "hot patterns" include Pecking caddis, Casual Dress, and Girdle Bugs.

When fishing nymphs deep, Anderson sometimes uses a split shot a foot back from the fly and a fluorescent cork indicator six or seven feet above the fly.

The Bighorn has some outstanding streamer and spin fishing waters. Some of the streamers mentioned by Anderson and Collins are olive Wooly Buggers, light and dark Spruce Flies, brown Matukas, Zonkers, black Nose Dace, and white Maribou Muddlers. However, a yellow streamer called the Bighorn Special might be the most popular fly of all on the river. Streamers for the Bighorn should be of the larger variety such as a size 2.

The Bighorn's moss can hamper spin fishing from April to mid-October. Otherwise, spin fishing can be dynamite. Haviland recommends Mepps, sometimes with feathered hooks. He thinks the smaller sizes are best. Brass is most effective; gold can be good, while silver, in Haviland's experience, does not do as well. Anderson adds that gold or silver Thomas Cyclones seem fairly popular. However, the lure that tops most recommendation lists is the

Rapala. "It's just awesome what they can do," says Collins.

Bait anglers plying the lower river almost always use worms. Navasio's record rainbow was taken in by the standard nightcrawler. The only other alternatives mentioned frequently were grey dead minnows. Even though sculpin do not reside in the Bighorn, they might work very well, especially closer to the Yellowstone. As mentioned before, bait anglers should be aware of special regulations.

Haviland has two unconventional strategies for anglers to consider. The first is a revival of the dropper rig, a traditional method earlier this century, but rarely practiced lately. At the end of his leader Haviland ties on a Muddler Minnow or a Bighorn Special. Two or three feet up the leader, he ties on a separate six-inch strand of leader with a black hair fly dangling at the end of it.

This dropper rig does not just present the trout with a choice of flies. The real intention is to make the hair fly look like an egg-laying caddis fly as it dips to the water's surface. The large streamer acts as an anchor. With a little practice, the angler can play the tension in the line so that the dropper fly will bounce, skitter, and tease any trout that is keying on one of the Bighorn's prolific caddis hatches.

The dropper rig method may sound complicated and too tricky to skeptical anglers, but it is a proven producer. In 1935, Charlie Cook caught an eleven-pound-plus brown on the Big Hole in western Montana employing this same tactic. When anglers see caddis flies fluttering just above the river surface, they might do well to try the dropper fly.

Haviland's other unconventional method will not appeal to the weak of heart nor to those who like to catch a suntan while they fish. Mature trout, especially browns, are notoriously nocturnal in the summer. Almost all anglers have witnessed the voracious feeding which so often takes place as the light dims after sunset. While most anglers head home at this time, Haviland finds nightfall a good time to start his fishing.

Haviland explains that as the light level drops, the big browns feel safe

Because of the shortage of access, most Bighorn River anglers use boats. Michael Sample photo.

enough to come out of their deep pools and into the shallow riffles. With the help of a full moon, he has seen big fish practically on the rocks, fins out of the water, looking like a pack of hungry sharks. Haviland feeds them something substantial like a Muddler Minnow on the end of stout, ten-pound test leader. He stresses that the night is a smaller world where you can catch fish right up to your feet. There is no need for ninety-foot casts at night provided a stealthy approach is made.

Obviously, it helps to know the section of the river very well from past experience. Falling into a river over the top of the waders at night could be scary, even dangerous. And there can be little surprises, such as one night when a startled beaver slapped his tail right next to Haviland. But the fishing can be prime; in a two-hour stand in one pool, Haviland once caught eleven fish between eighteen and twenty-two inches long.

What kinds of water do the experts fish on the Bighorn? Guide Mike Mouat likes the inside corners and the deeper banks. Anderson looks for the dropoffs as well as the faster riffles. Collins fishes just off the heavier water or where the heavy water hits the slack. The very slow, slack water itself should be avoided. Collins also keys in on the rare spots with gravel because the fish really seem to like it there. Haviland notes the drift lanes between the moss beds. Ames describes the Bighorn as a giant spring creek where all the water holds fish—"Some try to high-grade it, picking just what they think are the good spots, but I think they are fooling themselves."

The Bighorn remains ice-free and open for fishing year-round. March and April rate as the slowest months, but even they can be good. Summer and fall are the most popular times, but warmer winter days also bring local anglers to the river to cure their cabin fevers. Due to fluctuations in the release of water from the dam, the river seems to change frequently, even on consecutive days, let alone from one month to another.

Rivers with giant reputations sometimes have a way of disappointing anglers, especially neophytes. Collins sees lots of beginners with these "delusions of grandeur." Even though the Bighorn is an open river full of trout, it is not easy pickings for those who will not take the time to study its subtleties and learn the water. The fishing here especially favors the adaptable angler who, if he fails in his first try, goes on to try a different fly or lure or a different way of fishing them. While other anglers continue to flail away at the water uselessly in the same ineffective way, for the adaptable angler, good things can happen at any time.

Tributaries

The Montana section of the Bighorn has one tributary of note to anglers, the Little Bighorn. This large stream carries a heavy silt load at times, but the upper reaches in particular have some good fishing. However, the Little Bighorn runs entirely within the boundaries of the Crow Reservation and access to it is next to nil.

Access

"It is unlawful to go upon tribal, trust, or allotted lands on the Crow Reservation for the purposes of hunting, fishing, or trapping." (18-USC 1165) And thus it is imperative that anglers wishing to fish the Bighorn from Hardin to Yellowtail Dam reach the river either through FWP's fishing access sites or National Park Service land.

The uppermost of these is just below the bridge across the river from Fort Smith and immediately downstream from the afterbay. Next, about three float miles down, is NPS Lind Ranch Access. Twelve more miles down is FWP's Bighorn Access. These three sites currently receive the brunt of visitation.

A very long day's float (about 19.5 miles) down from Bighorn puts the angler at Two Leggins Access. From there, an eleven-mile float past Hardin to the edge of the Crow Reservation ends at Arapooish Fishing Access, just off Interstate 90.

Below the Reservation, there are two more developed sites on the west side of the river. Grant Marsh Game Management Area is about seven miles north of Hardin. And at the mouth of the Bighorn near the Interstate-94 bridge is the Manuel Lisa Fishing Access. Anglers can, of course, reach the river north of the Reservation by crossing private lands with permission. A map of the river and detailed information for floaters is available in *Montana Afloat #14, the Bighorn River.*

Power boats are currently prohibited on the Bighorn from the steel cable below Afterbay Dam downstream to Bighorn FAS. FWP has added two access sites, Mallard's landing and General Custer, to disperse fishing pressure more evenly along the river.

BITTERROOT RIVER

Rumor has it that Joe Brooks, the celebrated fisherman, world-wide traveler, and prolific writer, once penned his ten choices for the best trout streams in the world. The Bitterroot was one of the chosen few. Notwithstanding, the Bitterroot has not attracted the national publicity other Montana streams have. "Thank goodness," say some locals who regard the river as a hidden treasure.

Yet it has not been treated as a treasure. Extensive logging has increased the river's sediment load. Subdividers and developers carve the land along its banks into ever-smaller lots. And irrigators drain much of the summer water out of the river and across the fields of Montana's oldest agricultural valley. That's three strikes against the Bitterroot, but don't count it out. Up to the time of this writing at least, the river has accommodated these and other demands and still holds forth with some excellent fishing. A prime reason for this is the use of sportsmen's dollars to buy water from Painted Rocks Reservoir; releases keep water flowing in the river through the summer.

"Outstanding. And just amazing that it is so outstanding." That's the fishing assessment of Hank Fischer, veteran floater and fisherman of most Montana trout streams. Fischer enjoys fishing the Bitterroot so much that he has practically patented a three-day float trip, starting from the confluence of the East and West forks. In late June and July he's thinking rainbow as he canoes past riffles and down runs.

Rainbow and browns make up the bulk of the fisherman's quarry, but his creel may also contain brookies, cutthroat, and bull trout. Illegal plants of northern pike provide another game fish. And, much to the surprise of anglers who have never encountered them, some sizeable largemouth bass lurk in the backwaters. The chance of catching such a mixed creel is just one reason for the Bitterroot's popularity.

High on the list of reasons why people enjoy fishing the Bitterroot is its

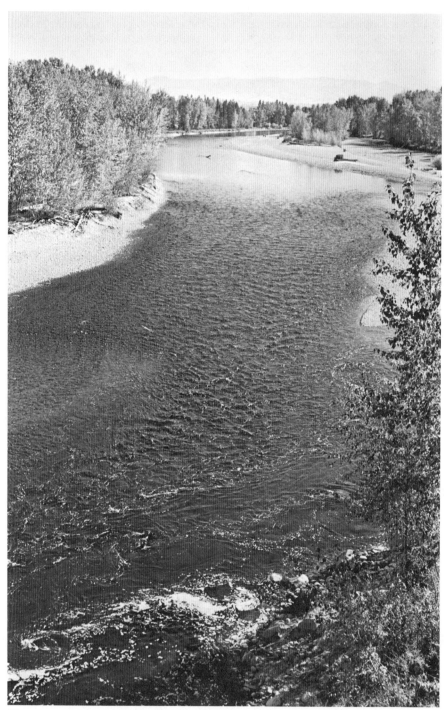

Bitterroot trout have a faster growth rate than the famous Rock Creek, with more trout in the upper river, but larger trout in the lower river. Michael Smaple photo.

scenic beauty. From the confluence of the forks near Conner until it joins the Clark Fork just west of Missoula, the Bitterroot flows on a northerly course along the base of the handsome Bitterroot Mountains. These mountains rise at so sharp a vertical angle that they appear to stand straight up from the river's west bank. They also seem to protect the valley from the high winds and severe weather that haunt other valleys such as the Yellowstone and Madison.

In the protective lee of the mountains grows a mixed forest of red-barked pine and tall, craggy cottonwood. When floating the river, the fisherman rarely sees the nearly solid swath of human occupation that stretches most of the way up the valley. This vegetative screen grants a feeling of isolation. The beautiful riparian greenbelt harbors amazing amounts of wildlife—deer, beaver, osprey, mink, even an occasional moose.

But it is the river itself that pleases the fisherman's eyes. Following the brief, but horrendous, runoff in late May and early June, the water becomes transparent. Every pebble and rock can be seen plainly, even in a six-foot column of moving water. Many an angler has snatched away his fly prematurely after seeing the start of a rise. Summer thunderstorms cause a quick show of muddy color, probably due in part to the logging in the watershed and poor streambank adjustment practices, but the water soon returns to cerulean blue.

The water of the Bitterroot is not only clear for the most part, it's also very readable. The fishy spots are obvious.

Frank Johnson, former owner of the Streamside Anglers shop in Missoula, describes the Bitterroot as "pool, riffle, pool, riffle, the whole way. Most of the river has well-defined fish habitat." Johnson points out that between Darby and Missoula, the angler can choose the kind of water he likes, whether it be big, heavy water; small side channel; riffle; or pool. He also notes the thousands of washed-down trees and cut banks and roots along the way, which serve beautifully to attract fish.

Don Peters, a fish biologist for the Montana Department of Fish, Wildlife and Parks (FWP), basically agrees with Frank Johnson's river description, but adds two additional comments. First, "The Bitterroot has a lot of slack, dead water which is really clear and offers no cover for fish, especially when the river is really low." He advises avoiding these "glassy sections."

Second, he recommends fishing old river channels, eddies, and oxbows. Here, among the log jams and debris, is excellent brown trout habitat. "Oftentimes these old river channels receive primarily ground water and have the appearance of a spring creek. These are haunts for big fish," he advises. These swampy-looking places are often bypassed by fishermen who never guess what they may be missing.

In selecting the better places in the Bitterroot to fish, the angler would be wise to watch for what Hank Fischer terms "the intact sections," where the river has not recently altered its course. As anyone who has built within its floodplain knows, the Bitterroot is a very unstable stream. Surviving the spring runoff is tough when most of a winter's worth of snow whooshes down the river in three weeks. Banks fold in and gravel bottoms shift radically. Peters describes this as a "bed load movement, where the bottom moves just like it's on a conveyor belt." Standing on the bank, one can almost hear the river grinding its teeth.

Peters suggest that, while brown trout spawners key into the new channels with their raw gravel beds, the best fishing generally is in areas with good

Clark Fork

90

Missoula

Kelly Island △
Maclay Bridge
Buckhouse Bridge

■ Weigh Station

12
Lolo Creek
Lolo

Private Bridge

93

△ Chief Looking Glass

Florence △

East Side Highway

Poker Joe △

Lee Metcalf National Wildlife Refuge

Bitterroot

Stevensville

△ Bell Crossing

Victor ● ↕ Victor Crossing

△ Tucker Crossing

Bitterroot Range

Sapphire Range

● Corvallis

Hamilton

River

38

Lake Como

Darby ●

HIGHWAY
COUNTY OR UNPAVED ROAD
△ OFFICIAL PUBLIC ACCESS
□ RANGER STATION
X BRIDGE
VVVV DIVERSION DAM

△ Hannon Memorial
● Conner

One inch = approx. 11 miles

473

West Fork Bitterroot

East Fork Bitterroot River

N

BITTERROOT RIVER

overhead cover, which generally are the established channels with trees and brush along the banks.

FWP is currently developing a good profile of trout numbers and sizes for the Bitterroot. "Trout populations are greatest in the upper river, yet the largest trout appear to prefer the haunts of the lower Bitterroot," Peters says. For Western Montana, the growth rates are excellent—about 4.5 inches a year, half again as fast as the growth rate of Rock Creek trout.

How big do trout eventually grow in the Bitterroot? No one has definitive figures about the biggest one percent of the fish population, but there are some big ones. A four-pound brown certainly wouldn't shock most local fishermen. There are hushed mentions of some big brook trout in certain places. Don Peters remembers a newspaper account of a fifteen-pound rainbow caught in one of the irrigation ditches off the main stem of the river. And because they are so rarely caught, bull trout may grow to very large size without anyone knowing. But then, that's one of the tantalizing parts of fishing.

Anyone assessing fishing in the Bitterroot eventually confronts a question: "How can this river, which by all accounts suffers from heavy fishing pressure, horrendous runoffs, and then sediment and other environmental problems, still provide such enjoyable fishing?

The answers vary: "Lots of bugs," responds Frank Johnson referring to the abundance of feed. Hank Fischer cites the superb riparian habitat. Don Peters explains that the high rough fish population means the river "apparently has the productivity because it is really supporting a large biomass."

Fishing Strategies

When the river is running bank-full in the spring, the best places to fish are along the banks and in the side channels. When the runoff subsides and the water drops away from the banks and retreats across the gravel bars to the main channel, the riffles are the hot spots. That, in a nutshell, is the advice of the experts who fish the Bitterroot.

As the river approaches peak flows, the currents in the main channels are powerful and unrelenting. Attempting to hold its position against such an onrush would be exhausting or even suicidal for a fish. The trout seek quieter water. Any place out of the main sweep of the current should be a favored place for both the fish and the fisherman.

Watch for the places where obstructions such as logs and boulders slow the water. Try the eddies where the water turns around. Check out the mouths of the numerous tributaries—fish often congregate there to eat the plentiful feed.

When the water has the consistency of chocolate pudding, the avid fly fishermen in this area will be testing their skills in the clearer waters of Rock Creek, just west of Missoula, or if they can gain access, in one of the choice spring creeks along the Bitterroot. Those people devoted to lure fishing are probably better off casting their shiny hardware into lake waters until the river flushes some of the mud out. However, anglers with worms or sculpins can take trout from the cloudy waters. Using lead to keep the bait down in likely spots should bring success, but the fisherman's patience may be tested by the Bitterroot's incredible population of squawfish and suckers.

Once the river begins to clear, lures and flies become useful again. Whichever piece of foolery the fisherman uses at the end of his line, the strategy is about the same. "Fling it to the banks," says Fischer, who catches good numbers of brown trout up against the banks. Johnson puts it this way: "More than most rivers, the six-inches-from-the-bank rule applies here."

Those places where the fisherman is most concerned about hanging up his line and losing his lure or fly are precisely the best places to find brown trout—fallen trees, tangled roots, and undercut banks. Naturally, fishing those places calls for accurate casting, some patience, and a few extra hooks, but the rewards are waiting around those hazards.

When the water comes down and retreats from the bank cover, the fisherman's attention turns to riffles. The urgency of the spring runoff is long gone in August and September. The Bitterroot becomes a slow stream, dropping an average of only twelve feet per mile. Clear, quiet water does not give enough protection to trout of catchable size. They seek a place where they can remain hidden from above.

The riffles offer just such protection. The bouncy, fractured surface of riffle water makes it difficult to see fish even in the shallows. The better oxygenated water in riffles grants trout some relief from the oxygen-poor water created by summer heat. And during warm months, trout find most of their food in the riffles.

The lower end of the Bitterroot from Lolo to the Clark Fork River has very slow water and few riffles. The areas just downstream from the major irrigation diversions, such as near Victor, are almost completely dewatered in later summer; trout die, stop feeding, or migrate to more hospitable sections. Thus, go upriver in times of low water.

The section from Conner to Hamilton, for example, has plenty of riffles and usually adequate water. Patient anglers await the first couple of frosts, when irrigating slows and water rises. Curiously, the river is almost deserted at this time, when the weather can be most hospitable and the fishing terrific. "It's amazing how ravenous the rainbow are at this time of the year," Fischer testifies. "They're storing up for the winter."

When wading, work each riffle carefully. In fast water, trout almost always face upstream. Approach from below the riffle and slightly to one side or from well above the riffle to avoid detection.

Work the fly or lure along the edge of the fast water. There is often a telltale, visible line between the fast and slow water to guide the fisherman. Trout wait just out of fast water, ready to dart at food as it tumbles by.

The same kind of feeding station exists around boulders in a riffle. A boulder buffers the current and provides trout a resting place even while whitewater cascades all around it.

For bait and spin fishermen, traditional Montana baits and lures work well in the Bitterroot. In addition to sculpin and worms, Peters suggests trying bottom insects which can be found in ample supply beneath stream rocks. Maribou jigs sometimes prove effective when worked along the bottom. Mepps and Panther Martins have also passed the test of time. If the silver hardware doesn't work, try the gold.

Peters has an interesting suggestion for those who would like to try their hand at catching bull trout. "The reason most people don't catch them is they don't know how to fish for them. We don't use big enough lures; they should be using salt water-sized lures like a Rapala."

The Rapala is normally considered a bass and pike lure, but Peters knows two fishermen who successfully used Rapalas for bull trout in Rock Creek and for big browns in the Clark Fork as well. It might be worthwhile sticking

Logjams and other obstructions slow the flow and produce excellent hiding places for trout. Michael Sample photo.

one in the tacklebox for those times when nothing else seems to work. It could make a big splash. FWP warns anglers that the bull trout population in the Bitterroot is in decline; catch-and-release for bulls of any size is encouraged.

The fly fisherman has plenty of bugs to imitate—good caddis hatches in early summer or late spring followed by the mayflies in mid-summer. Johnson gets roused just thinking of the stoneflies, which aren't as big as salmon flies but still make a good mouthful for big square-tailed trout. And although terrestrials may not be as important on the Bitterroot as some other rivers, grasshopper imitations still catch their share of trout in late summer.

In August and September, "fishing the riffles with attractor flies can be amazingly productive," explains Johnson. Fischer also likes to use big attractors such as Wulffs, which he casts downstream into the riffles and fast runs from his canoe. He also uses streamers about the time the leaves begin to fall. But perhaps his favorite, and that of many other fishermen, is the Muddler, that sculpin imitator. Whether or not trout think the Muddler is a sculpin is a topic of debate, but most fishermen who have given it a fair try will not debate its effectiveness.

"In all likelihood, I'll have a fly on before I even get to the stream and never change it," Johnson comments when asked for advice on flies. "I don't get excited about all these Latin names of all these insects. If it's a little green mayfly, then it's a little green mayfly. I fish about a half-dozen different fly patterns and that covers it."

Johnson conceded that this may be a contradiction, "because I innovate fly patterns, and I'm always writing an article about some hot dog fly. A lot of people thrive on that sort of stuff, and it's my job to give it to them. But because of the size of that fish's brain, I don't think the fly has much to do with it."

One may wish to take Frank's limit of six fly patterns with a grain of salt.

His point is that fishing the most productive places in a stream and presenting the fly well is more important than hair-splitting decisions between nearly identical feathered hooks.

A final suggestion: those backwaters warrant investigation. Whether it's with a bobber and worms, a Rapala, a copper spinner, or a big black Wooly Worm retrieved with a twitch, give it a try. There are some tackle-busting lunkers in those swamps.

Tributaries

The West Fork of the Bitterroot starts near Horse Creek on the southwestern edge of Montana and flows in a northerly direction through Painted Rocks Reservoir to its confluence with the East Fork near Connor. Above Painted Rocks, the West Fork supports nice populations of pan-sized rainbow, cutthroat, and brookies. Below the reservoir, anglers find a few browns and bull trout mixed in with the above cast of characters. Fish sizes run larger in this lower section. Some anglers float down from the reservoir, especially during high water when wading can be hazardous to one's health. Anglers gain access mainly through asking permission from private landowners, but also through some Forest Service land and in places where the stream runs right next to the road.

The East Fork curls around the southern end of the Sapphire Mountains and joins the West Fork at the Hannon Memorial Fishing Access, one of FWP's most beautiful streamside sites. The East Fork runs quite a bit smaller than the West Fork but has much the same size and species of trout. Peters finds that some sections have excellent numbers of fish while other stretches hold many fewer. Access is nearly all private.

Besides these two forks, the Bitterroot gathers its water from dozens of small streams, springs, and irrigation returns. Some have colorful names like Sweathouse Creek and Jack the Ripper Creek. The Burnt Fork and Blodgett, Lolo, Rock, Skalkaho, Rye, and Sleeping Child creeks, as well as a host of others, serve as important local fisheries and, in some cases, spawning areas. None of these would stand up long under increased fishing pressure and therefore are not hot-spotted here.

Most of these small tributaries suffer heavy irrigation demands during the summer months. Anglers generally do better heading upstream to Forest Service land, where irrigation withdrawals have not yet subtracted water from these streams' normal flows. Peters notes that the east side streams drain from a sedimentary rock watershed, which imparts more nutrients to the water than does the igneous rock watershed on the west side. Thus the east side tributaries tend to have more productive trout water. The exception to this rule of thumb comes when irrigation water sinks in on the west side's benches, then reappears down by the river in the form of very fertile springlets.

Access

Anglers currently have a choice of six FWP developed access sites on the main stem of the river. Hannon Memorial Fishing Access Site (FAS) enables anglers to enjoy the river where the East and West forks come together near Conner. Between Hamilton and Lolo, the next four are Bell Crossing, Poker Joe, Florence, and Chief Looking Glass. At the mouth where the river joins the Clark Fork just west of Missoula, Kelly Island FAS gives anglers access to this interesting area of many channels.

To supplement these formal accesses, anglers utilize at least eight bridges crossing the eighty miles of river. These include MacLays, Stevensville, Victor, Woodside, Hamilton, and Main Street bridges as well as a couple of unnamed bridges along U.S. 93. Several other spots, including the Lolo Sewage Treatment Plant, widen the choice.Actually the river never gets very far from Highway 93; anglers can reach almost any section they wish if they take time to ask permission. Anglers can also arrange float trips lasting anywhere from two hours to two days. Pick up a copy of *Montana Afloat #1, the Bitterroot River*, for a river map and more information on floating the Bitterroot.

BLACKFOOT RIVER

Winding its way through tall, dark timber in western Montana, the Blackfoot River beckons anglers to over a hundred miles of unspoiled, free-flowing water.

With six species of game fish, the big Blackie offers much more variety than most trout streams. Variety also marks the course of the river. Anglers can choose to fish meandering meadow stretches, dancing riffles, transparent pools, log-jammed stretches, and boulder-pocket water in the midst of thrilling rapids.

The Blackfoot tells a come-back story that is bound to become more familiar across the state as management techniques are refined and fisheries rise in the list of the state's priorities. The river's fisheries were in decline until recent efforts—primarily new regulations and habitat repair and protection—began to pay off.

A forward-looking coalition of private landowners, corporations, government agencies, and concerned individuals has blessed thirty miles of the Blackfoot with a "recreation corridor" that provides anglers, floaters, and campers with accesses, campsites, and conveniences while protecting both river and landowners. Such cooperation and intelligent management has been hailed nationally as a landmark project. The continued success of the corridor depends on how responsible the public is in observing the special regulations. As this type of arrangement is obviously vastly preferable to the locked-up, fenced-off, posted waters of some other rivers in the state, anglers are urged to be especially conscientious here. Hopefully, the concept will spread.

The Blackfoot begins as a small stream, populated mostly by cutthroat above the town of Lincoln. As with much of the Blackfoot River and its tributaries, the headwaters were hit hard in the flood year of 1964, but with the passage of time, the signs of the scouring are fading.

Paul Roos, who worked in Lincoln as a school principal and guided on the Blackfoot during the summers, does not recommend fishing from Lincoln up to where the Landers Fork joins the Blackfoot, as that stretch is characterized by poor fish numbers and habitat. But just below Lincoln, the Blackfoot receives an influx of water from several tributaries—Keep Cool Creek, Poorman Creek, Beaver Creek, and several others—which starts what Roos describes as one of the best fishing sections of the whole river. It is not,however, one of the best floating sections due to a profusion of logjams, some of which span the river like sieves to strain out unwitting floaters. Basically brown trout water, with excellent bank cover and undercuts, the Blackfoot here as elsewhere also harbors at least a smattering of brookies, cutts, rainbow, and bull trout.

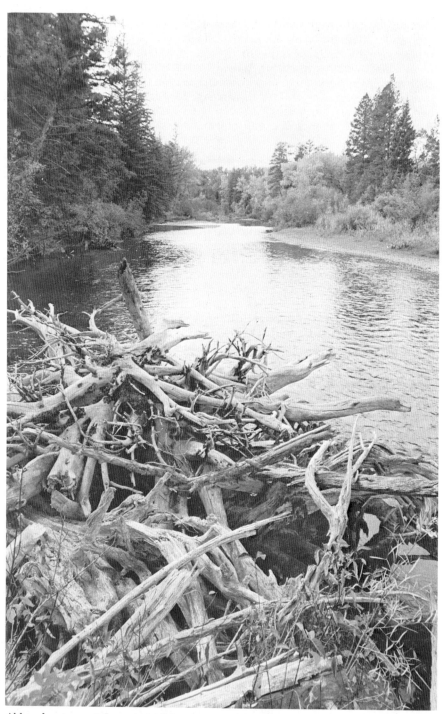

Although not as noted as a trout fishery as some other Montana rivers, the Blackfoot River offers more than 100 miles of unspoiled, free-flowing water, much of it filled with trout. Michael Sample photo.

From the Helmville bridge down to the confluence with the North Fork of the Blackfoot (a distance of nine miles by air, twenty-seven by river), the current flows very slowly over the mud-lined streambed and around uncountable bends. Some nice caddis hatches feed the resident brown trout, but Roos finds this section unappealing to most anglers and "sort of like trying to float a lake."

Below the confluence with the North Fork, the current and the fishing both pick up. Rainbow predominate. Some salmon flies, caddis, and mayflies along with plentiful terrestrials make for well-fed fish. Scenic values are exceptional, especially in the Box Canyon just below Scotty Brown Bridge.

Anyone wishing to float any section of the river between the County Line Fishing Access Site (FAS) and Johnsrud Park should consult Hank Fischer's *The Floater's Guide to Montana*. This rock-studded stretch has eaten more than its share of boats over the years. Even bank anglers find this section challenging. The fast and powerful current makes wading a chancy enterprise in places, especially when the water is still high. Moreover, anglers have more difficulty fishing pocket water around boulders than they do fishing standard riffle-pools. And because of the popularity of floating, anglers must put up with occasional disturbances. Nevertheless, the refreshing splash of whitewater, good numbers of trout, and the chance of hooking into a very rare lunker attract many anglers.

The last ten miles from Johnsrud Park to Bonner has much less hazardous water. Fishing that the Montana Department of Fish, Wildlife and Parks (FWP) rates as good to excellent comes mostly in the bends, at the mouths of little tributaries, and, especially, below the broad riffles.

Each year has its own peculiar flow pattern, but on average the Blackfoot produces a dramatic runoff starting in late April, peaking in late May, and dropping off sharply late in June and early July. As the water comes down, it usually clears remarkably fast. By August, it looks like the distilled water generally associated with Glacier Park's pristine streams.

Those anglers who relish getting out in the winter to catch whitefish find the Blackfoot to their liking. The lower river grows lots of whitefish, some of them very large. In 1977, the Blackfoot rewarded an angler with the state record mountain whitefish, a four-pound, nine-ounce fish. Although not generally thought of as a trophy fishery, the river has, in Roos's memory, produced five-pound rainbow and eight-pound browns. And Fred Tedesco, a fishing guide with the Western Rivers guide service in Helena, remembers a seventeen-pound bull trout being pulled out of one of the Blackfoot's tributaries.

Aside from some concerns about siltation from logging practices and the slim (but possible) chance of dam construction, the Blackfoot seems remarkably free of threats to its fishery. Irrigation withdrawals are negligible. Mining does not seem to pose a problem. Recreational cabin sites have not sprouted along the banks in any large numbers. Indeed, the Blackfoot is an intact trout stream, producing trout near its potential, harboring abundant wildlife along its flood plain, and dazzling visitors with its scenic beauty.

Fishing Strategies

Each river has its own physical makeup, its own flow characteristics, its own seasonal patterns, and its own type of trout food. These variables often weigh to the advantage of some fishing techniques while weighing to the disadvantage of others.

For example, anglers with spinning gear frequently find the Jefferson or the Yellowstone rivers more to their liking than the Big Hole. To bait anglers, the

Landers Fork

Lincoln

Blackfoot River

Nevada Creek

Scapegoat
Wilderness

North Fork

Blackfoot River

Browns
Lake

141

Aunt Molly

Cedar Meadow

Harry Morgan △

Ovando

△ River Junction

Garnet Range

Monture Creek

Scotty Brown Bridge △

Russ Gates
Memorial

Bear Creek

N

Sperry Grade

△

△ Clearwater Bridge

Clearwater Crossing

Salmon Lake

Clearwater River

200

△ Roundup Bar Bridge

83

Clearwater

Seeley Lake

Ninemile Prairie △

Riverbend △

Whitaker Bridge

Thibideau

McNamara Bridge

Johnsrud Park

K. Ross Toole △

Angevine △

Wisherd Bridge

Marco Flat △

Weigh Station

Clark Fork River

Dangerous diversion dam!

Milltown

BLACKFOOT RIVER

44

upper Beaverhead seems almost impossible, but the Missouri is another story. Dry fly aficionados find the upper Madison much more friendly than the Bighorn, but that same Bighorn smiles upon those using streamers and nymphs. And so on.

In contrast to these biased rivers, however, the Blackfoot is open to all comers. The Blackie will accommodate just about any trout fishing technique yet devised. Wherever an angler feels most comfortable operating, whether pool, run, riffle, boulder pocket, in a boat, from the bank, or wading mid-stream, the angler will find plenty of those friendly places somewhere in the Blackfoot's 100-mile length.

Because the Blackfoot has a relatively cold drainage, which stays in the grip of winter longer than most streams on the other side of the Divide, the trout are slow to become active. All methods of fishing can be intermittently good in April until the river muddies up, whereupon the river becomes the exclusive domain of the bait angler until July.

Becky Garland from Garland's Town and Country Store in Lincoln has been stocking and selling fishing tackle for years. Her customers who use bait usually go with earthworms, maggots (for whitefish), sculpins when the browns are running, sucker meat when trying for bull trout, and Pautzke's salmon eggs. She also sells Eagle Claw two-way spinners, small lures with colored beads or flashy metal pieces onto which the angler attaches a morsel of bait. As another alternative, some anglers use stonefly nymphs or grasshoppers with split shot.

As the river starts to clear, spinning gear becomes useful. Listening to her customers and noting what they purchase, Garland suggests that the smaller lures work much more effectively than the big hunks of metal. To stock a tackle box, she recommends Panther Martins (silver and gold), Mepps, Thomas Fighting Fish, and red and white Daredevles. If anglers wish to concentrate on bull trout, Frank Johnson, former owner of Streamside Anglers in Missoula, suspects that a sinking Rapala, fished deep, would be a good bet.

Depending upon the vagaries of a particular year's weather, the river may start to drop and become less turbid just as the salmon flies begin to emerge. Johnson rates the chances of finding a good hatch under fishable conditions as a long shot, perhaps one in four years. The smaller golden stoneflies hatch out a little later. The hatches start at the lower end of the river and progress upstream to the mouth of the North Fork, above which the hatch peters out due to heavy sediment on the riverbed.

Once the water clears, fly anglers watch for hatches of mayflies and caddis plus some terrestrials. Garland suggests trying red Ants, Mosquitoes, Humpies, and grizzly Wulffs in sizes 10 or 12. Johnson observes that, when fishing the riffles and pocket water "you can do better with attractors and larger-sized flies." Late in the summer, hopper patterns work well near the banks.

The late Joe Halterman once observed that one of the distinctive aspects of fishing the Blackfoot was the consistent surface action in the middle of the day, even during the heat of the summer. Dry fly anglers will generally do best working the shaded banks and places where trees and brush overhang the water.

One other fly pattern deserving attention here is the classic Muddler Minnow. Although the Muddler baffles outdoor writers who search for reasons for its success, clearly this fly works very well. Fished either wet or dry in the summer, the Muddler seems especially effective for autumn browns when kept under the surface.

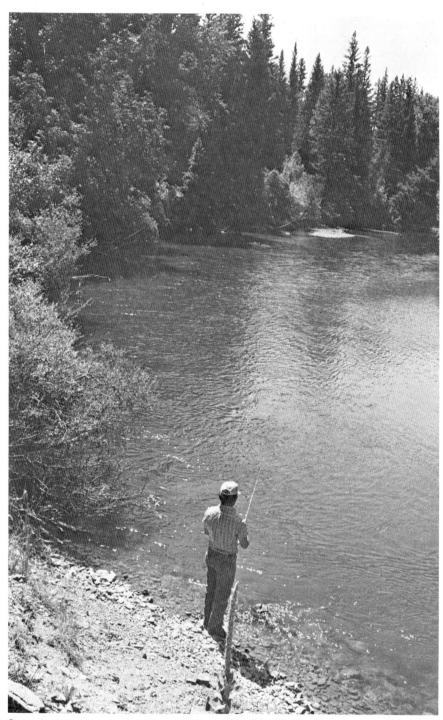

Some rivers require specific techniques, but the Blackfoot has such a variety of habitat that most types of fishing can be employed along the river. Michael Sample photo.

"For the average fly fisherman, bull trout are pretty inaccessible," says Johnson. He notes that an eighteen-inch bull trout eats six-inch minnows. Consequently, if he were concentrating on bulls, he would use a marlin fly (generally used in salt water) and get down near the bottom with a high-density sinking line.

While the Blackfoot has plenty of good trout water, it also has two types of places which could best be skipped by anglers. One of these typically shows up in the very slow stretches such as around Mineral Hill, where heavy deposits of sediment give the streambed a uniform color and consistency. Trout rightfully avoid these places because they are so easily spotted and thus vulnerable to predation. Anglers fishing these long, glassy slicks must analyze where the trout would feel safe.

For the same reasons, Roos recommends skipping places where the river crosses large slabs of bedrock, such as in several spots in Box Canyon. Trout do not find protective cover here, nor do they find much food.

One final suggestion comes from Davis: "When everyone is off chasing elk and deer in the hills during the hunting season, that's the best time to fish the Blackfoot." He sees very few anglers in the fall, but those he checks often report excellent angling. As a bonus, the brilliant fall colors along the Blackfoot would please even New Englanders.

Tributaries

Landers Fork lost much of its best holding water and vegetative cover during two recent flood years. Larry Davis, the FWP warden stationed in Lincoln, notes that few anglers do well in the bottom stretches of this geologically unstable stream, but as the anglers go upstream several miles from the highway, the fishing improves. Copper Creek, a tributary of Landers Fork, yields some nice cutthroat plus a few bull trout up to five pounds.

In the vicinity of Lincoln, a half dozen small streams and a few ponds sometimes provide exceptional fishing for those who can gain access, but that access is not always easy to come by. Make friends locally.

Nevada Creek "has some really good fishing for a little stream," in the opinion of Davis. Few anglers try this meandering stream, which holds some big browns and bulls in its somewhat murky water.

The North Fork of the Blackfoot has some of the most beautiful water in the state, thanks in part to its wilderness watershed. Several miles past the end of the road, a waterfall marks the top of the bull trout water. Above the falls, cutthroat and a few rainbow make up the fishery. Below the falls, larger cuts and rainbow mingle with bull trout up to fifteen pounds. The North Fork has its own access site, "Harry Morgan," not far from Ovando, as well as many miles of Forest Service access upstream.

Monture Creek is a long, rather small stream flowing through mostly private land, but with a nice FWP campground just off Highway 200. Most of the trout fall into the pan-sized category, but occasional larger fish provide pleasant surprises.

Cottonwood Creek has bushy banks and lots of undercuts, features which anglers find difficult but which brown trout relish. This small stream flows for about two miles through the Blackfoot-Clearwater Game Range. Tedesco remembers an eight-pound brown which rewarded one diligent angler here.

When springtime runoff has most area streams looking like chocolate pudding, the Clearwater River is a sight for sore eyes. With a chain of lakes

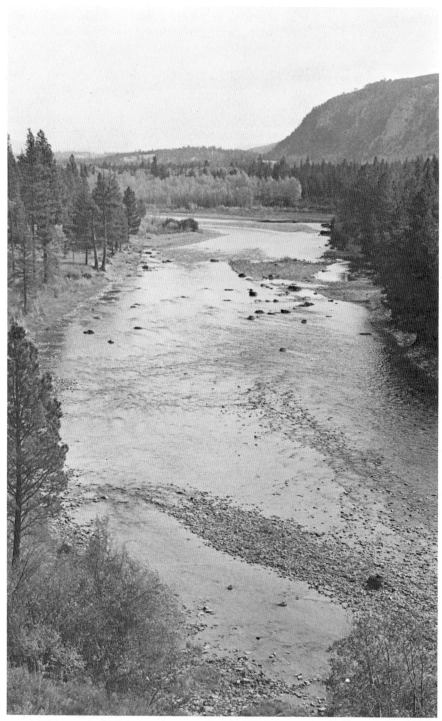

A good time to try for Blackfoot trout is in the fall when everybody else is up in the hills chasing elk. Michael Sample photo.

to settle out the sediment, the Clearwater runs high but clear from the foot of Salmon Lake to its junction with the Blackfoot, living beautifully up to its name. Although tough to fish because of innumerable willows and alders along undercut banks, the Clearwater provides some excellent fishing for sizeable browns before summer temperatures heat up.

The Blackfoot has more than a dozen other, smaller tributaries where adventuresome anglers sometimes try their luck at catching not only resident trout but also spawning lunkers.

Access

Anglers wishing to fish between Mineral Hill (where Helmville-Avon road—#141—crosses the river to join Highway 200) and the headwaters depend on casual access along the highway and county roads.

If interested in fishing the river from Mineral Hill downstream to Bonner, anglers would be wise to obtain a copy of the pamphlet *Montana Afloat #2, The Blackfoot River.*

"Aunt Molly" refers to a block of FWP land covering about five miles of the river frontage six to thirteen miles downstream from Mineral Hill. Road access is a county road leaving from Montana Highway 141 about two miles south of the Mineral Hill bridge.

Cedar Meadow, downstream from the Blackfoot's confluence with Nevada Creek, is more a boat launch spot than a place to fish extensively.

River Junction is an extensive camping and fishing spot that has no road access and thus is of use only to floating anglers.

Scotty Brown Bridge has no public land around it, but less than a mile downstream the recreation corridor begins, so some floaters launch here. County Line, just off the Highway, has campsites. Sperry Grade, two miles downstream, has good fishing above a series of rapids.

Clearwater Bridge is at the top of a two-mile section with two accesses and some casual road access.

The Roundup Bar Bridge marks the top of a sixteen-mile section loaded with access and including seven campgrounds. Anglers need to travel the gravel road which leaves the highway on the north end of the bridge and closely parallels the river down to Johnsrud Park, the end of the recreation corridor.

Below Johnsrud Park, river and Highway 200 rarely part company. Angevine Park is the last formal access site, but anglers can pull off at a number of spots. Floaters should not venture past the Bonner Weigh Station.

CLARK FORK

Think of the sure-fire titles for best-selling novels about this river: For those who love to cheer for the underdog, *The Comeback Story of the 1970s*. Romantics will swoon over *A Red River Goes Blue*, while Zane Grey devotees will surely snap up *Tough Trip From Hellgate to Paradise*.

No doubt about it, the Clark Fork is a river of many faces. An angler in the upper river who must drag his canoe across gravel bars might be skeptical, but the Clark Fork at Thompson Falls holds the undisputed title as Montana's mightiest river. If the angler were to canoe from Warm Springs all the way to Thompson Falls, he would paddle almost every conceivable kind of water, from a meandering, brush-choked brooklet to a powerful, full-fledged river with deep runs, fathomless pools, and whitewater.

Prior to 1973, no angler in his right mind would launch a canoe in the upper Clark Fork. A sickening mixture of municipal sewage and acidic and heavy metal wastes from the Anaconda Company's operations painted the river red and delivered a lethal blow to all aquatic life in the upper Clark Fork.

Once the Anaconda Company instituted an effective pollution abatement program and the river had a chance to cleanse itself, insects and fish slowly repopulated. At first only a marginal fishery, the upper Clark Fork now shows potential for becoming a first-rate trout stream.

Still standing in the way of complete health is an oversupply of nutrients, heavy metals in the floodplain, and an undersupply of instream water.

Frank Johnson, fishing guide and former owner of Missoula's Streamside Anglers, jokes about the taste of trout from the upper Clark Fork, knowing what happens in the headwaters. Butte, Anaconda, and Opportunity discharge sewage effluent into Silver Bow Creek, which then flows right through Anaconda Company's settling ponds.

But Montana Department of Fish, Wildlife and Parks (FWP) biologist Jim Vashro reports that, incredibly, the settling ponds function "almost as well as a tertiary sewer system," resulting in almost complete removal of even nitrates and phosphates from the water. Preliminary tests have shown that the liver and kidney tissues of fish in the Warm Springs area contain some heavy metals, but well below the federal Food and Drug Administration's suggested limits.

Just below the settling ponds, Silver Bow Creek combines with Warm Springs Creek to inaugurate the Clark Fork. From this point down for about twenty river miles, the stream supports bountiful numbers of brown trout. Short riffles separate a succession of deep pools and cavernous undercuts. Willows crowd the banks and lean over the water. Browns relish such cover.

Just below Deer Lodge, heavy local fishing pressure plus some pollution problems take their toll. Fish numbers and size drop off. The last few miles to Garrison Junction, the water "seems to grow tired," in the words of FWP biologist Don Peters.

However, when the Little Blackfoot River adds its clean, clear water at the junction, the dilution rejuvenates the Clark Fork and another good stretch of fishing ensues. Red-barked dogwood, aspen, and water birch create a distinctive riparian habitat here; foliage enthusiasts revel in autumn's red and yellows.

One of the Clark Fork's best fishing sections runs from Gold Creek to Drummond. Johnson ascribes this to "incredible, incredible habitat." Deep pools, eddies, and undercut banks, some a hundred yards long, present almost continuously ideal housing for browns.

Below Drummond, anglers begin to find a few rainbow and an occasional cutthroat. Trout populations in general decline severely, however, especially from Bearmouth to Rock Creek. This is due to critically high summer temperatures in the stream and to extensive channel alterations to accommodate the freeway.

Once again the Clark Fork benefits from its cooler, cleaner tributaries when Rock Creek adds its superb water. From the mouth of Rock Creek to Milltown Dam, trout abound again in impressive numbers and the aquatic life shows more diversity. Browns still predominate, but rainbow amount to thirty percent of the population. In contrast to the stream above Rock Creek, where relatively few anglers venture, many try their luck downstream to the dam.

Vashro and Peters think the condition of the brown trout in the upper Clark Fork has improved recently, but when the biologists electrofish, they still find some fish with large heads and skinny bodies. These "snakey" trout demonstrate that not all is right in the stream.

Curiously, the biologists also find an occasional large cutthroat, almost always in excellent condition. Peters thinks the cutthroat drop out of some tributaries when the fish reach such a size that the smaller water no longer seems secure. Yet cutthroat have a reputation for being finicky about water quality. As Hank Fischer says, "the Clark Fork's story doesn't add up quite right. No one has quite put the whole story together."

Unquestionably, the upper Clark Fork has a concentrated nutrient load. Municipal sewage plants, mining, and farming contribute an overly rich chemical balance to the water, which, in turn, triggers profuse algae growth.

Once nearly wiped out by pollution, the Clark Fork trout population has come back strong. Michael Sample photo.

During a sunny summer day, the algae (commonly known as moss) produces so much oxygen that the water can't get rid of it; oxygen builds to 150 percent of saturation. Then at night, algae and bacteria consume the oxygen so quickly that it drops to fifty percent of saturation. Peters notes that oxygen supersaturation has many of the same effects on fish as nitrogen supersaturation. "Moveover," he says, "the fluctuations are very hard on the trout."

Add yet another problem: summer water temperatures commonly reach critical levels, such as seventy-six degrees Fahrenheit at Bonita. Even the tolerant brown trout keel over during extended periods of such high temperatures.

Fish biologists and anglers agree that if the fishery on the upper Clark Fork is to improve, more of the stream's water must be kept within its banks, not siphoned off for irrigation during the summer. More water would not only dilute the nutrients but also keep temperatures at a healthier level. Less irrigation would result in less leaching of minerals from the soil, a benefit to ranchers as well as to the fishery.

The confluence of the Clark Fork and the Blackfoot marks not only a major transformation of the Clark Fork but also an interesting spot to compare the two rivers. While the Clark Fork above this juncture drains nearly twice as large a basin as the Blackfoot, the Clark Fork's flow is actually slightly less on the average than the Blackfoot's. While the Clark Fork carries a rich load of nutrients, the Blackfoot's water looks distilled by comparison. And while both rivers generally reach peak flow near the end of May, the Blackfoot has much the more spectacular runoff.

Below the confluence, the Clark Fork goes through a rapid transition. The water flattens. Riffles become more isolated. Deep pools alternate with runs. Instead of brush, boulders stud the shoreline.

Hordes of rough fish populate the river from Milltown Dam down through Hellgate Canyon. Peters reports that in all his electrofishing experience in rivers, he has never seen such a concentration of big suckers and squawfish. When the electrodes send their current across the section, the water turns white with rough fish, and the FWP crew has to hunt hard for the scarce trout.

The objects of much angling effort, a few brown trout and bull trout lunkers lurk in the big pool below the dam. Downstream, the trout population continues the shift from brown trout to rainbow. Below Kelly Island and the mouth of the Bitterroot, the browns practically disappear and rainbow rule the roost.

From Missoula to Superior, the average trout Johnson catches measures about sixteen inches. Peters concurs with this impressive estimate. Unfortunately, these big fish do not inhabit the river in big numbers. "The fish seem to be just in pockets," says Johnson. Peters describes the fishery as "real spotty in distribution, with lots of water between good spots." Fischer advises anglers to spend considerable time on the river to recognize "the subtle differences" between those places which house trout and those which prove to be empty residences.

In the late 1970s and early 80s, Peters found only about 250 trout per mile in the Superior area in his electrofishing surveys. More recent studies indicate trout numbers are up, closer to 500 fish per mile. He thinks now that the relatively low trout numbers are probably a result of past and present pollution. Juvenile trout are scarce, which also has FWP concerned.

Perhaps not by coincidence, the only truly fine tributary to the lower Clark

The big water of the lower Clark Fork—big trout, but hard to fish. Michael Sample photo.

Fork flows into the most productive section of the river below Kelly Island. Fish Creek joins the Clark Fork just after the river begins its way through Alberton Gorge (sometimes called Fish Creek Gorge), known primarily to whitewater rafting enthusiasts. Boulder-strewn rapids make hazardous boating for all but the most experienced rafters.

Anglers find it difficult to gain access to this section; even when they reach the banks, they still find the swift water a tough proposition to fish. But the effort may have its rewards, as good numbers of big rainbow find the gorge to their liking. Peters notes that the gorge marks the only section of the river below Kelly Island where electrofishing crews find more than spotty populations of trout.

An electrofishing survey near Superior turned up some cutthroat and bull trout as well as rainbow. While it may not appear to be classic cutthroat water, Johnson catches "some big and heavy natives" around Superior. Fischer reports that the stretch from Superior to Paradise doesn't get hit by fishermen at all. "I suspect that there aren't many trout," Fischer says, "but those that are there are bruisers."

Joe Huston, an FWP biologist, agrees that the section from St. Regis to Paradise, known locally as the "cutoff section," gets very little fishing pressure, primarily due to its distance from large population centers. In Huston's mind, the cutoff section should be termed a "real sleeper," because it holds good numbers of rainbow and bull trout as well as some browns, cutthroat, and whitefish. FWP's census shows about 400 fish per mile on this stretch, with an average size of sixteen inches. Anglers occasionally catch trophy-sized trout here, either in the riffle water of the upper section or in the pools of the last ten miles. The entire section is scenic, easily floated, and readily accessible from the highway.

At Paradise, the warmer water of the Flathead River mingles with the Clark Fork. Immediately a tendency toward more rough fish and few trout develops. Huston recommends one last productive area, the Weeksville rapids, a five-mile stretch west of Plains where some big rainbow enjoy the faster water. Other than that, the Clark Fork below Plains interests anglers primarily for its northern pike, some of which weigh over twenty pounds.

Fishing Strategies

Like most fish biologists, Vashro enjoys spending some of his leisure hours in pursuit of trout, not with the electrofishing gear, but with a fishing rod. In friendly competition with anglers he knows who fish from Warm Springs to Garrison Junction, he often compares notes on successes and failures.

Vashro acknowledges that bait users do well, generally with nightcrawlers. Oddly enough, sculpins work well too, even though they do not inhabit the upper reaches of the stream and must be imported. Anglers with gold Daredevles or Mepps catch fish here, as they do in most Montana waters.

Anglers using flies also do well, although they have a terrible time casting in close quarters with all the brush. He corroborates reports of massive caddis hatches ("just like a snow storm") and tells of finding 2,000 caddis nymphs per square yard of streambed. Montana nymphs and small, green Wooly Worms catch more than their share of fish; any small brown caddis imitation works nicely during a hatch. As an afterthought, Vashro suggests trying a Muddler or spruce fly under the banks.

However, Vashro thinks he has found a better way. It takes some practice to master. It's no secret—he will describe it to anyone who asks. He loves to tease fly and bait anglers about how well it works. For a pole, he wields an ultralight spinning rod, just perfect for in-close work around the willows. At the end of his monofilament line dangles his choice of enticements, a white Maribou jig.

How well does the jig work? Vashro proudly recounts four early mornings of fishing the Warm Springs area when he caught sixty fish between twelve and nineteen inches long. "And I only hooked about one in four that hit the jig," he says.

Any effective strategy on the upper river takes into account the scourge of moss. By mid-summer, both the green filamentous type of moss and the floating brown algae have bloomed in profusion. Bait and spin anglers quit in despair. Even those who fish dry flies spend a frustrating amount of time unwrapping the stuff from their feathered hooks. Some summers seem worse than others. Vashro suggests wading the middle of the river and casting to the edges with hopper patterns and Muddlers. "Fish them wet," says Vashro, "twitching them out into the current. And hang on—you'll get explosions." He can recall several fifty-fish days taking brown trout with this method in the Gold Creek area.

Fischer and Johnson try to avoid the floating gunk altogether, preferring to fish either early in the spring before runoff or immediately after the river comes back into fishable shape. Once the cold nights return in the fall, moss no longer presents a problem, and the fishing heats up.

Above Rock Creek, only a few mayflies and a handful of salmon flies struggle to continue their life cycles. Johnson reports that each year he sees a few more of each. But basically, this is caddis country. Like Vashro, Johnson recounts seeing clouds of caddis so thick that in a time-exposure photograph he took,

Legend:
- ━━━ HIGHWAY
- ---- COUNTY OR UNPAVED ROAD
- △ OFFICIAL PUBLIC ACCESS
- □ RANGER STATION
- X BRIDGE
- ∿∿∿ DIVERSION DAM

One inch = approx. 12 miles

Bitterroot River
12
Missoula
△ Brickyard
Milltown Dam
Sapphire Mountains
Turah △
Blackfoot River
Schwartz Creek
△
Clinton
Rock Creek Bridge
△ Beavertail
Rock Creek
Clark Fork River
John Long Mountains
Bearmouth
Garnet Bridge
Flint Creek
Drummond
Philipsburg
90
Jens
Georgetown Lake
Flint Creek Range
Gold Creek
Phosphate
Garnet Range
N→
Garrison
Little Blackfoot River
Warm Springs Cr.
Deer Lodge
Kohrs Bend △
12
Warm Springs
Anaconda settling ponds
Silver Bow Creek
To Butte
To Helena

CLARK FORK RIVER (Upper)

he could hardly see the water. Standard adult caddis patterns include the Henryville special, the Bucktail caddis, and the Elk Wing caddis. To boost the angler's arsenal, add a few hopper imitations as well as some Muddlers.

Vashro explored some undercut banks with a probe and found caverns going back under the banks as much as six feet. The current undercuts the stream banks much of the way from Warm Springs to Rock Creek. Brown trout favor the undercuts and the pool-eddy combinations; anglers should follow suit. Cast dry flies close to the bank; sinking flies, lures, and baits should go under the bank, if possible.

More anglers wet their lines between Rock Creek and the Milltown Dam than in any other comparable length of the river. Cold, fresh water from Rock Creek jolts the much warmer Clark Fork back to life. Insect life proliferates. Mayflies ride the breezes. Salmon flies, powerful magnets both for trout and anglers, crawl out of their cases and spend their short adult lives airborne before dropping to the water's surface as potential mouthfuls for waiting trout. The much-awaited hatch comes up the river from Missoula soon after peak runoff; the exact timing depends on the weather and water temperatures.

The river below the dam provides a tough test for the average angler. Instead of easy-to-read riffles, anglers will find long runs and pools that make fish habitat indefinite. Few places permit wading. The immense size of the river means the angler can only fish a small portion of any given stretch. Johnson comments, "There isn't a lot of character to it until you gain some experience. The inexperienced fisherman won't do as well here as on the Bitterroot."

Almost like a Florida angler cruising in search of a school of tarpon, Johnson either floats or drives in search of rising trout. He points out that between Missoula and Superior, about twenty places offer good lookouts not far from the highway. If one spot shows no hatch or feeding fish, he moves to the next one.

Johnson thinks matching the hatch meticulously is an unnecessary exercise. Feeding trout in the lower Clark Fork tend to be unselective and very active. "But," he says, "they may be in four-inch slots, and if you don't get your fly in that slot, they'll totally ignore it."

"It's a challenge on a really huge river," says Johnson, "to use techniques and flies which normally would be used on a spring creek." Johnson routinely makes eighty-foot casts with a sixteen-foot leader and size 20 flies. Admitting that anglers have slim chances of landing big fish with this equipment, he stresses the sport of trying anyway. "It's fun fishing."

Fischer also puzzles why some places hold fish while others don't but says that if you fish it enough, you find places where fish rise regularly. He cites an example, a place where the river speeds up and cuts into a bank. "It doesn't look any better than other banks," Fischer admits, "but I caught a fish there the last five times I've tried."

Fischer also recommends fall fishing. With different timing than Johnson, Fischer finds some large mayflies coming off the river in the afternoons and uses a big Wulff on the surface to fool the trout. Fischer thinks that the trout move into the shallow water with the advent of cooler weather. He especially likes a stretch that parallels a leaky irrigation ditch; the breaks in the ditch seem to aerate the water and make a good spot for trout.

Whether an angler chooses bait, lures, or flies, the same type of spots should hold his interest. Watch for deep banks, gravel riffles dumping into deeper water, and tributaries where they enter the main river. Work the pocket water

CLARK FORK RIVER (Lower)

Heron

Cabinet Gorge Reservoir

Noxon

Noxon Reservoir

Cabinet Mountains

Trout Creek

Idaho
Montana

Flat Iron Ridge△

Dam—Thompson Falls

Thompson River

Clark Fork River

St. Regis River

10

135

St. Regis

Plains

Paradise

Bitterroot Range

Superior

Perma

Flathead River

Flathead Lake

Lozeau
△ Forest Grove

Tarkio

Cy...

Natural Pier Bridge

200

Fish Cr

Petty Creek△

Alberton

Huson

Erskine△

Frenchtown

Harper Bridge

Maclay Bridge△

Kelly Island

△ Brickyard

Missoula

Milltown Reservoir

90

93

△ Turah

Bitterroot River

Blackfoot River

HIGHWAY
COUNTY OR UNPAVED ROAD
△ OFFICIAL PUBLIC ACCESS
☐ RANGER STATION
X BRIDGE
〜〜〜 DIVERSION DAM

One inch = approx. 20 miles

N

57

around boulders. Try to spot underground springs bubbling into the river. And skip the long, flat runs.

This river requires experience. Anglers unfamiliar with the river should not expect instant success. Try floating some sections; no other way provides such a fast education.

Bank anglers should enjoy the confusing channels around Kelly Island or the boulder-filled reaches in Alberton Gorge. For the adventurous who like to search out far away, relatively unknown water, the cutoff section promises a chance for a lunker.

Tributaries

Four major tributaries to the Clark Fork have chapters in this book devoted to them: Rock Creek, and the Blackfoot, Bitterroot, and Flathead rivers.

Warm Springs Creek provides very important spawning water but nearly runs dry in late summer. A number of other small tributaries (which shall remain nameless because they could not withstand much increase in pressure) support surprising numbers of trout. Peters recalls finding one that could be crossed in places without getting the ankles wet, yet harbored a three-pound brown and quite a few fifteen-inchers in the pools between the shallow riffles.

Peters rates the Little Blackfoot "a fine fishery, even though it has been abused by channel alterations." An FWP study found thirty catchable trout in a bulldozed section, but more than ten times that number in a comparable, but unaltered, section nearby. In addition to some good-sized browns, the Little Blackie also fosters some cutthroat and rainbow in its deep pools, undercuts, and logjams. Vashro suggests fishing from Elliston to Avon or below Avon in the intact sections. Quite a few local anglers, especially from Helena, already fish this stretch. The river flows through private land here; be sure to get permission from the landowners before crossing their property.

Excessive withdrawals, sediment, and some pollution problems hurt Flint Creek, but the stream still manages to support some nice browns. Peters says the access is mostly on private land, but the landowners normally grant permission.

Rattlesnake Creek is closed to fishing from its headwaters down to the Missoula water supply dam. From the dam to the mouth, local anglers work for spawning trout during the runs. Because the Clark Fork does not receive enough population recruitment from its tributaries, Peters thinks even the lower Rattlesnake may someday be protected for the spawners.

Most of Fish Creek's watershed lies within undeveloped public land, which makes for outstanding water quality. "I consider it the best potential cutthroat water in the region," exclaims Peters. Rainbow also favor the lower reaches.

"Someone has always been mucking around with the St. Regis River," notes Peters. After some mining, two railroads, and a superhighway ripped up the stream bottom, little fishery remains, although current efforts to improve the stream habitat may help in the future.

The upper reaches of the Thompson River attract Kalispell anglers for pan-sized brookies, rainbow, and cutthroat. The middle twenty miles hold mostly rainbow up to twenty inches plus some brookies and whitefish. Occasional browns and bull trout, or "char" as they are called locally, run with the predominant rainbow in the last fifteen miles. Huston finds some trout up to five pounds, probably out of the Clark Fork, in the lower reaches. He rates the salmon fly hatch on the Thompson "second only to Rock Creek." The

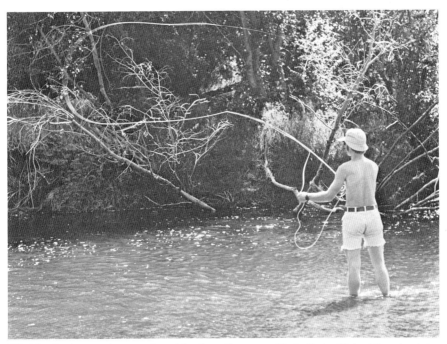

Working for browns in an undercut bank on the upper Clark Fork. Michael Sample photo.

hatch comes earlier here than on other streams, usually in mid to late May. Almost the whole length of the river below Thompson Lakes runs close to roads.

Access

Much of the Clark Fork runs just a cast or two from a highway. Because the river intertwines so much with the highway and railroad tracks, anglers have a wide choice of pull-outs. In many cases, the highway right-of-way includes the thin strip of land between road and river, providing undeveloped but convenient public access.

In addition to the informal accesses, passage to the river is granted by FWP fishing access sites (FAS), bridge crossings, and corporate landholders such as Champion International. Of these, some of the most important are mentioned below.

Leaving Interstate 90 at Warm Springs, anglers can reach the top of the river through FWP's Game Management Area. FWP has another access, Khors Bend, reached by the Beck Hill exit off I-90 east of Garrison. Vashro reports that the landowners between these accesses usually grant permission to fish. Floaters and anglers also utilize several bridges between Warm Springs and Garrison Junction.

Floating from the Gold Creek bridge to Drummond allows the angler to fish the most remote section of the Clark Fork, but at least one landowner along this stretch has some pronounced unfriendly feelings towards outsiders. Stay off the banks and watch for a strand of electrified wire stretched across the river.

Below Drummond's municipal park, anglers may wish to pull into the Bearmouth Rest Area for I-90 westbound travelers. The river borders the rest area beside a beautiful stand of quaking aspen. Also try the pond for some fair-sized stocked trout.

The fishing access at Beavertail Hill just above Rock Creek would best be used during the cooler portions of the fishing season. Below Rock Creek, water temperatures do not present such a problem. A private landowner currently allows fishing around the Schwartz Creek Bridge just upstream from Clinton, and FWP maintains an access site at the northeast corner of the bridge. FWP has another access near the tiny community of Turah.

The bridge at Milltown makes a good starting point for a float to the Sharon FAS in East Missoula, which also has a boat ramp. Anglers can reach the river almost anywhere in the city of Missoula. Just below Missoula, FWP has a major fishing access site, Kelly Island, which can be reached from either side. The boat ramp is on the south side of Kelly Island off Spurgin Road.

Other accesses between Missoula and St. Regis include Council Grove, the Champion land at Big Flat, Harpers Bridge, Petty Creek, Cyr FAS, and Forest Grove (upstream from Superior on the northside road). Access below St. Regis rarely presents a problem.

Almost all of the Clark Fork grants easy floating, but a few diversion dams (such as around Missoula) and some big rapids (as in Alberton Gorge) demand considerable skill and caution. For more thorough information on floating, see *The Floater's Guide to Montana* by Hank Fischer and the pamphlet, *Montana Afloat #4, the Clark Fork River.*

FLATHEAD RIVER

Anglers talking about the "Flathead" may be referring either to the magnificent lake or to the mighty river that feeds it. Together the lake and river make a complete system; the lake supplies the fish while the river supplies the spawning grounds.

The Flathead River and its forks make up a unique fishery in Montana because most large game fish are nonresidents traveling from Flathead Lake. Compared with some of the nutrient-rich rivers in southern Montana, the Flathead's pure, nutrient-poor water supports less aquatic life. Tough winters, cold water, and low chemical content combine to make water gorgeous to look at but less than hospitable for fish.

Thus, river anglers have Flathead Lake to thank for providing quarry on a seasonal basis. The lake acts like a giant heart, pumping pulses of fish into its arteries. In spring, cutthroat and bull trout start their spawning runs; in fall, major pulses of lake whitefish follow.

For the bulls and cutthroats, the eventual destinations are the tiny headwater creeks that branch off the Middle and North Forks. Some travel up to 130 miles before stopping to make their redds and deposit their eggs. The lake whitefish generally run only as far as Blankenship Bridge on the main Flathead.

Actually, the Flathead has three forks, but Hungry Horse Reservoir gobbled up much of the South Fork, and the dam cut off upstream migration from Flathead Lake. The short section of the South Fork below the dam holds few fish because of a lack of fish food and severe fluctuations in the volume of water released by the dam.

However, for the hardy angler who can solve the access problems, the upper fifty miles of the South Fork above the reservoir have much to offer. The river there not only has a spawning run of bull trout and resident cutthroat trout, but also a handsome setting in the pristine Bob Marshall Wilderness. As with most of the Flathead River system, the pleasure of being out in such beautiful country adds an extra dimension to fishing the South Fork.

In addition, the South Fork has the best catch rates of the three forks, due in part to "wilderness limits" recently established to protect the cutthroat

The Flathead River System has always been noted for its large bull trout. Scott Crandell photo.

fishery. Many anglers catch an average of ten cutthroat an hour; ten to thirty percent of these fish range from twelve to eighteen inches.

The best fishing on the South Fork is at Big Prairie, about thirty miles into the wilderness. Fishing is also good just below the Meadow Creek Gorge or two to four miles beyond the Meadow Creek wilderness portal.

The Middle Fork originates deep in the Bob Marshall Wilderness. Officially designated a "wild river" for the first half of its length, the Middle Fork plunges swiftly from the confluence of Strawberry and Bow creeks to Bear Creek. From Bear Creek, U.S. Highway 2 closely parallels the river for the second half of its course to the mouth of the North Fork.

The upper section of the Middle Fork provides fishing, floating, and spectacular backcountry experiences; the lower section offers floating but only marginal fishing. Pat Graham of the Montana Department of Fish, Wildlife and Parks (FWP) rates the fishing on the lower section "poor." Local anglers such as Gary Collier, however, like the section from Bear Creek to Coram for bull trout.

The Middle Fork marked the epicenter of the infamous 1964 flood. On an annual basis, the Middle Fork averages a discharge of less than 3,000 cubic feet per second (cfs), but on June 9, 1964, the river gushed 140,000 cfs and scoured its streambed so badly that the results will be obvious for years to come. Fortunately, such a flood should occur only once in about 200 years.

Much of the upper Middle Fork runs through steep-walled canyons with big, deep pools. After a muddy runoff in May and June, the river drops and clears rapidly. Anglers who want to float from Schaefer Meadows to Bear Creek try to time their trip to include the brief period when the water has substantially cleared but still runs in sufficient volume to carry rafts over the rocks. Each year has its own weather patterns, but this period generally comes between June 20 and July 15.

Because of the area's remoteness, the upper Middle Fork receives little fishing pressure. In the earlier part of summer, anglers work primarily for westslope cutthroat. In late July and August, anglers search for trophy-sized bull trout.

FWP's Pat Graham likes a description he heard of the North Fork: "a baby thrashing around in a cradle." He explains that, in the spring, the river runs high, throwing rocks and trees all over, while in the fall, the North Fork is a tiny river meandering through a big floodplain. The sides of the cradle include the Whitefish Range to the west and the awesome peaks of the Livingstone Range to the east. The North Fork marks the western boundary of Glacier National Park.

One of the unusual features of the North Fork watershed is that five of the drainages out of Glacier are interrupted by large, deep, fjord-type lakes. Referred to geologically as "sinks," these lakes trap many biologically important chemicals and release water with very low nutrient levels.

The first quarter of the North Fork hails from Canada. The United States portion runs fifty-nine miles to its confluence with the Middle Fork near the Blankenship Bridge. Although the two forks have some similarities such as size, wilderness watersheds, and low nutrient levels; the North Fork drains a larger area, has a more gradual gradient, and faces more serious environmental threats.The environmental concerns center on logging, residential development, and coal mining; although oil and gas exploration looms as a possible fourth problem. Frantic logging activity aimed at salvaging lodgepoles ravaged by mountain pine beetle has already partly denuded and ripped up some of the lower drainages on the west side.

More seriously, a multi-national mining company planned to develop open pit mines to recover reserves of high-grade coal. The plans include diverting Howell Creek, building a coal preparation plant, and developing the roads for the expected heavy use. FWP fears coal development would have serious impacts on water quality and on the trout's spawning and rearing success. An international joint commission studied the plans and recommended against development; for now, the plans are on hold.

Graham found records as far back as 1933 indicating that fishing on the North Fork has never been considered fabulous. Most of the cutthroats caught measure less than ten inches. Fishing for the elusive trophy-sized bull trout is rarely a fast and furious proposition because they usually number one or two to a hole.

Yet anglers who know the North Fork will think that this kind of creel census misses the point. Bill Schneider, who liked to cool his heels in the North Fork after working trail crew in Glacier Park, thinks the experience has more to do with the beautiful scenery, exceptional water quality, and the wildness of the country rather than with the fish numbers.

Born of glaciers, running free and wild, the North Fork has a lore about it. The exceptional can, and often does, happen. An angler recounts seeing a grizzly sow and cubs feeding on camas along a bank. A rafter enthuses about running Fool Hen Rapids. In a stroke of unbelievable luck, a biologist recaptures a tagged cutthroat that has just traveled seventy miles from British Columbia to below Columbia Falls in under twenty-four hours.

At their meeting just upstream from Blankenship Bridge, the North and Middle forks normally carry about the same amount of water. This confluence marks the beginning of the main Flathead. In about ten miles, the unpredictable flows of the South Fork join in. At times the South Fork hardly moistens its streambed, but at peak discharges it may more than double the size of the main Flathead.

For its fifty-five-mile journey to Flathead Lake, the big river meanders broadly through an increasingly populated floodplain. With a gradient of less than four feet per mile, the sluggish water languishes in sloughs and backwaters and braids around islands. In the marshy country near the outlet, the river and lake become almost indistinguishable; the exact division depends on the season and on releases from Kerr Dam at the south end of the lake.

The last few miles of river not only make a thoroughfare for the migrating fish, they also hold some good numbers of nonmigrating fish year-round. Many of the big cutthroat spend the winter in this section of the river. Because of this and the section's proximity to Kalispell, anglers pressure this stretch more than any other.

The main Flathead below the lake continues to hold its picturesque qualities but holds little promise for the trout-seeker. Larry Petersen of the U.S. Fish and Wildlife Service blames the poor spawning streams for the dearth of trout. Most available streams either dry up due to diversions or silt over so badly as to be unsuitable for fishing.

The lower Flathead does have a few cutthroat, rainbow, brown, and bull trout; but in such a large river their small numbers make them few and far between. Another game fish, the northern pike, provides most of the piscatorial excitement, especially in the backwaters and below Dixon. Petersen found

Cabin Creek

Canada
Montana

Kintla Lake

North Fork Flathead River

Ford Creek

Ford

Whale Creek

Bowman Lake

Quartz Lake

Riverfront

Polebridge

Whitefish Range

North Fork Road

Logging Lake

Glacier National Park

Coal Creek

Camas Creek Bridge

Big Creek

Cottonwood Point

N

Canyon Creek

Middle Fork Flathead River

West Glacier

Blankenship Bridge

County Road

2

93

Hungry Horse

Columbia Falls

40

South Fork Flathead

424

Hungry Horse Reservoir

HIGHWAY
COUNTY OR UNPAVED ROAD
△ OFFICIAL PUBLIC ACCESS
☐ RANGER STATION
X BRIDGE
〰 DIVERSION DAM

One inch = approx. 14 miles

NORTH FORK OF THE FLATHEAD RIVER

he could tag a pike, release it, and return to the exact same place in the river weeks later to find the pike again. The northerns often weigh in at over twenty pounds.

The Northern Plains Resource Council hopes to restore kokanee and boost populations of cutthroat and bull trout in the main Flathead to offset losses incurred by the construction and operation of hydroelectric dams. The council's plans call for enhanced habitat, improved fish passage, regulated water temperatures, and stocking with hatchery fish.

Fishing Strategies

On most other rivers, anglers can usually approach their favorite holes anytime during the season confident that fish will be there. Not so on the Flathead.

Graham states that "the harsh and relatively unproductive nature of the upper river system has favored the development of migratory fish forms." When those fish aren't migrating past a particular hole, that hole may well be empty of fish. As biologist Laney Hanzel puts it, "Timing is the key. People just don't understand that the fish are here today and gone tomorrow." Thus knowing the fish, and when they do what, is helpful—even critical—to the Flathead angler.

The westslope cutthroat move out of the lake first. Before completion of Hungry Horse Dam, the cutthroat apparently waited until April. Now, fooled by the relatively warm releases from the reservoir, the cutthroat sense spring has sprung as early as February. By the time runoff has reached full tilt, cutthroat are spawning in the tributaries, some as far as 136 miles from the lake.

While the slow journey upstream takes several months, the trip back may be accomplished overnight. Graham thinks most come back to the lake while the full tide of runoff still swells the river. He has tagged fish to back up his theory.

Yet, anglers report catching some big cutthroat even into August. Schneider proudly remembers a beautiful nineteen-inch cutthroat he caught in a backwater pool late in the summer. Collier has photographs he took on float trips in July that show whole strings of what he calls "red bellies"—big cutthroat with pronounced red undersides and a little orange around the gills. Graham notes that the upper Middle and South forks produce more large fish during the summer than does the North Fork.

Fishing season on the Flathead traditionally opens in the latter part of May, when the river runs pell-mell with snowmelt and dirt. Collier waits for the time when the river starts to clear but still has a murky green color to it. He thinks many people mistakenly wait for crystal clear water. When he sees the green water, he fishes with split shot and scrap pieces of beef. Other anglers use worms or hellgrammites, but beef has worked best for Collier.

Once the water completely clears, Collier turns to flies to catch the cutthroat, which he finds not very choosey about different patterns. "They're hungry, and anything halfway close to what they're looking for is good enough." Two patterns he personally favors are the Royal Coachman and the Irresistible.

Fish biologists rate the cutthroat as the least predacious of the trout family. Oddly enough, the Flathead cutthroat share the river with the highly predacious bull trout. Early in its life, the bull trout turns to a fish diet; for this reason bulls grow big. Collier recalls a twenty-three-pounder that decorates the wall of a local tavern.

MIDDLE FORK OF THE FLATHEAD RIVER

SOUTH FORK OF THE FLATHEAD RIVER

FLATHEAD RIVER

Like the cutthroat, the bull trout begin their spawning runs in spring, but their runs tend to be slower and more spread out. Graham reports finding bulls in the Canadian section of the North Fork while others are still straggling out of Flathead Lake. Generally, he found only one or two in each appropriate hole, but later in the summer the bulls sometimes congregate at the mouths of certain tributaries. The fish wait until fall to actually spawn on their distinctive redds, usually in the small streams and headwaters of the watershed.

When Collier floats the Flathead and its forks, he often has two rigged rods at hand. One stands ready for the cutthroat while the other, heavier rod stays in reserve for likely looking spots to try for bulls.

At the end of the bull trout rod dangles a Wilson Wobbler, a four-inch wooden plug available locally. The handmade plugs derive their back-and-forth action from curves filed into their sides. To be effective, the plug must go to the bottom where the bulls lie. Collier notes that some plugs stay on the surface. "Throw them out," he advised, "they're worthless."

Collier looks for "bars" about four or five feet deep to work for the bulls. Water that either rushes or lies almost motionless will not impart the right wandering motion to his plug.

For bull trout, Collier prefers the North Fork. He hasn't found as many in the upper Middle or South forks, but at times he has done well in both. Although he doesn't fish it as often, he knows a number of local anglers who favor the Middle Fork between Bear Creek and Coram.

Other anglers have different methods of catching bulls. Fred Nelson from Bozeman, for example, likes flies. Using large, colorful streamers, he once caught eight bulls in three days' fishing. He feels the most important factor is getting the flies down in front of the bulls.

All three forks of the Flathead have sizeable populations of cutthroat trout, a species requiring high water quality. Michael Sample photo.

Schneider and many others prefer a bass plug known as a Bassoreno. Painted red and white, the Bassoreno imitates a cutthroat.

FWP figures anglers fish an average of ten hours per bull trout caught. Because FWP currently regulates the Flathead as a trophy fishery, allowing anglers to keep only one bull, some might think bull trout too time-consuming to pursue.

When asked why he fishes for bulls, Collier replies, "I'm always looking for the big one." So far his biggest weighed seventeen pounds, but he wants one over twenty. A twenty-five-pound, ten-ounce bull caught in 1916 still stands as the state's record.

In the meantime, Collier will continue to enjoy the thrill of having his line stripped from his reel and marvel at the big ones that have straightened his stout hooks.

A new addition to the Flathead fishery is a run of lake whitefish in the fall. Lake whitefish generally do not spawn in rivers, but the Flathead population apparently has not read the textbook. They crowd into the river by the hundreds of thousands from the mouth of the Stillwater to Blankenship Bridge. These fish are the alter egos of their cousins, mountain whitefish. They range from 1.5 to three pounds and prove as tasty as they are hard-fighting.

Anglers jostle shoulder to shoulder around the popular holes near Kalispell to vie for a bucketful of whitefish. The standard set-up is a green or chartreuse jig fished on the bottom in calm eddies.

Until recently, the Flathead also produced a spectacular fall run of kokanee. Anglers lining the banks would snag more than 100,000 salmon, and another 100,000 fish would squeeze between the banks of McDonald Creek in Glacier National Park to spawn. Their dying throes attracted hundreds of bald eagles, which in turn attracted thousands of tourists who came to watch the drama.

Now the salmon runs are gone, the victim of a combination of dam construction and operation, overharvest, predation, and the accidental introduction of mysis shrimp, which compete with kokanee for food in Flathead Lake. The collapse of the Flathead salmon fishery offers a dramatic lesson in the dangers of tinkering with complex ecosystems.

Tributaries

All three forks of the Flathead derive their water not from one or two major tributaries, but from a myriad of small streams. An angler walking along the banks of these tiny streams would expect to find only pan-size fish. Imagine the surprise of seeing hefty two-pound cutthroat and bull trout so big they may be mistaken for logs, swimming in water hardly deep enough to cover their backs.

Fish as far along in their spawning cycle as those found in the tributaries rarely feed until after spawning is completed. Graham reports that the bulls probably don't feed at all once they begin making their redds, but they may strike at annoying flies and lures.

Mortality rates for the spawning bulls may run as high as fifty percent, Graham estimates. The exhausting run up the river, lack of food, predation, and the stress of spawning in tiny streams takes a heavy toll on the big fish. For this reason, FWP closes certain tributaries to fishing to protect the bulls from harassment. Check current regulations closely before fishing.

Glacier Park feeds the North Fork through streams coming out of Kintla, Bowman, Quartz, and Logging lakes. The fish in these streams are under the

Going after a big one—as usual. The Flathead River System has fishing for all anglers. Michael Sample photo.

jurisdiction of the National Park Service, not FWP, but angling in the park is also closely regulated. Check with rangers at any of the major ranger stations before wetting a line.

The Whitefish and Stillwater rivers combine and flow into the main Flathead not far upstream from Flathead Lake.

Bob Domrose reports that the Whitefish River leaves Whitefish Lake with very little gradient and only a few trout but with a lively population of northern pike. Eight or ten miles down, the gradient picks up, and with it, the trout fishing. Where streambank alterations haven't disturbed habitat, pools and riffles harbor cutthroat and some dandy 1.5- to three-pound rainbow. But the last stretch of the river flattens out again, and fishing is often disappointing here unless the angler hankers after trash fish.

Belying its name, the upper Stillwater rolls out of the Whitefish Range on a steep gradient and slows down only after it hits the valley floor. Domrose recommends the upper sections primarily for cutthroat; he recommends the section around Stillwater Lake and down to the mouth of Logan Creek for rainbow, brookies, and cutthroat. Below this, the river becomes much too slow and heavily silted for trout; the challenge here is northern pike, some in the twenty-pounds and up range. The last segment from Highway 93 to the Flathead provides a minor exception, offering a few pools and riffles that furnish acceptable trout habitat.

The Swan River empties into Flathead Lake right in the midst of the town of Bigfork, but it begins in some of the most rugged, wild, and strikingly beautiful country in Montana—the Mission Mountains Wilderness. Tumbling out of cold, pristine lakes such as High Park, Grey Wolf, and Crystal, the headwater streams drop rapidly until the Swan nears Montana Highway 83. Thereafter, it meanders with a riffle, pool, riffle pattern to Swan Lake.

Below the lake, the Swan sprints four miles, then flattens out for a very slow ten miles to the small impoundment near Bigfork. Below the dam, the Swan goes through one last frenzied rush—"the wild mile"—over a boulder-strewn streambed before calmly running into Flathead Lake.

Anglers catch a few rainbow and lake trout below the dam, some rainbow below Swan Lake, and cutthroat, rainbow, and brook trout above Swan Lake and in the tributaries.

But much of the angling interest in the river centers on the big bull trout that run out of Swan Lake. Trout in the five- to fifteen-pound class are not to be sniffed at anywhere, but when caught in what ordinarily would be called small-fish water, they look monstrous. It happens every summer in the upper reaches of the Swan and stirs up plenty of excitement. For the angler who prefers to catch one very large fish instead of a whole creel of little ones (and who has the necessary patience), Swan River bull trout fishing could be the highlight of a summer.

The tributaries of the lower Flathead suffer badly from irrigation diversions. Of the possible streams, Larry Petersen of the U.S. Fish and Wildlife Service singles out only the Jocko River for passable fishing. Petersen reports that a run of rainbow comes up the Jocko during high water. Anglers also find a smattering of cutthroat, browns, and a few bull trout.

Access

To fish the North Fork, most anglers utilize the North Fork Road, which runs about fifty-five miles from the Canadian border to Columbia Falls. The

Glacier View Ranger Station in Columbia Falls has information and a helpful map for the whole North Fork area.

The road closely parallels the river, giving anglers considerable casual access, especially for the southern third of the river. Major points of access include Blankenship Bridge, Big Creek Campground, Camas Bridge, Coal Creek, Polebridge, a campground three miles north of Polebridge, and the Ford Station.

The North Fork can also be reached from Glacier National Park by two roads. One is the paved Camas Creek Road from Apgar to the Camas Bridge, where it joins with the North Fork Road. Aside from the Camas Bridge, this road gives no other access to the river.

The second road is a narrow, twisting dirt road that also departs from the Apgar area and forks at Polebridge to either Bowman or Kintla lakes. From Logging Creek to Kintla Creek, this monster of a road stays close to the North Fork. Anglers who don't mind short hikes through timber can reach many otherwise inaccessible spots via this road but must count on very slow driving.

Above Bear Creek, the Middle Fork flows through the Great Bear and Bob Marshall Wildernesses. To fish the upper Middle Fork, the angler faces an unusual choice—hike, ride a horse, or go by plane to the Schaefer Meadows airstrip. Those who do make the effort think it well worth the rewards. Fishing in a beautiful wilderness area is the peak experience of a lifetime for some, but reaching the river obviously requires more effort and planning than just pulling off the highway into a developed access area.

From Bear Creek down to the confluence with the North Fork, river and road stay close together. Several access points exist. Anglers need only cross the railroad tracks or negotiate some steep hillsides to reach the river.

Like the Middle Fork, the South Fork has wilderness beginnings. Anglers hike or pack in from Seeley Lake or Holland Lake to the headwaters in the Bob Marshall Wilderness. Another route is to drive around Hungry Horse Reservoir to Spotted Bear Ranger Station or to Bunker Creek, and then hike along the river.

The main Flathead is accessible at the Blankenship Bridge at the mouth of the South Fork, along a small park next to U.S. Highway 2, at Kokanee Bend and Pressentine Bar accesses, from the old Steel Bridge, and at the mouth of the Stillwater.

The lower Flathead flows through the Flathead Indian Reservation and has no formal, developed access sites. However, it can be reached right in Polson, at Buffalo Bridge, at Sloan Bridge, and from Highway 200 most of the way from Dixon to the confluence with the Clark Fork. Within the Flathead Indian Reservation, anglers must have a tribal recreational use permit. Inquire locally.

For information about floating anywhere on the Flathead River system, and especially on the forks, read Hank Fischer's *Floater's Guide to Montana*. The North and Middle forks contain stretches of highly technical and dangerous whitewater that should be avoided by all but experienced rafters. The Middle Fork boasts several reaches of class IV to VI rapids, notably from Schaefer Meadows to Bear Creek and just above West Glacier. Float maps are available from the Flathead National Forest.

GALLATIN RIVER

The Gallatin drainage offers a diversity of trout fishing opportunities unmatched by Montana's other major rivers. The angler working the forty-mile canyon of the Gallatin River can choose among mountain stream riffles, boulder-dotted pocket water, surging runs, and deep pools. Below the canyon mouth, the Gallatin braids and spreads out to provide a selection of readily wadeable channels for the fisherman. The East Gallatin River represents a totally different fishing experience—a serpentine hay-meadow stream, lined with deeply undercut willow banks. Finally, the main Gallatin River, formed by the junction of the East and upper Gallatin rivers, hosts a full complement of steady runs, long pools, and gravelly riffles, along with an opportunity for solitude not often experienced on southwestern Montana's other major rivers.

The quality of trout fishing within these sections of the Gallatin drainage depends on the angler's ability to adapt his approach to differences in flows, habitat features, and fish populations. Armed with the proper techniques at the proper time and place, the angler can have the opportunity to see the true colors of the blue-ribbon Gallatin River.

The Gallatin River heads in the remote northwest corner of Yellowstone National Park and, after exiting the park, parallels U.S. Highway 191 for its northward journey through Gallatin Canyon. From the park boundary downstream for about fifteen miles to the mouth of the West Fork, the Gallatin hosts a trout fishery of primarily pan-sized rainbow, although occasional browns and cutthroat are taken. Lack of deep holding areas and snowmelt-cold water temperatures are the major factors limiting trout numbers and growth rates, with most fish less than a foot long. Still, some of the biggest fish in the river lurk in this upper section below Yellowstone National Park.

Whitefish thrive in the shallow riffles that characterize this stretch of the Gallatin, and the angler can enjoy good action on "whities" and feisty rainbow. This upper part of the Gallatin is a particularly good place for beginning fly fishermen because of the open channel, generally manageable wading conditions, and the agreeable nature of whitefish and rainbow to take a fly.

Near the confluence with the West Fork, the rocky substrate of the Gallatin becomes peppered with numerous large boulders. The trout take advantage of the protection from the current and hold in the pockets behind the midstream rocks. Picking these pockets with either flies or lures is the most successful technique, especially when water temperatures have warmed enough to put fish on the feed. An occasional big rainbow can be taken here, particularly by anglers who work some of the less obvious or difficult-to-reach holding areas.

The waters of the West Fork boost both the flow and the trout population of the main river. For twenty-two miles below this largest tributary, the Gallatin surges through a series of powerful runs and swirling pools. Submerged boulders and large rapids give rise to some of Montana's best whitewater. The final eight miles of the canyon below Squaw Creek lose the whitewater but retain a swift flow with good deep holding water.

Trout populations in the canyon section of the Gallatin are estimated at about 1,300 fish over ten inches in length per mile of river. Most of the trout are rainbow, the majority less than fourteen inches long. The shortage of big fish relates to cold water temperatures and relatively slow growth rates; it takes about five years for most rainbow to reach a length of fourteen inches in the rushing canyon waters. Nevertheless, rainbow and occasional browns in the three- to five-pound class are caught in the canyon each year, not to mention the "ones that get away" in the strong current.

The most productive section of the Gallatin runs from the mouth of the canyon to the bridge at Gallatin Gateway. Here the river tames to a series of riffles, runs, and pools; and undercut cottonwood banks replace the rocky, pine-dotted slopes of the canyon. A few fish over two pounds inhabit this stretch, with brown trout becoming common. Fish in the ten-pound class are reported almost every year.

Below Gallatin Gateway, the river spreads across the valley floor into a network of channels. Here the waters of the West Gallatin are coveted by more than trout fishermen. Agriculture is king in the Gallatin Valley; and pumps, canals, and diversions start claiming their share of the flow for irrigation. Banks altered by bulldozers compound the problem of water withdrawals in some locations. Some sections in the river literally go dry each summer, and most of the remainder is dewatered enough to keep trout populations far below their potential.

The entire Gallatin, from its headwaters in Yellowstone National Park to its junction with the East Gallatin near Manhattan, is closed to float fishing, by order of the Montana Fish and Game Commission. This closure, designed to prevent conflict between floaters and bank fishermen, has been generally well accepted because of good public access to the river throughout the canyon and because the stream is relatively narrow and thus can be fished effectively by a wading angler.

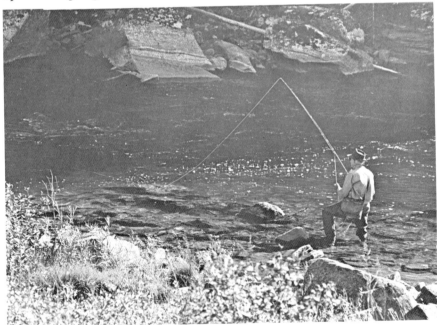

The Gallatin River offers good fishing spiced with outstanding scenery and easy access. Michael Sample photo.

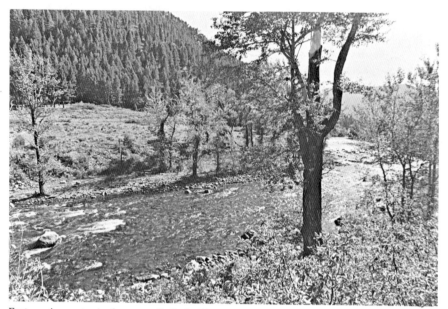

Fast-moving water in the upper Gallatin River can make fishing a challenge. Michael Sample photo.

The East Gallatin River flows in countless tight meanders over a course of about twenty air miles from Bozeman westward. Its smooth-flowing runs, sinuous channels, and often impenetrable willow banks bring to mind a miniature Beaverhead River—and the potential for lunker browns in the East Gallatin makes the comparison even more valid.

"The East Gallatin is kind of a sleeper around here," notes Dave Kumlien of the Montana Troutfitters Orvis shop in Bozeman. Kumlien says many local anglers overlook this river because of its small size. The river can be knee-deep for a long stretch, with seemingly little ability to hold decent fish. As a result, fishermen won't take the time to work the river and discover those ten-foot deep undercut bends where the big fish hold.

Another reason the East Gallatin is overlooked is its recent history of pollution. Although the East produced many large trout (up to a recorded seventeen-pounder in the mid-'60s), the river went into a precipitous, fifteen-year tailspin with the opening of the Bozeman sewage treatment plant and resultant discharge of ammonia-laden effluent into the river. Since the late 1970s, however, the pollution problem has been substantially alleviated and trout populations have recovered tremendously.

The new problem on the East Gallatin is access; virtually the entire stream-bank is in private ownership, except at bridge crossings. A new FWP access for wading anglers is being developed just off of Highway 10 north of the railroad overpass on the outskirts of Bozeman. This site will straddle the river, allowing anglers access from both banks. Floating the East Gallatin is possible, although the narrow channel; slow, winding flow; and occasional cross-stream barbed-wire fences must all be considered before launching.

The East and main Gallatin rivers meet about two miles north of Manhattan, and the resulting main stem Gallatin is a marvelous hybrid. On its ten-mile journey to join the Madison and Jefferson, the Gallatin River passes through some of the wildest bottomland habitat remaining in southwestern Montana. Moose, otters, and nesting herons and cormorants join the normal complement of white-tailed deer, beaver, mink, and Canada geese as the river channels its way through cottonwood forests.

The abundance of wildlife is nearly matched by the abundance of trout. Biologists report that the Gallatin holds about 750 browns and rainbow over eleven inches long per mile. Most of the rainbow are less than thirteen inches long, while the browns run quite a bit larger. A recent estimate puts the number of browns over sixteen inches long at eighty per mile, and many of these fish weigh from three to ten pounds.

The main stem Gallatin is a large river, best fished by floating. The deep undercut banks provide holding water for big browns, while the riffles host rainbow. Water conditions are the key to success on this part of the Gallatin. Spring runoff puts the Gallatin out of shape in terms of both color and flow beginning in early May, and the water can remain cloudy for several months due to bank erosion and silty return flows from upstream irrigation. In midsummer, dewatering for irrigation can drastically reduce the flows in the main Gallatin, causing the river to warm and the fishing action to slow down. Fall is the most predictable time to find clear water and active fish on the main stem Gallatin, although the periods just before and just after spring runoff can be very good.

Fishing Strategies

The diversity of fishing techniques necessary for the Gallatin mirrors the diversity of the river system. The angler's choice of naturals or artificials, time of day, season, and type of water to fish all change in relation to the section of the river being fished.

The riffly uppermost section of the Gallatin is perhaps least demanding, as it is readily wadeable and shallow enough to ensure that fish will be accessible. One key here is fishing when the water is warm enough to get the trout active. In the well-shaded Gallatin Canyon, fish are most active from midday through early evening during the mid-summer period. The standard high-floating attractor patterns will work well for fly fishermen, while any number of small spinning lures will also produce. Before you start casting take some time to look for the smooth surface slicks or submerged rocks that mark holding water for the better fish.

The pocket water sections farther down the canyon call for quick, pinpoint casts, whether the tackle is spin or fly gear. The trout will be holding behind the rocks, watching for a potential meal in the slower current along the edge of their protected lie. Cast repeatedly, as the fish won't be readily spooked from these prime holding areas.

The powerful flows in the canyon from the West Fork of the Gallatin downstream are among the most challenging waters to fish. The runs harboring the best fish should be fished deep unless the fish are working the surface during an insect hatch. The successful fly fisherman will generally have to cast a heavily weighted nymph upstream and allow it to bounce on the bottom. You'll need short line to keep control of the fly and to be able to detect a strike. Lure fishermen should cast upstream, allowing time for spinner or spoon to drop near the bottom before beginning to retrieve. The retrieve should be just slightly faster than the current, to give the lure some action but not to raise it much off the bottom. Size 2 and 3 lures are recommended, as smaller sizes won't get down quickly enough. Bait fishermen will do best bouncing the bottom of the runs and pools with stonefly nymphs or worms, especially during high water.

Although Gallatin Canyon has a very good salmon fly hatch, it doesn't draw the crowds that descend upon the Madison and Big Hole rivers during their hatches. This fortunate circumstance is in part due to the ban on float fishing on the Gallatin; despite their enthusiasm for salmon flies, most anglers don't relish the prospect of wading in Gallatin Canyon during high spring flows. A related factor is the frequently coincidental timing of muddy water and the emergence of salmon flies. The Taylor's Fork is an infamous sediment producer, and in most years it will color the Gallatin brown during at least part of the mid-June hatch.

Nevertheless, fishing can be good during the hatch, especially during low runoff years. The bushiest, highest-floating salmon fly patterns will work for fly fisherman in the swift current. Work the banks, as they provide the best holding water for trout and the most likely spot for natural salmon flies to fall into the water.

Throughout the summer after the high-water period, Gallatin Canyon hosts good evening caddis hatches, along with sporadic mayfly activity. Royal Wulffs, Royal Trudes, elk hair caddis, and Humpies are all dependable patterns. Grasshopper patterns—or live grasshoppers for the bait fisherman—can be very effective producers in any of the grassy bank areas of the canyon from late August through mid-September. Fall fishing in the canyon is primarily a nymph proposition for the fly fisherman, while lures and bait will continue to be successful for the spin fisherman.

The section of the Gallatin just below the canyon mouth provides excellent nymph and spinner fishing just prior to high water. During the hatch, dry salmon fly patterns will bring up large fish if water conditions provide at least a foot or two of visibility. After high water, concentrate on the deeper runs with large, dark nymphs and on the banks with Muddlers, Woolly Buggers, or other streamers. Lures fished on the bottom of runs and under the cut banks will also produce. Evening caddis hatches, mid-day stoneflies, hoppers, and other terrestrials will provide some good dry fly action throughout the summer.

During the warmest periods of summer, work the riffles carefully. Dave Kumlien notes, "In the fast waters of the Gallatin, the bottom is very uneven. Good fish can hold in the depressions or behind the rocks—the biggest rainbow I've ever caught have come out of these pockets surrounded by water only six inches deep."

Sculpins and other small fish, along with caddis, mayflies, and some crane fly larvae, are the major food items for browns of the silty-bottomed East Gallatin. Streamers, rubber-legged nymphs, and spinning lures fished beneath the undercut willow banks will provide the best opportunities to move a big fish. Water clarity is a key on the East Gallatin, as irrigation returns can cloud the river well after runoff has finished. Bait fishermen concentrate on the deep, quiet pools and the back eddies where the river turns.

The main stem Gallatin provides the greatest range of habitats, including deep runs, riffles, undercut banks, and quiet banks. Here again, fishing to the deep, protected lies offers the best chance of success. Dry flies are most effective during late summer evenings when the water is clear but not too

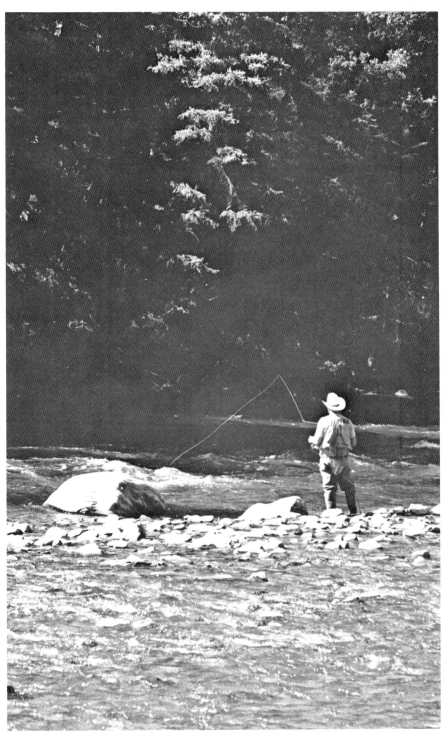

Working the mid-day shadows in the scenic Gallatin Canyon. Michael Sample photo.

GALLATIN RIVER

warm. Fall streamer or lure fishing can be excellent, offering the chance to catch resident fish and some of the huge browns moving up from the Missouri River. A weighted fly line is a good idea for getting the streamer deep, and the float fishing angler would be advised to stop and carefully work the three- to five-foot deep runs.

Tributaries

Squaw Creek and the West Fork of the Gallatin are the largest tributaries in Gallatin Canyon. Both offer good fishing for trout up to a foot long. Many other swift canyon streams hold pan-sized rainbow, and brook trout are well established in the small meadow streams.

The best stream fisheries in the Gallatin Valley below the canyon are the spring creeks which run through fertile agricultural lands. These waters, however, are entirely private and not available to the visiting angler.

Access

Access to the Gallatin River is excellent, with numerous pullouts and Forest Service campgrounds throughout Gallatin Canyon. Below the canyon, access is provided by a series of seven county bridges, beginning with Williams Bridge a few miles below the canyon and ending with the highway bridge east of Manhattan. A good local road map is the best guide for finding these bridges, which provide the only public access to the lower part of the Gallatin.

The East Gallatin is also surrounded by private land, with county bridges providing access. These access sites are located near Bozeman, north of Belgrade, and northeast of Manhattan.

The main stem Gallatin is accessible from bridges at its sources north of Manhattan and at Logan, five miles downstream. Missouri Headwaters State Park just north of Three Forks provides the final access point. The floating angler can take good advantage of the access set up on the main stem Gallatin River and plan a whole day ten-mile float or a half-day five-mile float at either the upper or lower end. For more information on floating the Gallatin, pick up a copy of *Montana Afloat #11, the Gallatin River.*

JEFFERSON RIVER

Much of the Jefferson River remains as wild and remote as the day Lewis and Clark first encountered it in 1804. Cottonwood bottoms, thick shrub fields, and expansive hay meadows isolated the river from civilization along much of its length. Abundant wildlife and waterfowl use the river and its banks, adding to the Jefferson's appeal.

The Jefferson flows for about seventy miles northeast from its origin near Twin Bridges to its confluence with the Madison and Gallatin rivers at the headwaters of the Missouri River outside Three Forks. A broad, multichan-neled river, the Jefferson has a gentle gradient and deep water.

The broad, beautiful Jefferson Valley provides the backdrop for the upper half of the river. The Tobacco Root Mountains tower over the river to the east and south, while the gentle Highland Range dominates the western scene. Autumn colors are particularly spectacular along the Jefferson during the first

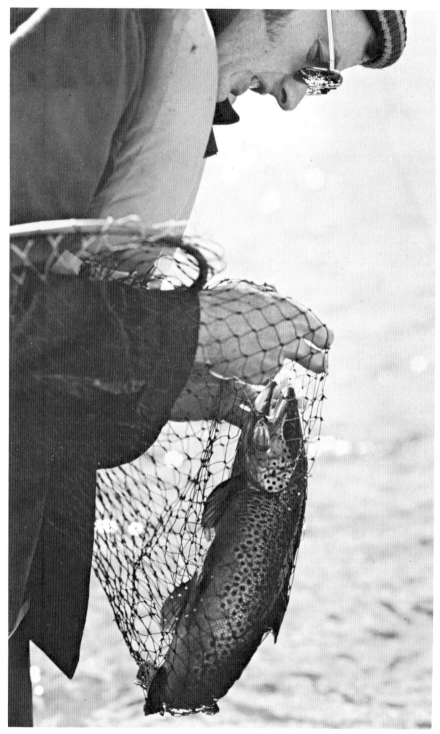

The Jefferson River has a few lunker browns, especially in the backwaters. Michael Sample photo.

weeks of October. After flowing through a picturesque rock-walled canyon east of Cardwell, the Jefferson opens into another broad valley north of Three Forks. Ringed by a series of small mountain ranges, this scenic valley typifies the arid southwestern Montana region.

For the angler, the big, lumbering "Jeff" provides a peaceful escape and a change of pace from the fast-paced float-fishing on the Beaverhead, Madison, and other southwestern Montana rivers. However, because the Jefferson is large, and more private than most rivers, it takes more time and patience to master.

Along the Jefferson, the brush banks and deep runs and pools provide good fish habitat and good fishing opportunities. Brown trout are the dominant trout species, though an occasional rainbow is taken, particularly on the upper end of the river. Thanks to catch-and-release regulations and a habitat improvement effort by the Montana Department of Fish, Wildlife and Parks (FWP), the rainbow population is on the upswing and gaining toe holds throughout the river. While the Jefferson is well known for its trophy five- to nine-pound browns, these are not common. More characteristically, the river produces trout in the ten- to fifteen-inch range, averaging about a pound.

A variety of factors, including high water temperature, low flows, and altered streambanks, keep trout populations well below their potential. Consequently, populations of trout on the Jefferson are substantially lower than on other rivers in the area.

Whitefish are abundant in the Jefferson's shallower runs and provide a popular fishery. A variety of rough fish are also adapted to the waters of the Jefferson. While not generally appreciated by anglers, these fish comprise the principle diet of river otters, which are fairly common—although seldom seen—on the Jefferson and its numerous sloughs.

While all of the Jefferson has good fishing potential, the river is naturally divided into three distinct sections, each providing different fishing conditions: the upper river, between Twin Bridges and Cardwell; the canyon section; and the lower river, downstream from Sappington Bridge.

The upper Jefferson has the steadiest current, though only in high water would the word "swift" apply. Deep pools and riffles intermixed with some long, sluggish runs characterize this section of river. The river is braided in many places, especially between Waterloo and Whitehall, where there are also a lot of sloughs and backwater areas. Habitat and water conditions on the upper river are the best on the Jefferson—trout in this section average better than fourteen inches. Trout populations are also best in the upper river where rainbow comprise about fifteen percent of the population. This is the most popular area of the Jefferson for guided float-fishing trips.

In the canyon east of Cardwell, the Jefferson is mostly a single channel river running deep and slow. Early afternoon shade in the summer helps cool the water and provide some good evening fishing. A paved road and railroad tracks on both sides of the river detract somewhat from the aesthetics and solitude of this area. The canyon has the poorest trout population on the river, but an occasional lunker is still taken from these waters— particularly by bait fishermen working some of the deep holes by the railroad tracks.

Downstream from the canyon, the Jefferson is mostly a single channel, pebble-bottom river lined with cottonwoods and hay meadows. Between Three Forks and the Missouri Headwaters State Park, the river braids extensively. This is the wildest reach of the Jefferson, where moose are sometimes seen, and good trout habitat is widespread.

The lower stretch of the Jefferson ranks as intermediate in fishing quality. Low water flows and warm water temperatures keep the trout population below its potential, but fishing can be good for eleven- to fourteen-inch browns.

Fishing on the Jefferson fluctuates widely and is notoriously unpredictable. Fish move around depending on season, time of day, weather, and water conditions. Timing is therefore all important. "Wait for a cloudy day and clear water with at least two feet of visibility," says Scott Waldie, owner of Four Rivers Fishing Company in Twin Bridges, "and you'll have a long wait for an evening of fishing that will rival it." This combination can result in some 50-fish days for the catch-and-release angler, Waldie adds.

Unfortunately, clear water is often a scarce commodity. High water from spring runoff (mid-May into June) brings the first of the muddy water conditions but lasts only a short time. The lower Beaverhead's murky waters contribute silt to the upper river throughout the summer. Irrigation return flows on the Jefferson compound the problem, and the summer rainstorms can muddy the river overnight·by further eroding unstable banks.

Despite these problems, most of the Jefferson does have fairly clear water during the summer and fall. Late June and July generally offer good fishing conditions. During the hot summer weather of August, the Jefferson is great for lazy recreational float trips but is not noted for good fishing. However, the fish do concentrate in riffles on hot, sunny days; and fishing can be quite good, although you may encounter lots of whitefish.

Severe dewatering becomes the major problem on the Jefferson later in the summer. During peak irrigation season, between mid-July and mid-September, the river's flow may drop to less than half of the level that fisheries biologists believe is necessary to support optimal trout populations. The drought of 1987-89 hit the Jefferson particularly hard, reducing some reaches of the river to a trickle between stagnant pools. Juvenile trout are most affected by such dewatering, and the numbers of big fish may not decline until several years after the drought.

As a result of low flows, water temperatures rise dramatically. In one area of the lower river, water temperature has been measured at seventy-four degrees Fahrenheit; ideal for swimming but not good for trout. Warm water reduces growth rates and trout activity. As a result, cooler periods of early mornings and evenings are the best bet for fishing.

In the fall the Jefferson regains its character, and the big browns begin their spawning runs. The fish move into shallower runs and riffles, where they are more easily accessible. This provides some of the best fishing the Jefferson has to offer.

Guide Tony Schoonen thinks the Jeff "...underrated. And I'd like to see it stay that way," he says. "Unlike the Big Hole, you can always catch some fish here."

Fishing Strategies

Trout on the Jefferson River are not dainty eaters. Crayfish are abundant on the Jeff; sculpins and small fish comprise a majority of the trout diet. Consequently, the angler must generally use flies and lures that imitate small fish.

The Jefferson does not have the variety and abundance of aquatic insects found on other southwestern Montana rivers. Among the aquatic insects,

Typical brown trout water in the Lower Jefferson River. Michael Sample photo.

caddis are available throughout the summer. Large stoneflies, once abundant on the upper river, have been virtually eliminated from the Jefferson over the past twenty years due to siltation of the river bottom.

Grasshoppers provide a source of food for trout in areas near hay meadows in the fall, and a variety of small terrestrial insects supplement the trout diet during the summer. Imitations of these insects offer anglers opportunities for surface action.

Accurate casting to the best trout habitat is one key to success on the Jefferson. Good trout habitat lies under the undercut or brushy banks and also near the riprapped banks. In the spring and fall, Schoonen also likes to work the mouths of sloughs where trout congregate to eat the abundant food.

"Areas with clean, rocky bottoms where the sediment has been washed away are particularly good," according to Al Troth, nationally recognized fly tier and Dillon area outfitter. "Avoid the slow, muddy bottom waters; they are generally unproductive."

"During the summer, work streamers or Yuk-bugs (a large block rubber-legged concoction) along the deep banks and dikes," says Waldie, "but in fall work the shallow water and riffles."

Wading can be difficult on the Jefferson due to steep, brushy banks and deep water. Mid- to late summer provides the best wading during low water. Rarely is the best fishing water found near access points so be prepared to walk a long way to reach good areas.

Spin-fishing is popular and effective on the Jefferson. The broad, deep water allows each cast to cover a lot of water. Cast to the banks and let the lure sink before retrieving it. Heavier Panther Martins and Mepps that will get down quickly are standards on the Jefferson, but most lures and spinners are likely to work if cast to the right spots and presented properly. Good spin casters are reported to have landed over 100 trout in a day when the fish are

Legend:
- ▬ ▬ HIGHWAY
- ----- COUNTY OR UNPAVED ROAD
- △ OFFICIAL PUBLIC ACCESS
- ☐ RANGER STATION
- X BRIDGE
- ∿∿ DIVERSION DAM

One inch = approx. 8 miles

Gallatin River

Missouri River
Headwaters State Park

Missouri River

Trident

Madison River

Three Forks

△ Drouillard

90

Jefferson River

△ Williams Bridge

Sappington Bridge △

10

287

Lewis and Clark
Cavern State Park

Harrison

Boulder River

LaHood Park

359

Cardwell

△

Mayflower Bridge

Tobacco Root Mountains

Kountz Bridge △ Parrot Castle

Whitehall

Renova

55

Parson's Bridge

Beaverhead
River

Ironrod
Bridge

Twin
Bridges

Silver Star

41

High Road △

Highland Mountains

Big Hole River

JEFFERSON RIVER

86

hitting. The Jefferson is one southwestern Montana river where the spin fisherman often out-fishes the fly fisherman.

Schoonen, who caught a 7.5-pound brown, observes that a lot of people think the bigger the fly, the bigger the fish. "No way," declares Schoonen. "Those folks just do a lot of hard casting and a lot of cussin'."

Troth backs him up with documentation from the fishing diary he keeps. "In one season, my clients caught and released fifty-eight trout over four pounds; fifty-five of these were caught on 10- to 14-sized flies." Troth goes on to point out that smaller flies catch fish more consistently because there are more small life forms in a river than large ones; small flies can be fished more naturally in low water; and "there is less of a fraud to be suspicious of." He also finds fishing a dropper fly to be very effective at times.

The fly fisherman will generally do best using weighted streamers or wet flies that imitate the sculpins and small fish on which Jefferson brown trout feed. Girdle bugs, Bitch Creeks, Yuk-bugs, and black or white Maribou Muddlers are commonly and effectively used. A heavy leader facilitates retrieval of flies from the brushy banks.

In the mornings and evenings, Royal Wulffs, Royal Trudes, and Humpies can be effective throughout the summer. These flies are suggestive of the beetles, bees, flies, and ants that fall into the water along the banks. Late in the summer, grasshopper and caddis patterns bring the trout to the surface.

On hot, sunny days when the fish are concentrated in riffles, the fly fisherman can find surprisingly good action. A bushy dry fly pattern often brings trout up for some of the best dry fly fishing on the Jefferson, but a medium-sized nymph (size 6 to 10) is apt to be the best producer.

Floating provides the best access to good water, if you have the time and equipment. While it's possible to cover a lot of river floating, the slow Jefferson current generally requires a minimum of four to six hours even for a trip of relatively short mileage. More often, a float trip on the Jefferson is a full day's undertaking, requiring frequent stretches of serious rowing to move through slow, unproductive water. Strong headwinds can slow progress to almost a standstill, so it's wise to plan plenty of extra time for a trip to avoid being caught on the river after dark.

Traditionally, the Jefferson has been a bait fisherman's river. The long, slow, deep pools are well suited to dangling a line on a peaceful summer evening. Bridges on the Jefferson are conveniently located near the deep holes well suited to the casual bait fisherman. Bouncing bait off the bottoms of riffles and into the heads of deep pools is also a successful technique for the Jefferson, however. Bullheads and sucker meat are the commonly used baits.

Fran Johnson, who owns a well-known tackle shop in Butte, notes that bait anglers catch most of their big ones in the springtime; and not only in deep pools, but also side channels, backwaters, and overflow areas.

Tributaries

The Jefferson River has only a few noteworthy tributaries, although there are numerous lakes and creeks containing fish throughout its mountainous headwaters. In its upper reaches, Hells Canyon Creek provides good fishing for an abundance of small rainbow trout. The lower five miles of the creek are in a canyon with rattlesnakes and rugged terrain, but a Forest Service road joins the creek a few miles upstream. Rainbow trout from Hells Canyon Creek move into the Jefferson and contribute to the substantially higher percentage

Much of the Jefferson is relatively flat water, broken by only a few riffles. Michael Sample photo.

of rainbow on the upper Jefferson as compared to the lower river.

The Boulder River north of Cardwell was once a prime fishing stream, but years of abuse have diminished its quality drastically. Past and present mining activities have contributed excessive levels of heavy metals to the lower half of the river. The metals, still found in the riverbed substrate, are blamed for eliminating the willow bank cover in some areas, thus reducing trout habitat. Stream alteration and streambank grazing contribute to siltation problems, while excessive irrigation withdrawals dry up the stream annually. The result is poor fishing in the lower Boulder River. The uppermost twenty miles of the Boulder, however, with more difficult access and less habitat degradation, still produce a good population of small brook trout. The lower end of the Boulder is closed to fishing at the end of September (check current fishing regulations for exact date) to protect a vulnerable population of spawning brown trout.

The South Boulder River flows from high in the Tobacco Root Mountains to its confluence with the Jefferson east of Cardwell. The lower end is bordered by private land, but the upper stretches are on public forest land. Access is by a good gravel road that follows the stream. Fishing is good for small rainbow and brook trout, though an occasional fifteen- to sixteen-inch brown is taken from the lower reaches.

Willow Creek flows from Harrison Reservoir in the Tobacco Root Mountains to its confluence with the Jefferson near the town of Willow Creek. Despite low flow releases from the Harrison Reservoir during the winter, Willow Creek supports a healthy population of rainbow and brown trout. The upper end is far better than the lower stretch but is surrounded by private land, so ask for access permission. The middle section flows through a canyon reported to be a haven for rattlesnakes—a major deterrent for many anglers—

Fishing the head end of large pools common on the Jefferson often brings good results. Michael Sample photo.

but fishing can be very good for those willing to hike in. Willow Creek has become a popular fly fishing spot over the past several years due to its proximity to Bozeman.

Access

Although surrounded by private land, the Jefferson River nonetheless has good fishing access. Bank fishermen may have to walk to reach the best water, but boat fishermen have numerous choices for their floating.

The only access to the uppermost reaches of the Jefferson is by way of the Beaverhead or Big Hole rivers in Twin Bridges. Either place provides a good starting point for floaters but only difficult access for bank fishermen.

Downstream between Twin Bridges and Silver Star, you'll find both boat and bank access on the Hells Canyon road north of the Ironrod Bridge. This is a popular fishing area, especially for whitefish in the winter. Twin Bridges to Ironrod Bridge is a good four-hour float, but many people take out at Hells Canyon to cut a few miles off the downstream end.

County bridges cross the Jefferson at Silver Star and about six miles up the road near Waterloo. At the Parsons Bridge on the road to Waterloo, a major water diversion requires portaging. Between these two bridges it's a long, slow float, providing plenty of solitude.

An FWP fishing access site is available downstream at Parrot Castle. This spot does not provide boat access, however, unless you are willing to carry your boat across a slough and several hundred yards to the river. Boat fishermen interested in access to this section of river can use a small section of Bureau of Land Management (BLM) land abutting the river on the east side near the remains of the Parrot Castle smelter. Check the maps to be sure you're not trespassing.

Southeast of Whitehall, Kountz Bridge and Mayflower Bridge both provide boat and some foot access. Only three river miles separate these bridges.

Another FWP fishing access site is maintained outside of Cardwell. Downstream at LaHood is the last official access to the Jefferson before the river enters Jefferson Canyon. Throughout the canyon, there is walk-in access across the railroad tracks.

Outside the canyon are several access sites before the Jefferson ends at the Missouri Headwaters State Park. Sappington Bridge, Williams Bridge, Willow Creek Bridge, Drouillard, and the Old Town Bridge east of Three Forks provide good access; though not all have easy boat access.

Access is limited to float-fishing between Three Forks and the Missouri Headwaters State Park. This stretch of river is braided and excessively brushy, making wading difficult. A river map and additional information for floaters can be found in the pamphlet, *Montana Afloat #10, the Jefferson River.*

KOOTENAI RIVER

Half of Montana's ninety-nine-mile share of the Kootenai River was flooded by Libby Dam; the other half tempts power companies with at least two potential dam sites. So what remains of interest to anglers? A trophy rainbow fishery that deserves more recognition.

Because the river just clips the northwestern corner of the state, most Montanans never see the Kootenai. Pat Graham, a fish biologist for the Montana Department of Fish, Wildlife and Parks (FWP), remembers some Kalispell anglers who were accustomed to catching eight-inch cutthroat in the streams around their area, until they drove the 100 miles to the Kootenai and were astonished by the big rainbow.

In his study of the Kootenai, Graham found that the average creeled rainbow—usually in excellent condition—measured between twelve and thirteen inches. And anglers catch fish from the Kootenai at about the same rate as from other more highly touted blue-ribbon streams of Montana. "In my mind, it's clearly the best big-river trout fishery in northwestern Montana," concludes Graham.

No dainty, intimate trout stream is this. Anglers do not wade back and forth across the Kootenai as they do the Big Hole. The Kootenai's annual flow exceeds that of even the Flathead or the Yellowstone. A visit to the rim of Kootenai Falls provides dramatic proof of the river's immense power.

The river rises in a long, broad Canadian valley, fills Koocanusa Reservoir behind Libby Dam, then flows past the communities of Libby and Troy to join with the Yaak River before exiting the state bound for the Columbia.

In the forty-nine miles of river from the dam to the state line, four distinct segments of water stand out. Most reminiscent of the lost, inundated river beneath Koocanusa Reservoir, the first segment, from Libby Dam to the town of Libby, features some big bends, islands, gravel bars, and a clear progression of riffles and pools.

Just downstream from Libby begins the section known locally as "the rocks." Many boulders imbedded in the cobble streambed resist the powerful current

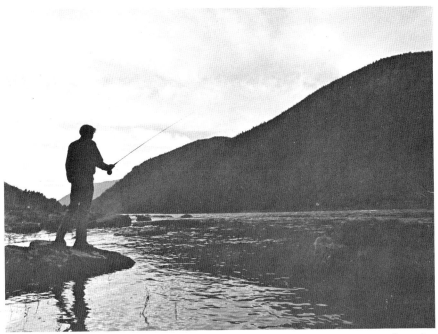

Although not highly touted, the Kootenai River produces large trout at a rate equal to other famous Montana rivers. Michael Sample photo.

of the river's westwardly flow. Near the lower end of this section, the turbulent water pours through China Rapids, a challenging hazard to floaters.

At Kootenai Falls, the river cuts through the bedrock of the Purcell Range. Fault lines in the bedrock make a spectacular stair-step series of falls. Below, the river races through a tortuous, confined canyon, then subsides into a deep gorge.

The last Montana segment of the river flows placidly through a heavily timbered valley to the state line. After the Yaak River adds its volume to the already ponderous river, the Kootenai meanders more in its last five miles; riffles, gravel bars, and islands become few and far between. Long, deep runs merge into pools. At the Idaho border the Kootenai flows just 1,820 feet above sea level, Montana's lowest elevation.

Libby Dam has had a profound effect on the river. Perhaps most important, the Army Corps of Engineers exercises control over the river's flow. Winter discharges are high. In the spring, when most rivers swell to several times their normal size, the Kootenai remains low while the reservoir fills. In the summer and fall, the flow fluctuates sharply from 4,000 to 24,000 cubic feet per second (cfs), depending on power demand. The water level can rise a foot an hour, which has left more than one unwary angler stranded out on a rock.

From 1972 to 1975, when the Corps was filling the reservoir and releasing water by spillway instead of through turbines, gas supersaturation killed many fish and upset the aquatic balance. Torrent sculpins almost disappeared from the river above Kootenai Falls. The population of whitefish dropped drastically. Whether from gas supersaturation or flow fluctuations, some insects became more numerous while others vanished.

Gas supersaturation diminished once the dam started functioning normally. A positive aspect of the dam soon became clear; the temperature of the river could be held at ideal levels to foster trout growth throughout the summer and fall. Grow the rainbow did, both in numbers and in average size. Graham estimates that when the young rainbow leave the tributaries where they spend the first year or two of their lives, they grow between seven and eight inches their first year in the Kootenai.

Always noted for its large rainbow, the Kootenai has in recent years rewarded anglers with many two- to five-pound trout. Lunkers up to eighteen pounds have shocked an occasional lucky angler, and even bigger fish have found their way into the record books. The Kootenai garnered statewide attention by producing rainbows weighing twenty-six and twenty-nine pounds, shattering the previous state record of twenty-one pounds—even more remarkable that these fish came out of a river.

These record-breaking fish were the end result of good water temperatures and a "chum line" of dead and dying kokanee churned out by the turbines at Libby Dam. Although an impressive number of big rainbow have shown up in the Kootenai, FWP biologists recommend catch-and-release on everything except trophies and pan-sized trout.

While the rainbow have fared fairly well, Montana's only known white sturgeon population seems to have had greater trouble adapting to the new conditions imposed by the dam. This giant, prehistoric fish once swam in sizeable numbers up the Kootenai to the deep gorge below Kootenai Falls. Biologists assume the sturgeon spawned there, but efforts to learn more about the mysterious fish have so far turned up little information except that very

A walk across the suspension bridge near Kootenai Falls gives a full impression of this river's size and strength. Michael Sample photo.

few sturgeon still return. Graham surmises that the new flow fluctuations may confound the sturgeon.

Although rainbow reign supreme as the most desired game fish, three others deserve mention. Cutthroat trout occasionally drop from the reservoir and move downriver in search of other impoundments. The cutthroat comprise only four percent of the catch. A few bull trout seasonally run below the falls. Much more numerous, whitefish have rebounded in great numbers since 1975, to the concern of local trout fanciers who fear the whitefish may be competing heavily with the rainbow. Before the dam, local anglers caught many whitefish through the winter ice, but the river no longer ices over, leaving the whitefish population unchecked.

Already chopped in half by Libby Dam, the free-flowing Kootenai would be cut another twenty percent if the Corps gets approval for a re-regulating dam. As an auxiliary to the main dam, the re-reg dam would allow more peaking capability. But it also would impound a prime stretch of river. The Northwest Power Planning Council states that this region already has more peaking capability than can be used in the foreseeable future.

Still another dam project looms at beautiful Kootenai Falls. The Rural Electrical Cooperative proposes to build a "run-of-the-river" dam just upstream from the falls to divert up to ninety-seven percent of the river through a tunnel to drive generators before returning the water to the river channel a mile downstream.

Aside from reducing the falls to an unsightly trickle, this dam would back up water for three miles, ruining some of the best fishing water in the "rocks" section. Graham thinks this section would become "an unnatural habitat"—

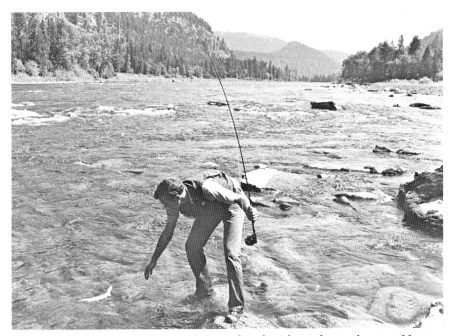

Kootenai River rainbows run consistently larger than those from other northwestern Montana streams. Michael Sample photo.

British Columbia

N

Yaak River

Leonia

Purcell Mountains

△ Yaak

Koocanusa Reservoir

Eureka

37

Kootenai Falls

China Rapids

Kootenai River

Troy

2

Libby

Libby Dam

Lake Creek

Fisher River

Cabinet Mountains

Idaho

Montana

━ ━ ━ HIGHWAY
- - - - - COUNTY OR UNPAVED ROAD
△ OFFICIAL PUBLIC ACCESS
□ RANGER STATION
X BRIDGE
∿∿∿ DIVERSION DAM

One inch = approx. 11 miles

KOOTENAI RIVER

too slow to be called a river but too fast to be a lake. Trout do not succeed in such an environment, but chubs and suckers might. As for the fishing downstream and the few remaining white sturgeon, no one can venture more than a wild guess about what the dam would bring.

Fishing Strategies

This is rainbow country—no brown trout. Don't waste time looking for undercut banks. The rocks and the riffle pools harbor the rainbow. Stu Swenson has fished most of Montana's rivers and many in Canada, but he chooses to live beside the Kootenai partly because the fishing is "just plain fantastic." Swenson and river guide Gary Evans point out two different strategies for fishing the Kootenai. "Some fishermen are very successful setting up in a hole," says Swenson, "but I especially enjoy working around the rocks."

But Evans notes that the river from the Libby Dam to Libby and from below Kootenai Falls to the old Troy Bridge has some very fine fishing holes. Distinguish the productive holes from the unproductive by looking at the stream bottom, according to Graham. The big rainbow avoid sandy bottoms or flat bedrock. They seek broken backgrounds like cobble and gravel or, especially in the Kootenai, the cover of macrophytes (or, as it's called locally, "moss").

Typically, water from a riffle dumps into the slower water of a pool. Evans positions himself to one side and casts a weighted line above the pool to let it drift down and go deep. If necessary, he adds split shot. He also watches for eddies where the foam collects off to one side of the pool; here, too, he sinks his line in and lets it swirl around.

Swenson explains that in the past he fished like Evans does, but now he thinks the river has changed to favor the surface fisherman. "It's the best dry fly fishing I've had in all of Montana," he claims. Naturally, Swenson likes to fish when a hatch comes off the river. Instead of fishing the big pools, Swenson prefers the "rocks" section between Libby and the Kootenai Falls because "that's where the biggest fish are." He casts his flies above, below, and around the boulders; but he believes the upstream side is the best feeding station for trout.

Anglers who prefer bait generally gravitate to the pools. Nightcrawlers, fire red salmon eggs, and sucker meat are the most popular enticements. Graham adds a tip which might be useful: the rainbow gorge themselves on whitefish eggs in the fall after the whitefish spawn on gravel beds both in the Kootenai and in some tributaries.

When Evans first started guiding anglers on the river, he didn't believe lures would be very effective, but some of his clients have since changed his mind. Graham believes lures work well in the upper reaches of the river, where less turbulence favors hardware. Thomas Cyclone tops the list of favorites.

"Fly fishermen do well," explains Graham, "especially during hatches of small mayflies in spring and caddis flies in the late summer." The most successful fly anglers float the "rocks" section and cast toward the banks, because hatches usually begin there.

Graham found in his aquatic samples that stonefly numbers have declined since the advent of the dam, but Swenson insists there are still plenty of stoneflies to excite the fish. A brown stonefly nymph imitation with a little grey coloring catches more than its share of Swenson's creel.

When a caddis or mayfly hatch brings trout to the surface, Swenson uses the old standby patterns like Irresistibles, grey Wulffs, and Adams. He cautions that matching the size of the natural insects is very important.

Whatever the angler chooses to fool the fish, the most favorable conditions for fishing come when the dam releases lower flows. Graham found that fishing success was fully fifty percent higher when the flow ran less than 10,000 cfs. Local anglers know simply by watching rocks in the river when the water is down, but for the inexperienced, the Army Corps of Engineers has a phone number listed under "U.S. Government" for flow information. During the summer, the Corps has an informal policy of dropping the water for weekend fishing when feasible.

Special regulations designed to protect spawning rainbow may prohibit spring fishing in the Kootenai until the opening of the general season. Check with a local sporting goods dealer or FWP to be sure.

By mid-May, turbidity from the Fisher River may slow fishing down until early June. From then on the water has excellent clarity, and fishing can be good at any time the river is low. Graham notes that few anglers still on the river in the fall have very high catch rates.

Swenson likes fishing in the earlier part of summer, from the end of May to early July, "if they aren't jacking the river up and down yet." He remembers some exciting fishing in early afternoon and fishes wet until he spots a hatch or fish working on the surface. In Swenson's mind, evening fishing is best.

Tributaries

Anglers looking for a change of pace from the big river may wish to try some of the feeder creeks or the Yaak River.

Of the streams flowing onto the Kootenai River, Graham picks a trio of especially appealing creeks to investigate. O'Brien, Callahan, and Lake creeks all join the river near Troy. O'Brien has good numbers of brookies and some spawning rainbow in the spring. Steep Callahan Creek proves difficult to fish, but it supports some good-sized natives and rainbow plus occasional bull trout. Lake Creek proves popular due to its nice rainbow and cutthroat and pan-sized brookies.

The Yaak River and its forks harbor multitudes of rainbow and cutthroat. Above the Yaak Falls anglers can easily see their quarry in the clear, slow water. A parallel road for most of the length of the upper river provides good access.

The steep, confined canyon below the falls propels the water far faster than the lazy stretches above. "You have to be a mountain goat to fish it," testifies Swenson. The only heavy fishing pressure on the Yaak comes at its mouth by the campground.

The larger tributary streams of Lake Koocanusa have been planted with fish by FWP in hopes of establishing spawning runs up these streams. The success of these ventures swings on the ability and willingness of the trout to cross mud flats and steep banks created by the huge draw-down of the reservoir.

Access

With a few hazardous exceptions, the Kootenai presents little difficulty to the floating angler. China Rapids should not be attempted by anyone without prior experience in whitewater and the foresight to study the water first before attempting it. This holds true especially during high flows.

Kootenai Falls stand as an absolute barrier to floaters. If the first fall didn't kill, the tumble into the maelstrom below would.

The standing waves where the Yaak pushes into the Kootenai might pose an upsetting problem to those with little freeboard or navigational skills. Otherwise, the river runs nearly flat and hazard free.

No formal access sites presently exist along the river. However, you can easily gain casual access to the section from Libby Dam to Kootenai Falls from the parallel highways. Below the falls, access is through private land except near Troy and at the Yaak River Bridge. The road access at the state line has recently been chained on occasion, so check locally before anticipating access here.

MADISON RIVER

The Madison is, in many people's opinion, Montana's river of superlatives, with a list including highest trout density, most consistent action, best dry fly fishing, and most spectacular scenery. Not surprisingly, this southwestern Montana jewel is also the most heavily used fishery in the state, growing more popular annually.

The Madison River heads at the junction of the Firehole and Gibbon rivers in Yellowstone National Park. (This book covers the park section of the river in the Yellowstone Park chapter.) From here, it flows for over 100 miles to its confluence with the Jefferson and Gallatin rivers at Missouri Headwaters State Park near Three Forks. The Montana section of the Madison begins just inside the park boundary. After a few meandering miles, the river collects in Hebgen Lake, a sprawling reservoir created by a Montana Power Company dam built in 1916. Only two miles downstream from the Hebgen spillway, the Madison is again confined. Quake Lake, a striking testimony to the continued geologic unrest of the Yellowstone Plateau, was formed on an August night in 1959, when a major earthquake shook loose a mountainside of rock across the river. This natural dam has since been civilized, courtesy of the Corps of Engineers, and is now operated for flood control.

Just below Quake Lake, the Madison turns from its westward course and begins a fifty-mile run due north to Ennis Lake. The upper Madison, as this section is termed, flows between willow-lined banks, bordered on either side by miles-wide grassy "benches" so flat that many tourists think they were leveled by man. Above the benches to the west rise the jagged 10,000-foot peaks of the Madison Range; to the east are the timbered slopes of the Gravelly Range. In *The Living River*, angler supreme Charles Brooks aptly describes the upper Madison as "one of the loveliest river valleys anywhere."

The flow characteristics of the upper Madison are almost as distinctive as the scenery. Through nearly its entire course, the river is broad, rapid, and shallow, a veritable "fifty-mile riffle," as it has so often been described. Gravel and cobbles compose the substrate, and occasional boulders rise above the water surface. The upper Madison is primarily a single channel from Quake Lake down to Varney Bridge, but between the bridge and Ennis Lake, the river braids freely, undercutting banks and separating scores of cottonwood-dotted islands. Riffles still dominate the flow in this "channels" section of the river.

Three miles north of the town of Ennis, the upper Madison empties into Ennis

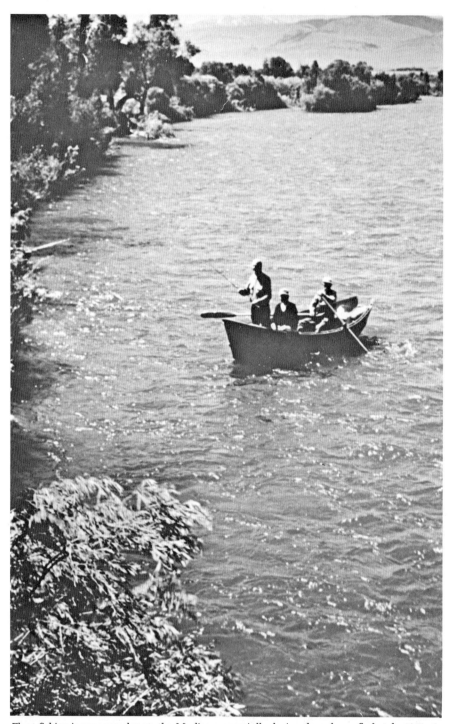

Float fishing is very popular on the Madison, especially during the salmon fly hatch. Al Troth photo.

Lake, the product of another Montana Power Company dam. Ennis Dam is the dividing line between the upper and lower Madison.

From the outlet of Ennis Lake, the lower Madison roars through the rugged Beartrap Canyon Wilderness Area. The seven-mile canyon is one of the most challenging whitewater stretches in Montana, with powerful runs and rapids over six feet high. At the mouth of the canyon, the river broadens and slows for its final thirty-mile journey. The river continues northward, lined by dense willow thickets and productive pastureland. The 105-foot-high Grey Cliffs form a distinctive border to the middle reaches of the lower Madison.

The Madison's fame and exceptional fishery stem to a large degree from the river's role as a living laboratory for wild trout management. In 1968, the Montana Department of Fish, Wildlife and Parks (FWP) initiated a two-year project to assess the effects of its artificial stocking program on trout populations in the upper Madison. The results of this pioneering research led to the revolutionary but inescapable conclusion: The addition of thousands of hatchery-reared trout each spring was actually reducing the number of fish in the river. Fisheries researcher Dick Vincent reasoned that the influx of hatchery fish was displacing the resident population from the limited number of holding areas in the Madison, but the hatchery fish were unable to survive more than a short time in the demanding river environment.

The fallout from this study rained on rivers throughout Montana; in less than a decade, most rivers and streams in the state had been converted to wild trout management (natural reproduction only) with spectacular improvements in the quality of trout fishery.

For the Madison, elimination of stocking was only the first of a series of steps designed to bring the river to its fishery potential. The second item to be addressed was harvest. Creel surveys and population censuses indicated that anglers were keeping so many of the larger trout that, despite good reproduction, only small fish remained. The average fish size had dropped to about ten inches, a sorry state of affairs for a river with the exceptional water quality, habitat, and food supply of the Madison.

Backed by mountains of Dick Vincent's data and scores of sportsmen demanding the restoration of quality fishing, the Montana Fish and Game Commission designated the thirty miles of the upper Madison from Quake Lake to McAtee Bridge as a "catch-and-release" section for artificial flies and lures only. This stretch became the longest such special management section in the nation, and the results have been remarkable. Total trout populations have more than doubled since the advent of the special regulations in 1977. Numbers of thirteen- to eighteen-inch fish have risen even more sharply; they are now estimated at more than 800 per mile.

The success of the catch-and-release regulations have created a new problem on the Madison, namely, "handling mortality." Vincent documented this occurrence by comparing trout populations in the catch-and-release section to those in a research area of the Madison which had been closed to fishing for five years. Populations in the closed section were about twenty percent higher than in the catch-and-release area, indicating that many of the trout handled by fishermen were not surviving after release. Biologists now recommend that fish be brought to net or hand quickly, not played to exhaustion. A tired fish will have extreme difficulty regaining its equilibrium in the swift Madison current, especially when the water is at summer temperatures. If a fish has been played out, it should be held upright in calm water and moved back and forth gently until it has recovered its strength. The cavalier "fish drop" release so commonly seen may prove a death blow to trout in the rushing waters of the Madison River.

After dealing with wild trout management, catch-and-release regulations, and handling mortality, you might think Dick Vincent and his crew would rest on their research laurels. Hardly. "Species management" is the next phase on the Madison, as biologists attempt to adjust harvest regulations in the river below Varney Bridge to increase the number of rainbow trout. Anglers are advised to keep posted for additional improvements in the Madison fishery.

Populations in the upper Madison are now estimated at about 4,500 trout over eight inches long per river mile. In the upper sections the mix is about two rainbow for each brown; close to Ennis Lake, the relative populations are reversed.

Surprisingly, the years of protective regulations have not resulted in great numbers of trophy trout in the upper Madison. Even in the section which had been closed to fishing, biologists report relatively few trout longer than eighteen inches. The shortage of fish over three pounds, particularly rainbow, probably results from the cold water temperatures, short growing season, and, for rainbow, lack of a major food source. Browns, which readily become fish-eaters, will continue to grow even after reaching sixteen inches, while rainbow tend to maintain this size once it's attained. Another factor may be that the large population of trout and even greater number of whitefish are simply dividing the food resource between too many mouths. Below Varney Bridge, where brushy banks and slower channels provide better brown trout habitat, trout up to four pounds are not uncommon.

The special regulations have brought the upper Madison close to its potential for producing trout. It hosts an exceptional number of one- to two-pound fish, offering the knowledgeable angler the opportunity to experience a forty- or fifty-fish day. As Dick Vincent wrote, "At times, catch rates on the upper Madison can average about three fish an hour. That's fantastic fishing, especially when you consider how many novices are included in that figure." The lower Madison, on the other hand, is far from its potential as a fishery. Trout fishing here suffers from "thermal pollution"—a fancy way of saying the river just gets too darn warm.

During the summer, daily maximum water temperatures over seventy degrees Fahrenheit are the rule in the lower river. At these temperatures, trout feeding—and angling success—can come to a screeching halt. Temperatures over eighty degrees have caused local fish kills in the lower Madison. Trout growth rates are well below normal levels, and veteran anglers report that numbers of fish over three pounds are only a fraction of what they used to be.

The thermal problem stems from Ennis Dam and its reservoir, Ennis Lake. Since dam construction in 1900, the lake has silted in to an average depth of nine feet, about half its original depth. During summer, the shallow reservoir acts like a six-square-mile solar collector. Upon discharge at Ennis Dam, Madison waters have warmed by about eight degrees. Montana officials are now evaluating the feasibility of various engineering options to channel the flow quickly through the reservoir and thus alleviate the summer warming problem. A successful resolution of the lower Madison temperature problem could readily transform the lower Madison into one of the best trout fisheries in the nation.

Despite temperature problems, the lower Madison still holds a very respect-

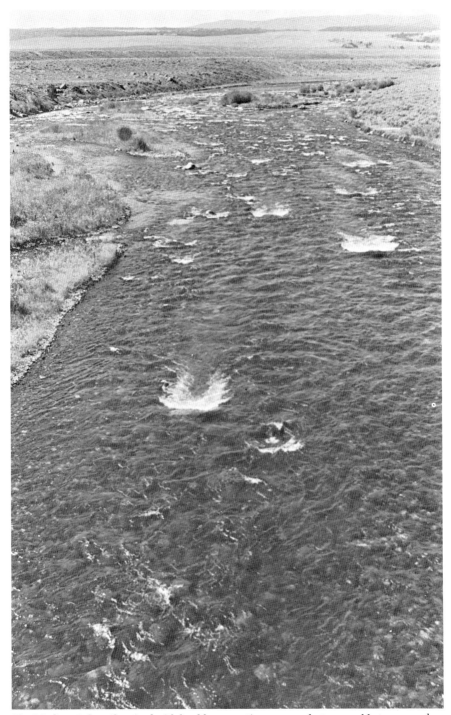

The Madison is heavily spiced with boulders, creating a somewhat unusual but very productive habitat. Michael Sample photo.

Missouri Headwaters State Monument

Gallatin River

Three Forks

90

10

Jefferson River

Cobblestone

Greycliff

287

Black's Ford

84

River

Bozeman

Norris

Madison

Bear Trap Canyon Primitive Area

Madison Dam

Ennis Reservoir

Valley Garden

Ennis

Ennis **Bridge**

287

Burnt Tree

Eight Mile Ford

Varney

Varney **Bridge**

287

McAtee Bridge

West Madison

Wolf Creek

South Madison

West Fork Madison

Madison River

West Fork

Madison River

Reynolds Pass

87

Hebgen Dam

Quake Lake

Hebgen Reservoir

West Yellowstone

Tobacco Root Mountains

Madison Range

Gravelly Range

Yellowstone National Park

N

- - - HIGHWAY
······ COUNTY OR UNPAVED ROAD
△ OFFICIAL PUBLIC ACCESS
□ RANGER STATION
X BRIDGE
VVVV DIVERSION DAM

One inch = approx. 12 miles

MADISON RIVER

able trout population—in fact, trout numbers can equal those in the Varney Bridge section of the upper river. The key for the angler is to fish when the temperature conditions are conducive to trout activity. In general, this means April to June and again in late September to November.

Most early season fishing on both the upper and lower Madison is done from rubber rafts or drift boats, as high-water conditions make wading difficult. Float fishing is restricted in some sections of the river, so check current regulations before starting a trip. The Madison is floatable year-round, although the late summer flows can occasionally cause some bottom bouncing.

After the water drops, wading becomes feasible, and the best spots can be found between Varney Bridge and Ennis Lake. The exceptional number of channels at the Valley Garden fishing access site near Ennis, for example, provides a great opportunity for the walking fisherman to find a private place to fish.

Ennis Lake also harbors a rebounding population of grayling. A recent FWP study determined that these grayling may be a native, fluvial strain, one of two remaining populations in the state. To protect this unique resource, fishing for grayling is catch-and-release only for the entire length of the Madison.

Fishing Strategies

For most anglers, the annual fishing agenda on the upper Madison begins in May prior to spring runoff. At this time, the fish are concentrating on the black, two-inch-long nymphs of Pteronarcys californica. This large stonefly, known as the salmon fly for the orange color of the winged adult, is abundant in the riverbottom cobbles. Large Bitch Creek nymphs, Yuk bugs, Girdle bugs, and similar heavily weighted, rubber-legged concoctions in sizes 2 to 6 are the most reliable patterns. These flies should be worked right against the banks—just where the trout are waiting for the clumsy crawling naturals that stack up along the shoreline before emerging. The float fisherman should cast slightly downstream to allow the fly to sink before it begins to drag behind the boat. An upstream mend of the belly of the fly line will extend the drag-free drift, and the quick movement of the fly will often entice a strike. As soon as the fly does drag, pick it up (carefully—you'll remember once you've hit yourself in the head with a size 2 weighted nymph) and cast again. If this technique brings few results, test your patience and drift a big nymph along the bottom about ten to twenty feet from the shore.

The wading fisherman should quarter his cast upstream, allowing the fly to sink in the swift current and dead drift along the bank. As the water warms through the spring, the fish will also chase gold, silver, and black spinners; again, cast right against the bank in the pre-hatch period.

Runoff flows typically last from late May through June. Fishing can remain good during the high-water period if the river retains at least a foot or two of visibility. Forget the days when the river has risen more than about six inches in a twenty-four-hour period. The West Fork of the Madison is a major sediment producer, and at times the angler can find fishable water upstream from the confluence.

Adult salmon flies begin to emerge around July 1 in the channels just above Ennis, and the hatch works its way upstream for the next three weeks. Fly fishermen from across the nation converge on the Madison in the hopes of catching many and large fish on the big dry salmon fly patterns. Sometimes this scenario plays out; at other times, fishing is only fair or poor in the face of high, turbid water or trout already gorged on naturals. Persistence is the key during the hatch. An angler who puts in long days of floating has the best chance to have those magical few hours when virtually all the two- and three-pounders go on a feeding frenzy.

A number of salmon fly patterns are effective, and it's a good idea to have both tight-silhouetted patterns (like the Sofa Pillow or Bird's stonefly) and bushy patterns (like the fluttering stone or other well-hackled elk hair ties). Alter your tactics frequently during the day, and don't be timid about switching to nymphs or wet patterns if the dries won't produce.

Dry fly action on the upper Madison is remarkably good from the end of the high water through the summer. The clear, shallow, fast water probably accounts for the willingness of trout to work the surface. Even inexperienced fly fishermen can find some excellent action on most afternoons. The consistent success of a variety of attractor patterns—especially the gaudy Royal Wulff—belies the purist's match-the-hatch credo on the upper Madison.

Despite the relative ease of dry fly fishing on the upper Madison, the ability to cast to the right spots will make a tremendous difference in the number of fish taken. Reading the water is the key—even though at first glance the famed fifty-mile riffle may seem indecipherable.

"Look for a change in speed or a change in depth," advises Bud Lilly, founder of the famous Trout Shop in West Yellowstone. "If you can identify a feeding station where the trout don't have to work so hard, that's where they'll be." These stations can be along the banks, on the edges of the faster runs, behind visible or submerged boulders, or in small gravel depressions. A good pair of polarized sunglasses is a necessity for reading the streambottom subtleties of the upper Madison.

The famed Madison caddis hatch is the bread and butter of summer fishing.

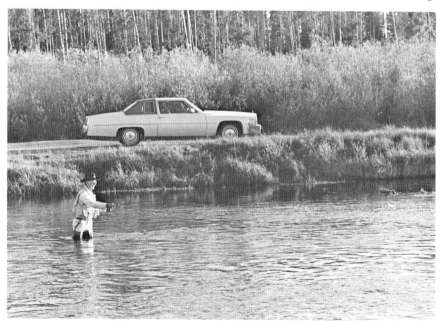

The Madison not only offers world-famous fishing, but easy access. Michael Sample photo.

Light brown caddis in sizes 10 to 14 hatch throughout July and August; clouds of the moth-like adults can be seen along the shoreline willows, particularly on warm evenings. Elk hair caddis, Humpies, Royal Trudes, and Royal Wulffs are the top dry fly producers, while hare's ears and other soft hackle patterns will take trout feeding on the emerging caddis pupae just under the water surface.

By late August, terrestrials dominate the trout diet. A trout creeled on the upper Madison (below the catch-and-release boundary at McAtee Bridge, of course) is likely to have ants, grasshoppers, bees, spiders, and half a dozen different species of beetles in its stomach. The message here is opportunism—both on the part of the trout, who will take nearly anything, and on the part of the angler, who should select a visible, high-floating attractor pattern in size 12 or smaller. Royal Wulffs are the favored pattern; their white, upright wings provide excellent visibility in the surface glare and chop. For the sharp-eyed angler, a size 12 Adams can also turn the trick when the attractors don't.

By early September, the grassy edges of the upper Madison are jumping with grasshoppers, many of which are considerately deposited in the river channel by the afternoon winds. Trout take greedy advantage of this "wind-fall," and anglers do likewise. Any of the standard hopper patterns will bring enthusiastic strikes; many of the fish that strike will also be in the fourteen-to eighteen-inch class. A muddler fished just under the surface can also be very effective.

The grasshopper period coincides with the highest floating pressure and the lowest water levels. These are prime conditions for boats or wading fishermen to spook fish from their bank holding areas. Fishermen might do well to try some of the mid-river holding areas behind boulders in addition to the typical bank spots.

Fall in the upper Madison Valley brings subfreezing nights and a sharp decline in surface insect activity. Trout begin keying in on aquatic nymphs and sculpins. Black or olive Woolly Buggers, dark Maribou streamers, and brown sculpin imitations all can be effective stream patterns, while nymphs will also produce well. Fall is a good time for the lure fisherman as well, because fish are no longer looking to the surface for food.

Anglers interested in working hard for big autumn browns might consider the section of the Madison above Hebgen Lake and on into Yellowstone Park. A good spawning run leaves Hebgen in October, and deeply laced streamers and nymphs will take fish.

Even winter can provide some good fishing on the upper Madison for the angler willing to brave the cold temperatures and work weighted black nymphs along the streambottom. The trout might be a bit sluggish in the near-freezing water, but they will feed, as will scores of the more cold-adapted whitefish.

With the many attractions of the upper Madison now firmly in mind, a fisherman should also consider a few cautions. The strong summer afternoon winds in the valley can make casting—and even floating—extremely difficult. Use a heavier rod to counter the wind. The heavy current and slippery cobbles will limit the range of the angler on foot, especially during high water or where the river flows into a single channel. To avoid slipping, try cleats on the bottoms of your waders. Finally, the summer fisherman needs a tolerance for crowds. During a typical summer day, as many as forty guided drift boats from Ennis and West Yellowstone, along with a good number of private trips, will float the catch-and-release section. The bank angler may see a flotilla pass

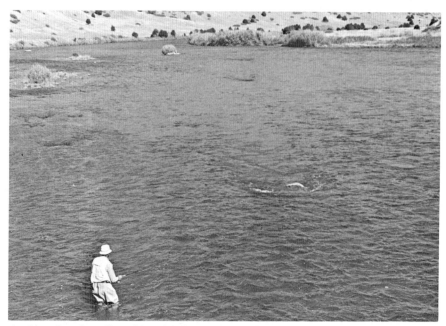

Anglers often do well working the slower water in front of the many big boulders in the Madison. Michael Sample photo.

before him, while the floating fisherman will be sandwiched between "dudes" flailing the water. Most of the guide boats put in between 10 and 11 a.m.

On the lower Madison, the basic tactic for early season (March through June) success is to cast large, dark, rubber-legged nymphs tight to the banks. As in the upper river, trout are looking for the natural salmon fly nymphs getting ready to emerge during high water. Spinners, along with streamers giving the impression of a darting sculpin or crayfish, are also effective. Bait fishermen focus on the deep runs and occasional holes along the cliff faces or beneath the cut banks. Dead-drifted sculpins or salmon fly nymphs are the most effective baits throughout the year on the lower Madison.

The dry fly fisherman on the lower Madison has his heyday in April and early May, when a thick mid-day caddis hatch blankets the smooth-flowing portion of the river just below the mouth of Beartrap Canyon. Typically, water temperatures are ideal, and trout rise freely to the naturals and to size 12 elk hair caddis imitations.

The salmon fly hatch on the lower Madison is sporadic, as nymph populations have been decimated by the warm summer water temperatures. Some dry fly action is possible, but most anglers continue to work the weighted nymphs along the banks. Again, high roily water can interfere with salmon fly fishing.

The hatch in Beartrap Canyon is more consistent and can provide good dry fly fishing. The turbulent waters of the canyon, however, are a radical change from the rest of the river, and the angler must adjust his tactics. Floating is restricted to the expert oarsman, and during highest flows, the canyon can be impassable. The fisherman on foot should ignore the midstream torrent. Instead, he should work the back eddies, bank edges, and spots behind or

Wading out and then working back toward the banks also works well on the Madison.
Michael Sample photo.

in front of boulders. A well-hackled elk-hair pattern is best suited to imitate the dry salmon fly in the rushing canyon waters.

The lower Madison has generally warmed by late June, and trout activity tapers off. Thick mats of green algae carpet the streambottom and wave in the current, making it almost impossible to fish with bait, spinners, or weighted nymphs. Dry caddis patterns can still provide some morning and evening action if the weather remains cool. During July and August, however, the knowledgeable anglers head for the upper river, conceding the lower Madison to the inner tube set.

Cool temperatures can put the trout on the feed again by the end of September, and fishing can remain good into November. Dark streamers and spinners are the best producers in the fall.

Tributaries

The area between Hebgen Lake and Yellowstone Park contains three of the most important tributary fisheries to the upper Madison. The South Fork of the Madison is a clear narrow stream meandering through brush fields and meadows just outside of West Yellowstone. The undercut banks and deep holes of this stream do hold some very large brown trout, but getting in a good cast without spooking the fish is a tremendous challenge.

Grayling Creek and Duck Creek are shallow, willow-lined streams holding good numbers of brookies, cutthroat, and rainbow, a few grayling, and occasional large spawning browns moving up from Hebgen Lake in the fall.

From Quake Lake to Ennis, the West Fork of the Madison is the most productive tributary fishery to the upper Madison. The West Fork's lower section is the classic free-stone mountain stream, with good fishing for rainbow

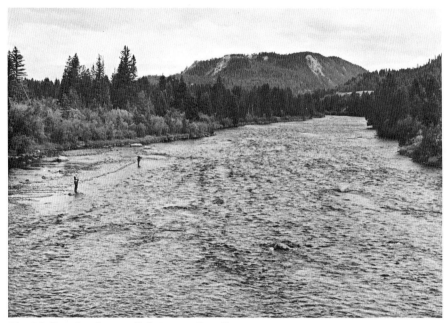

The Madison has been called "a 50-mile riffle." Al Troth photo.

averaging about twelve inches. Further upstream, the West Fork becomes a meandering, silt-bottomed stream with many beaver ponds and pan-sized trout. The West Fork is paralleled by a Forest Service gravel road and is readily accessible.

The dedicated dry fly fisherman on the lower Madison might want to try Darlington Spring Creek, a crystal clear stream flowing within an irrigation levee through Cobblestone fishing access site. Darlington has been improved greatly through a stream rehabilitation program by the Bozeman-area chapter of Trout Unlimited; the stream now offers good dry fly fishing for wary browns under a catch-and-release regulation.

Access

Public access to the upper Madison is generally excellent, as U.S. Highway 287 parallels the river from Hebgen Lake to Ennis. Where the road borders the river, you can simply park at a pulloff and start fishing. At other places, the river can be as much as three miles from the highway, so the angler should use one of the many public access points along the way. Lyon Bridge just below the West Fork; BLM's Palisades and Ruby Creek campgrounds; McAtee Bridge; and FWP's fishing access sites at Varney Bridge, Eight Mile Hole, Burnt Tree Ford, Ennis Bridge, and Valley Garden near Ennis provide an excellent south-to-north chain of access sites for floaters and waders.

Access to the lower Madison is very good from the mouth of Beartrap Canyon for the next five miles downstream. The canyon itself can be reached by trail, starting from the mouth or from the powerhouse below Ennis Lake. The final eighteen miles of the lower Madison are surrounded by private land, with public access provided at about six-mile intervals by the Grey Cliff and Cobblestone fishing access sites and by the U.S. Highway 10 bridge near the river's mouth. Floating anglers should be forewarned that taking a boat out at Cobblestone requires a trek of about 100 yards over two levees and across a shallow canal. A map of the entire river and details for floaters are found in the pamphlet, *Montana Afloat #15, the Madison River.*

MISSOURI RIVER

In the past twenty years, anglers from Helena to Great Falls and elsewhere around the state have learned the Missouri's secret: There are big fish in that big water! Not many out-of-staters know this yet, but the river has garnered some publicity in the big sporting magazines, and news of lunker trout has a way of spreading.

Ask a fisherman what he thinks of dams and he will probably respond, "It depends on which river." Anglers bitterly oppose some potential dams, such as the Allenspur Dam on the Yellowstone and the Kootenai Falls Dam on the Kootenai. But in other cases, anglers must admit that some blue-ribbon trout streams owe their excellence to dams. The Yellowtail Dam, for example, transformed a muddy, troutless Bighorn River into one of the nation's fine tailwater fisheries. Trout fanciers also benefitted with the advent of several dams on the Missouri.

For a hint of what the Missouri looked like before dams, regard the upper Missouri today. No dams impede the river from the confluence of the Gallatin, Madison, and Jefferson near the town of Three Forks down to the Toston Dam Reservoir. As with the other sections of the river, the upper Missouri is flat and very big, a football field or two across. But unlike the rest of the river, this stretch has a horrendous runoff. Even when the high waters have run their course, the water remains somewhat turbid through the irrigation season.

Make no mistake about it, this upper section holds thousands of trout averaging a very respectable size, with a few in the lunker and trophy classes. But if biologists had a ratio of number of trout to volume of river water, the trout density in this section of the Missouri probably would rank rather low. This part of the river is simply not as loaded with trout as other sections. Those trout that do live here don't, with minor exceptions, concentrate on any one area of the river. Anglers find that they need to cover a lot of river to do well here.

Because of its reputation as a good, but rarely spectacular, fishery in desolate-looking country quite distant from Montana's major population centers, the upper river does not see its just share of anglers. A few anglers poke in around Clarkston, gamble on the back roads and rattlesnakes around Lombard, or run their power boats up from Toston Dam, but these people certainly don't return with complaints of elbow-to-elbow fishing. For those who value solitude, the upper Missouri waits.

At Toston Dam, the picture changes radically. While it's only a low diversion type of impoundment, the dam stops migratory trout from proceeding up river any further. Because of the migratory rainbow and browns coming from Canyon Ferry Reservoir, FWP biologists find it difficult, if not impossible, to come up with solid population estimates of just what fish lurk in this section of river. But from their studies, several key facts do come clear.

First, some rainbow and browns stay in the river most, if not all, of the year. FWP's Bruce Rehwinkel notes that the number of resident fish drops when especially big influxes of migratory fish come up the river, much like what used to happen to the wild trout of the Madison when hatchery fish were stocked alongside them.

Second, brown trout from Canyon Ferry and the Missouri make spawning runs in the late fall. These browns concentrate in the upper section of the Missouri, mainly between the Deepdale access and Toston Dam. Based on the records Rehwinkel has examined, each November a few brown trout in the eight- to fourteen-pound class will be in the river below the dam. He remembers one incredible day of electrofishing when he handled forty-seven browns over twenty inches, the largest weighing over twelve pounds. Clearly, the brown trout is doing very well there.

Third, the spectacular fall rainbow runs witnessed in the 1970s no longer happen in comparable numbers. FWP biologists suspect that two factors account for this drastic decline: a mysterious change of some sort in Canyon Ferry Reservoir and the unique characteristics of the Arlee strain of rainbow. Traditionally, FWP stocked the fall spawning Arlee rainbow in Canyon Ferry because the strain has some good characteristics. They are very catchable and fast-growing. A five-incher planted in July will grow to ten inches by November and thirteen or fourteen inches by the following summer. As Rehwinkel points out, this amazing pace matches the growth rate of fish that are hand fed in a hatchery.

But Rehwinkel thinks this fast growth carries a price. At 2.5 years of age, eighteen inches long, and weighing about two pounds, Arlee rainbow not caught by anglers may soon die of old age. Moreover, biologists think that

The Missouri is known for its large trout such as this four-pound brown that fell for a five-inch bucktail. Al Troth photo.

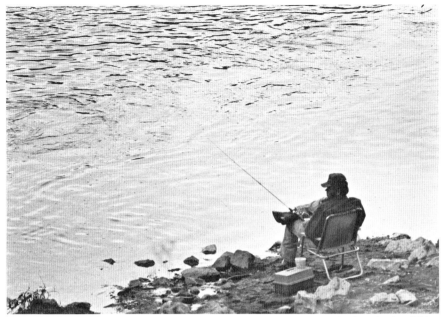

Perhaps more than other rivers, the Missouri attracts anglers in search of a relaxing fishing experience. Michael Sample photo.

few Arlee rainbow spawn successfully in the Missouri River. Thus there is little, if any, recruitment of future generations, and FWP had to keep up the never-ending cycle of stocking new fish.

Consequently, FWP is experimenting with plants of De Smet and Eagle Lake rainbow in Canyon Ferry. Spring spawners which grow more slowly, but live much longer, the De Smets may prove a valuable addition to the reservoir and the river above, especially if they spawn successfully.

Rehwinkel notes that the upper Missouri receives more than half its water from the Madison, water that has been heated by Ennis Lake. Peak temperatures in the mid-70s make trout lethargic. Rehwinkel suggests the cooler seasons for more lively action.

The cooler season of spring brings anglers out to muck through the mud and fish for the rainbow moving in and out of the river just above Canyon Ferry. Most of these fish measure twelve to eighteen inches, but Rehwinkel has found a very few in the three- to four-pound class.

The next section downstream on the Missouri is a one-mile stretch between Canyon Ferry and Hauser Lake. Though short in length, the river here supports kokanee and tremendous numbers of trout, both resident and migratory, and survives equally tremendous fishing pressure. FWP's Al Wipperman testifies that it runs about 13,000 angler days a year for just that one mile.

Ten- to twenty-inch rainbow comprise most of the catch year-round but most of the anglers who fish here have hopes of a trophy brown. Every year sees a few browns in the ten- to twelve-pound size brought to bay, though catch rates have dropped off from those of the early 1980s. Wipperman recalls a twenty-eight-pounder. Some optimists even suspect the presence of a forty-pounder below either Canyon Ferry or Hauser.

Missouri River

87

Carter
Carter Ferry
Fort Benton

80

Sun River

Dams

Dearborn River

Ulm
Great Falls

Highwood Mountains

Cascade

226

330

Eden

Hardy Bridge

Craig

Smith River

Belt Creek

Wolf Creek

Holter Reservoir

Lake Helena

Hauser Reservoir

Helena

Big Belt Mountains

Canyon Ferry Reservoir

Indian Road

Elkhorn Mountains

Townsend

Deepdale

Toston

Toston Dam

287

Missouri Headwaters State Monument

Fairweather

90

Logan

Three Forks

Jefferson River

Madison River

Gallatin River

N

HIGHWAY
COUNTY OR UNPAVED ROAD
△ OFFICIAL PUBLIC ACCESS
☐ RANGER STATION
X BRIDGE
〰〰 DIVERSION DAM

One inch = approx. 31 miles

MISSOURI RIVER (Upper)

To Harlem

191

Fred Robinson Bridge

James Kipp Recreational Area

Fort Belknap Indian Reservation

66

Charles M. Russell National Wildlife Refuge

Cow Island Landing

Cow Creek

Area

Missouri River

Woodhawk Creek

To Chinook

Badlands

N

McClelland Ferry

To Lewistown

Judith Landing (PN Ferry)

Judith River

Eagle Creek

Slaughter River Campsite

Arrow Creek

Area

236

White Rocks

Hole-in-the-Wall

LaBarge Rock

Citadel Rock

Big Sandy

Coal Banks Landing

To U.S. 87

Virgelle Ferry

80

Loma Ferry

HIGHWAY
COUNTY OR UNPAVED ROAD
△ OFFICIAL PUBLIC ACCESS
□ RANGER STATION
X BRIDGE
〰〰 DIVERSION DAM

Marias River

Teton River

Fort Benton

One inch = approx. 13 miles

To Chester

223

87

MISSOURI RIVER (Wild and Scenic)

113

Fort Union

North Dakota

Sidney

Montana

16

Culbertson

Yellowstone River

201

N

Poplar River

Poplar

Redwater River

Wolf Point

13

Missouri River

HIGHWAY

COUNTY OR UNPAVED ROAD

△ OFFICIAL PUBLIC ACCESS

□ RANGER STATION

X BRIDGE

〰〰 DIVERSION DAM

Fort Peck
Indian Reservation

Big Dry Creek

One inch = approx. 31 miles

Fort Peck

Glasgow

Fort Peck Reservoir

Charles M. Russell
National Wildlife Refuge

Milk River

2

UL Bend National Wildlife Refuge

Musselshell River

191

Turkey Joe

Fort Belknap
Indian Reservation

△ James Kipp Recreational Area

Fred Robinson Bridge

MISSOURI RIVER (Lower)

Anglers find the monster browns mostly during their fall spawning runs which peak in late November. Fishing for these browns tests the dedication of any angler. Catch rates are very low. November winds and temperatures can make fishing miserable. But for those who persist, fishing fantasies can come true.

Much the same situation exists below Hauser Dam. Here anglers have several miles of free-flowing river to work. Most anglers congregate around the mouth of Beaver Creek, but FWP's Jim Vashro suggests hiking to other excellent spots up or down the river. This stretch is more broken than the mile below Canyon Ferry. Anglers can wade the shallows to reach more of the river. And a notable run of rainbow up to six pounds can make this section an early season hot spot in addition to the autumn action.

Right below Holter Dam, anglers and fish again congregate in large numbers. Good under ordinary circumstances, fishing is red hot when the dam spills over the top, dropping lake fish on top of the river trout already at the bottom. When the word gets out, angling here becomes a shoulder-to-shoulder affair.

Below Holter Dam, the river runs free of dams for ninety miles until it reaches the city of Great Falls. FWP rates the river down to Cascade as class 1, blue-ribbon class. Rainbow outnumber browns six to one from Holter to the mouth of the Dearborn River. From electrofishing surveys, FWP estimates 2,674 catchable trout per mile, including a hundred fish eighteen inches or larger. The number of big trout drop off below the Dearborn. Around Cascade, the river starts changing to deeper water and fewer riffles. When the Smith dumps its heavy load of sediment into the river near Ulm, the trout become few and far between.

As a sidelight for anglers who know how to fish for them, some walleyes up to ten pounds swim in these waters. Walleye fans think their fish taste better than any other caught in the state.

Wipperman notes some good walleye fishing below Cascade, too. He knows some boating anglers with sonar who find and work some twenty-foot-deep holes for the walleyes and even some ling. The good news for this stretch of the Missouri is that the Montana Power Company intends to continue using Hauser and Holter dams as baseload power generators, which means the water gets released in relatively steady fashion over the course of a year. Unfortunately, Canyon Ferry Dam is operated by the Bureau of Reclamation as a peaking generator, causing wide fluctuations in flows downstream. Such fluctuations can disrupt fish spawning and rearing habits, and on this reach of the Missouri the changes in flow have a ripple effect far downstream. Hauser and Holter are "run-of-the-river" dams, meaning they cannot store excess water, and releases from these two dams must mirror releases from Canyon Ferry. Montana Power has been working with FWP and hopes to stabilize flows, as much as is possible under the circumstances, below Hauser and Holter to better protect spawning and rearing habitat.

Below Great Falls, anglers still have a few hot spots to try out. Wipperman reports some trout fishing below each of Great Falls's five dams, especially Morony Dam, although access is difficult. Sauger also swim below Morony Dam, but catch rates have declined since a peak a few years ago. And FWP's regional office reports that a small population of big rainbow averaging four pounds spawn below Fort Peck in the spring. These rainbow have "oddball genes" quite different from normal strains of rainbow. They started showing up in a side channel below the dam in the late 1970s, but the origin of this population is unclear. Some proposals for a re-regulating dam would inundate the spawning beds, ending what is currently an interesting, but fragile, fishery.

Fishing Strategies

Successful Missouri River anglers use a wide variety of baits, lures, and flies. Success does not hinge on what an angler ties on to the line so much as where the bait, lure, or fly is fished. And the advice of everyone, except dry fly anglers, is to fish the hooks down near the bottom of the river. Rarely does advice from so many anglers come so unanimously. As Rehwinkel puts it, "To catch big fish on the Missouri consistently, you must be willing to lose lots of tackle on the bottom."

Local bait anglers like the Missouri. The river is not littered with dead tree limbs or boulder fields to snag their hooks. It has lots of deep holes. And bait anglers do very well along the banks during the spring. Worms do work here. Unfortunately, they work not only for trout, but also for suckers, carp, and other trash fish. Unless the angler wants to catch these trash fish, worms are not the best bait.

Vashro suggests using a strip of sucker meat, about the size of a thumb, with the skin attached to keep this chunk of bait together. Then suckers, for understandable reasons, will not bother the bait. Carp, too, seem to avoid sucker meat.

Another effective bait, to the dismay of some anglers, is the spawn bag, a glob of fish eggs held together by nylon netting. To obtain these eggs, an angler usually must kill a hen fish. The eggs are then kept fresh in a solution of Borax or sugar water. For those who hate to kill a fish unnecessarily, Vashro points out that commercially available salmon eggs work well also.

Throughout the Missouri's length, sculpins and their imitations do well for anglers. This holds true especially below the dams, where the trout are looking for injured sculpins and minnows which have come through the turbines. In the latter half of the summer, grasshoppers fished near the banks also fool many a fish, especially on windy days.

Bait and fly anglers face a problem with getting their baits or flies down near the bottom without fouling up too often. Father Charlie Gorman, who has a winning way with fish as well as with congregations, finds the solution is to add sinkers near the hook and then a bobber adjusted to keep the hook off the bottom. Just how well the angler adjusts the distance between hook and bobber does much to determine how successful the angler's day will be.

Vashro recommends that anglers stock up with the larger sizes of spinning gear for the Missouri. Popular choices include different patterns of hammered brass lures and Rapalas. But on the Missouri, perhaps more than on any other Montana river, anglers use lead head jigs. Vashro prefers the white or black Maribou over the Bucktail type. Retrieve with lots of little twitches to simulate an injured minnow.

The Missouri below Holter Dam is noted for its dry fly fishing and produces some large caddis hatches in the summertime. Anglers keyed into these hatches report excellent action in the magic hour just before dark. These July and August hatches are usually matched with the familiar caddis imitations such as Humpies, Goofus, and elk hair caddis. And if you can't match the hatch, Fred Tedesco, who runs the Western Rivers guide service in Helena, declares that the Royal Wulff is absolutely the best attractor fly on the Missouri, especially below Holter. Hopper patterns also fool their fair share of fish. Tedesco uses a hopper or the Wulff when there is no hatch on the river.

Tedesco also comes armed with leech imitations, some caddis emerger patterns, some pheasant tail nymphs, and perhaps some big Royal Coachmans to fish wet.

Tedesco guides quite a few clients on the river below Holter in August and September, when the mayflies hatch. During this time, he uses about a size 18 fly, such as Red Quill, Olive Dun, Polywing Spinner, or Adams. He stresses that this section of the river "has a different scheme than most. To catch fish consistently on flies, you have to learn the river, learn the places where the rainbow hang out and the places that just hold hundreds of whitefish." One way to learn these places is to observe carefully how the fish rises. "The rainbow makes a white flash, tends to make a swirl, and may show the dorsal fin; with a whitefish rise, the forked tip of the tail comes out," reports Tedesco. Once Tedesco finds a pod of rainbow, often in the weed beds or along the islands and side channels, he finds he can catch several fish in that one spot.

In the spring and fall, most fly fishermen use large nymphs and streamers in combination with basic steelhead tactics. When light levels are low, the trout will be out on the shallower gravel beds and at the riffle-tails; when the light is bright, the fish stay in the deeper pools and runs. With large rods and sink tip or high density sinking line, the casts should go quartering upstream to allow the weighted flies a chance to sink. Once the river takes the slack out of the line, the angler strips the line back in. After a couple steps downstream, the process is repeated.

Tedesco observes that, although the method is basically simple, many anglers make the mistake of not letting the fly get down to the bottom. And he finds a lot of people disappointed with how hard it is to fish this way. "The average

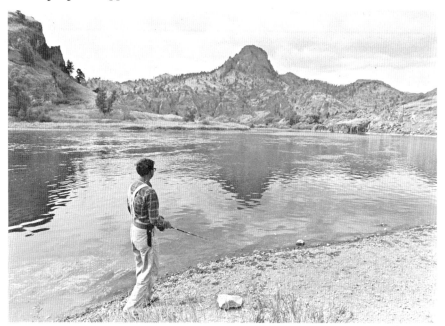

Even though it has a series of impoundments, the Missouri has maintained excellent trout fishing. Michael Sample photo.

person would be better off somewhere else. This dredging the bottom is not casual; it's trophy fishing, and you pay the price of hours on end with nothing."

In three years of very hard fishing in this manner, Tedesco has caught two rainbow over four pounds and a number of lunker browns, including an eleven-pounder. He notes that success in the fall depends on the flow—the lower the flow, the better the fishing. Other than that, he has not found any reliable indication of how the fishing will be from one day to the next. "You just keep plugging and hoping," he says.

In addition to traditional patterns, such as dark and white Spruce flies, Maribou Muddlers, and Wooly Buggers, several local favorites also reportedly catch the fishes' fancies: Road Kills (tied with rabbit), Happy Hookers, and perch imitations tied with yellow and orange color. These are generally tied on with beefy leaders. Tedesco remarks that the need for flimsy, light leaders "is a great big myth perpetuated by outdoor writers."

When fishing for big browns, whether by fly, lure, or bait, anglers should keep in mind the nocturnal habits of these fish. Take a flashlight to watch for hazards. Night anglers may not have great suntans, but they do have plenty of excitement.

Tributaries

Anglers who know Sixteenmile Creek regard it as a mixed blessing. As a fishery, it is exceptionally productive. A relatively small stream, it harbors large numbers of brookies nine to thirteen inches, rainbow ten to seventeen inches, and resident browns up to twenty-two inches. These fish hang out in the boulder pockets, under the heavy streamside brush, and in the riffle-pools. The stream provides consistently good action just about any time of day and throughout the fishing season.

However, the stream runs almost entirely through private lands. Road access is difficult. And the helpful railroad tracks have been abandoned and may also become private ranch land.

Sixteenmile Creek also has the dubious distinction of being fabled rattle-snake country. Vashro, who loves fishing but hates rattlers, declines to try Sixteenmile after a friend killed seventeen rattlers in the first mile above the Missouri. While this was undoubtedly an exceptional experience, anglers should be cautious, especially when walking through the brush.

Little Prickly Pear Creek, despite all the alterations to its streambed, still grants very good fishing for its lively population of ten- to fourteen-inch rainbow and occasional browns. The creek joins the Missouri a couple miles below Holter. Anglers will find easy access along old U.S. Highway 191, now officially a "recreation road."

With its canyon, limestone cliffs, and deep holes, the Dearborn River looks like a smaller version of the Smith River. The lower section from the Highway 287 bridge down to the Missouri has much of the best fishing and the only floatable water, in Wipperman's opinion. Again the predominate rainbow run ten to fifteen inches, and the holes house some browns up to five pounds.

Unfortunately, the floating season does not coincide well with the summer fishing season. By July, just when the fishing is picking up, the water drops to such a degree that anglers must drag their canoes or rafts across the shallow riffles.

Downstream, the Sun River joins the Missouri at Great Falls. A sluggish, muddy river at the end, the Sun has pristine beginnings in the Bob Marshall

Wilderness. Anglers willing to hike to the headwaters find good fishing for unsophisticated trout in the usually crystal-clear water. Wipperman terms the river below Gibson Reservoir a sleeper, because it gets little fishing pressure. Rainbow provide the bulk of the catch along with a smattering of browns. Wipperman rates the section between Simms and the town of Sun River as best. Here, the access is only through private lands except for the FWP access at Fort Shaw. Anglers can float the Sun, but they should watch for some mean diversion dams and cottonwood snags. Wipperman notes that some of the slower sections above Muddy Creek yield some exciting fishing for northern pike from five to fifteen pounds, as well as winter ice-fishing—when the wind is taking a day off.

In a very attractive park right in Great Falls, FWP stocks catchable rainbow in Giant Springs. As the springs are right next to the hatchery, this fishery is something of a pet project of FWP's. Many families enjoy the fishing in this beautiful spot.

The first ten miles of the Marias River below Tiber Dam yield some good fishing for rainbow. Local anglers try for some lunkers up to six pounds.

Trout fanciers need not pay much attention to the Judith River, but one of its tributaries, Big Spring Creek, deserves a lot more attention. Although the 1975 flood tore up Big Spring Creek, the fishery has made a tremendous comeback. FWP found more than 1,800 catchable trout in less than a mile, astounding for a medium-sized stream. For a comparison, note that the best sections of the mighty Missouri have about the same number of catchables per mile. Wipperman reports lots of rainbow from one to two pounds and a fair number of browns in the three- to four-pound range. He also recalls that, in 1968, an angler caught a nineteen-pounder just below the big springs—proof of what this phenomenal fishery can grow.

Big Spring is gaining in popularity among anglers, but fishing pressure is still low to moderate. FWP has three accesses: Burleigh, about four miles above Lewistown; and two currently unnamed spots below Lewistown. Fishing this fast-moving water buffaloes some anglers. Try fishing along the edges or down in the six-foot-deep holes.

The last trout-inhabited tributary of the Missouri is the unheralded

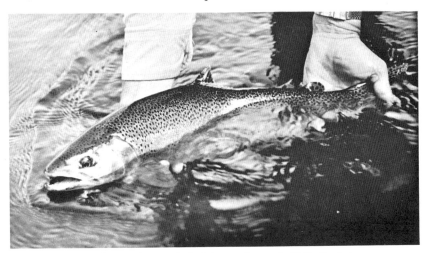

Releasing a big one for another angler's future enjoyment. Al Troth photo.

Musselshell River. The lower river runs too silty and warm for trout but FWP recently made an experimental planting of smallmouth bass near Roundup, and Wipperman thinks the plant has taken hold. Trout anglers head upstream of Harlowton where some big browns lurk in the cleaner water, especially in the twenty miles upstream of the town of Twodot. Recent dry years have hurt the Musselshell's fishery, but trout populations are at least holding their own. The Selkirk Fishing Access Site (FAS) helps anglers reach the river in an area otherwise privately owned. Or anglers can go further upstream into the headwaters in the Castle and Little Belt mountains where the Forest Service owns some riverbanks. Here, anglers encounter a mix of pan-sized brookies and some rainbow that wouldn't fit into most pans.

Like the Shields River to the south, the Musselshell grows fish quickly but runs out of the way of major highways and the travel routes of most anglers. Thus, anglers along the Musselshell do not bump into each other often. Miles of excellent river fishing await the more adventuresome anglers.

Access

Anglers can first reach the Missouri right where it starts, at Missouri Headwaters State Park. This informative facility is reached from a well-marked exit off Interstate 90 just east of Three Forks.

The Fairweather FAS is more elusive. FWP's Recreation Map describes the usual route starting at Logan, going west a mile on U.S. Highway 10, then 3.5 miles north on the Logan-Trident Road, then ten miles northeast on the Clarkston Road. As with all FWP's fishing accesses above Canyon Ferry, Fairweather has a good boat ramp.

Near the town of Toston on Highway 287, anglers are directed to the Toston Dam FAS by an obvious sign. Or anglers can reach the east side of the river by a county road running southeast from Toston. This road, if passable, will eventually bring the angler to Lombard, where Sixteenmile Creek joins the river.

Below Toston, anglers reach the river when it bends over to U.S. Highway 287, at Deepdale FAS four miles south of Townsend; and at Indian Road FAS a mile northwest of Townsend, also just off Highway 287.

About six miles east of East Helena, on Highway 287, Montana Highway 284 leads to Canyon Ferry Dam. A campground just downstream gives both bank and boat anglers access to this short, but intensely fished, section. Entry fees are now charged at these sites.

To reach the river just below Hauser Dam, drive from Helena past the Lakeside Resort and across the river to York, then turn northwest to Beaver Creek, then west on County Road 138 down to the river. Or drive eight miles north of Helena on Interstate 15 to the Lincoln Road exit, then four miles east on County Road 453, then three miles north to Black Sandy and White Sandy state recreation areas.

Anglers wishing to fish between Holter Dam and Ulm get off Interstate 15 and onto a recreation road which intertwines with the river and the interstate. A short spur road leads to the base of the dam from the Wolf Creek exit. Below, some nine fishing access sites and state recreation areas, plus considerable casual access where river and road come together, give the angler lots of choices.

Anglers interested in the river below Great Falls can launch their boats at Fort Benton, the Loma Ferry, Coal Banks Landing near the mouth of the Judith

River, at the PN Ferry due north of Winifred, and at the Fred Robinson Bridge where U.S. Highway 191 crosses the river. The section just above Fort Peck Reservoir offers good fishing for sauger in early spring and catfish in late spring.

Last of all, for fishing just below Fort Peck Dam, anglers should check out the Fort Peck Dredge Cuts FAS.

ROCK CREEK

For many residents of Missoula, the road to paradise begins only twenty miles east of town at Interstate 90, Exit #126—the Rock Creek Road. A drive along Rock Creek offers an escape from the sprawling metropolis of 50,000 inhabitants into a wild and beautiful mountain valley. It also provides access to one of the most delightful and challenging fishing experiences in Montana.

Throughout its fifty-mile length, Rock Creek is a classic fast-water trout stream. The riffles, runs, and occasional pools host five species of trout, all of which have the agreeable disposition of being where they're supposed to be. Literally any place that offers hiding cover and some relief from the current will harbor trout.

Rock Creek is one of the most studied streams in Montana. The Montana Department of Fish, Wildlife and Parks (FWP) has monitored fishing pressure, harvest, and fish populations during the past thirty years.

During the 1970s, intensive fish population sampling through electro-

The close proximity to Missoula brings large numbers of anglers to Rock Creek. Michael Sample photo.

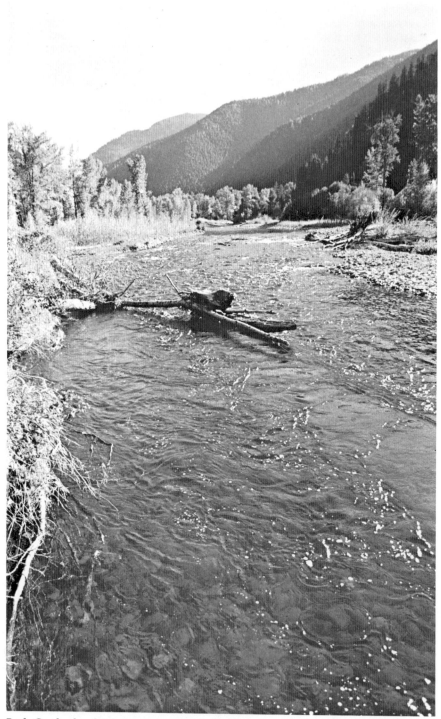

Rock Creek, the classic trout stream, all 50 miles of it. Michael Sample photo.

shocking confirmed what Rock Creek fishermen had long suspected—the good-sized fish were disappearing. By 1978, few rainbow beyond sixteen inches were being caught; and the biggest brown taken was twenty inches, down from the twenty-three- to twenty-four-inch fish of earlier years. Cutthroat, typically the easiest trout to catch and thus the most susceptible to overfishing, were all but eliminated from the population.

In 1979, the Montana Fish and Game Commission followed the recommendations of fisheries biologists—and the desires of local sportsmen—and instituted new regulations designed to let Rock Creek again reach its potential as a quality trout fishery.

The new regulations restrict the use of bait to children under fifteen years of age to minimize fish mortality. All other anglers may use only artificial lures. The middle reach of Rock Creek, between Butte Cabin Creek and Hogback Creek, is catch-and-release only, with no bait fishing allowed at all. As a result of these restrictive regulations there has been a significant increase in larger-sized trout and an improvement in the populations of cutthroat and rainbow trout.

Although Rock Creek provides excellent angling throughout the season, the annual salmon fly hatch provides its single biggest drawing card. The cobble bottom of Rock Creek supports an amazing density of the two-inch-long Pteronarcys californica nymphs. The flights of thousands of these bright orange, winged adults make for a fascinating natural spectacle.

Adult salmon flies begin emerging at the mouth of Rock Creek around June 1. During the month of June, the hatch gradually works its way up the fifty-mile stream course. A mid-day drive along the Rock Creek Road is the best way to locate the hatch, as the ungainly, helicopter-like adults are impossible to miss when they hover over the stream or land on the roadside bushes.

The proximity of Rock Creek to Missoula means intense fishing pressure throughout the summer, a situation compounded by the numerous Forest Service campgrounds along the stream's upper and middle reaches. "Opening day, holidays, and weekends are good days to avoid," cautions Don Peters, FWP fisheries biologist in Missoula.

Be sure to check the special regulations before fishing.

Fishing Strategies

The sparkling, clear water and a wide variety of aquatic insects contribute to Rock Creek's proven ability to produce trout. These same factors also force the angler to refine his techniques to achieve consistent success. In general, overdressed fly patterns or large, gaudy lures will not do the trick, especially on Rock Creek's sophisticated browns and larger rainbow. For the fly fisherman, this means reasonable imitations of whatever adult insects are hatching or of the nymphs crawling along the streambottom. The hardware fisherman must give his lure realistic action and careful placement in order to attract a strike rather than spook the fish.

The angler will find a good, diverse insect population on Rock Creek every day during the season. Aside from the major salmon fly hatch, there are caddis, mayfly, and small stonefly hatches throughout the summer. A size 14 to 16 chartreuse-bodied stonefly is ideal during the summer evening hatch. The spruce moth adult emerges in August when the water is low and clear. An elk hair caddis is effective during this mid-day hatch. With such an abundance of aquatic insects for trout to feed on, the spin fisherman will often do best by fishing a bubble and fly set-up.

During the salmon fly hatch, conventional wisdom says to go to the head (upstream end) of the hatch for best fishing. However, trout often continue to look for salmon flies where the hatch has passed over, sometimes for weeks.

Floating has become increasingly popular as a way to combat the difficult high-water conditions in the early season, especially during the salmon fly hatch. However, conflicts between floating fishermen and bank fishermen have arisen due to Rock Creek's small size and narrow channels. After monitoring the situation, FWP set restrictions prohibiting fishing from boats after June 30 until November 30. Anyone wishing to float Rock Creek should consult the pamphlet, *Montana Afloat #3, Rock Creek*, for a map and detailed information on the stream.

In the early season, wading Rock Creek provides both a challenge and an opportunity to the angler. The challenge is to make your way safely amid the swift currents and slick cobble bottoms. The opportunity is that hard-chargers can reach water—and fish—that most anglers only give a passing glance.

By mid-summer, anglers can wade most sections of the stream without too much difficulty. The best crossing points, where runs become shallow at the head of a riffle, are usually not more than a couple hundred yards apart. Rocks grow slicker with algae throughout the course of the summer, so felt-soled waders are recommended.

Subtle changes in topography and stream habitat divide Rock Creek into three sections, each from ten to fifteen miles in length. At its upper end, immediately below the confluence of the east and west forks, Rock Creek hosts gentle pocket water, which twists its way through a .5-mile-wide valley. Relatively small and unsophisticated cutthroat dominate the trout population here. Both flies and lures will produce reasonable catches of eight- to twelve-inch fish if cast into the likely spots behind midstream rocks and at the heads of the few deeper pools.

The middle section of Rock Creek begins where the canyon walls constrict just above the mouth of Big Hogback Creek. From this point downstream for the next fifteen miles, Rock Creek's swift flow becomes that much swifter, and holding water becomes a thing to be cherished. Although the continuous, swift riffles look somewhat unpromising, by all means stop the car, put on your waders, and start fishing. The trout are here—in excellent numbers. And don't forget your polarized sunglasses. They're a must for reading the rushing water and allowing you to distinguish the one- to two-foot-deep runs where fish can be found from the less-than-a-foot-deep stretches where they can't.

Rainbow trout constitute about sixty percent of the fish population in the middle section of Rock Creek, but the special "slot-limit" regulations that cover most of this water have sparked a veritable cutthroat renaissance. These scrappy, but vulnerable, natives now make up about twenty percent of the population, after having dwindled to negligible numbers when the former liberal limits were in force. Most rainbow will go twelve to fourteen inches, with cuts averaging a little smaller. The slot limit regulations—requiring catch-and-release for trout between twelve and twenty inches—have helped increase the number of rainbow larger than fourteen inches.

The middle and upper sections of Rock Creek also host a remarkable, but seldom encountered, bonus for the angler—one of the best stream populations of bull trout in Montana. This native fish attains weights of up to fifteen pounds by virtue of a diet consisting almost exclusively of other fish. A prime

To Missoula

I-90

Bonita

To Drummond

Clark Fork

LOLO
NATIONAL
FOREST

Rock Creek

Grizzly Point

Footbridge

x

Dalles

Harry's Flat

two miles

102

Bitterroot Flat

Hutsinpilar

Rock Creek

Bighorn

To Philipsburg

Squaw Rock

Gilles Bridge

N

West Fork

Highway 1

HIGHWAY
COUNTY OR UNPAVED ROAD
△ OFFICIAL PUBLIC ACCESS
☐ RANGER STATION
X BRIDGE
〜〜〜 DIVERSION DAM

ROCK CREEK

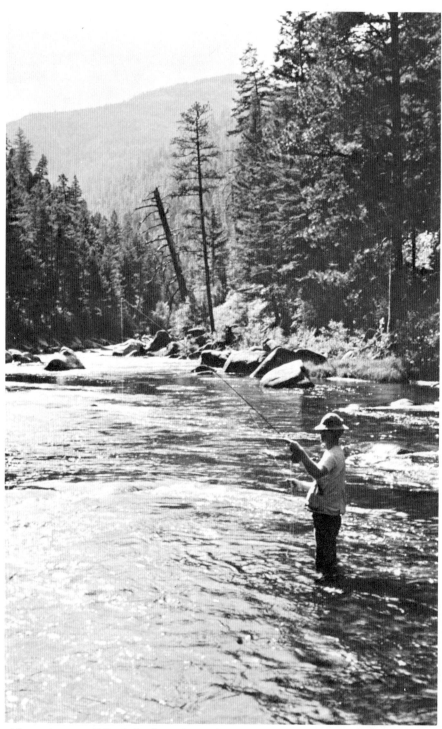

After spring run-off, Rock Creek can be easily waded throughout most of its 50-mile course. Michael Sample photo.

specimen of a Rock Creek bull trout can be viewed on the wall at Streamside Anglers fly shop in Missoula. For those who'd like to view one on the end of their line, prospecting the deeper runs or pools with big spoons or large streamers offers the best—but still slim—chance of success. Most bull trout taken are in the one- to three-pound range, and most come as a considerable surprise to the anglers who catch them.

The lower section of Rock Creek offers the greatest variety of trout habitat, with logjams, undercut banks, deep runs, and deeper pools. Brown trout and rainbow predominate here, with good numbers of fourteen- to eighteen-inch browns and ten- to fourteen-inch rainbows. Typically, the browns hold in the most protected lies; consequently, they prove hard to catch, making up only half the reported catch. Big spawners from the lower Clark Fork River show up in late fall, including some over five pounds. The deep pools and swift runs hold a few rainbow up to 2.5 pounds.

Successful fishing on Rock Creek requires diligent wading and careful reading of the swift water. "This is hard fishing for the novice fisherman, who often believes the fish aren't there," Peters claims. A ten-year creel census found that nearly half the anglers on Rock Creek don't catch any fish, while a small minority of anglers get most of the catch. Rock Creek is one stream where experience really pays.

Tributaries

Rock Creek has two major tributaries that provide fishing. The East Fork of Rock Creek flows through pasture and haylands with natural brushy banks. A small creek, the East Fork has good fishing for nice cutthroat and brookies. Permission must be gained from private landowners for access, however.

The West Fork of Rock Creek has easy access through National Forest land, but due to a sediment problem, it has a low fish population. There are some nice cutthroat, though, and the creek receives only light fishing pressure. The West Fork is small, running through low meadowlands with brushy banks.

Access

The Rock Creek Road follows Rock Creek closely along much of its length, providing good stream access. This is a narrow gravel road requiring slow travel. Area residents like it this way, because it helps minimize the road traffic. Fishermen get too impatient with the slow, bumpy pace and pull off early to hit the river.

The lower fifteen miles of Rock Creek are bounded by National Forest land, with private lands along the road. There are several access sites where you can walk in to the river as well as various points where the road meets the river. Once on the streambank, the angler has unlimited access to the river.

The middle stretch of river offers the easiest access, as it is bordered by the road for almost fifteen miles.

The upper river has the toughest access. Private lands between the road and stream limit access. Permission may be sought from any of several landowners, whose large ranches can provide access to long stretches of river. The road from Philipsburg is the best way to reach the upper river.

The Lolo National Forest maintains eight small campgrounds along the length of Rock Creek. They are open from late May through September, with a maximum fourteen-day limit on use. Needless to say, these are popular recreation spots on weekends.

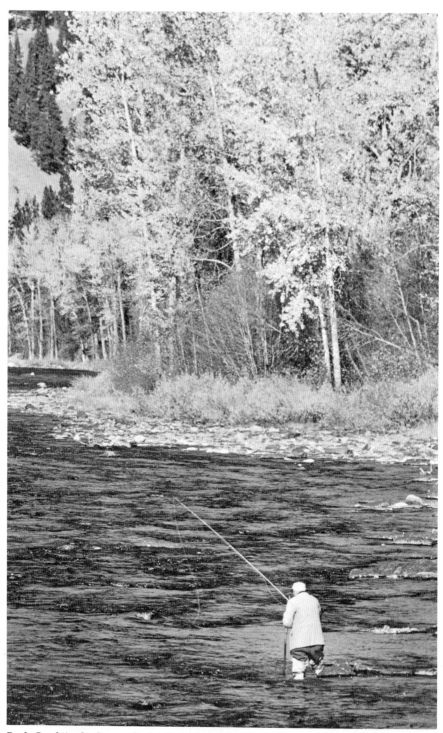

Rock Creek is also known for its slippery streambed which is why some anglers use wading sticks. Michael Sample photo.

SMITH RIVER

In the long list of reasons why people fish, one of the most frequently mentioned is "getting away from the rat race." Even an hour or two of fishing refreshes the spirit and puts the world in the right perspective. Imagine the tonic of a fishing trip lasting several days through the spectacular Smith River Canyon. As a getaway experience, floating and fishing the Smith certainly ranks among the best.

Like the forks of the Flathead and the wild Missouri, the Smith float appeals even to those who don't own a fishing rod. The usual float trip starts at the Camp Baker Fishing Access and ends nearly sixty miles downstream at the Eden Bridge. In between, the river bounces from one canyon wall to the other. Rarely does the river head in any one direction for long. The fairly swift current and thousands of boulders combine to make innumerable minor rapids. Other than a few clusters of cabins and an occasional fence, floaters see few signs of man.

Fishing guide Frank Johnson from Missoula describes the canyon float as a progressive learning experience for the beginning angler. In the upper section, large numbers of rainbow (few of them big) provide fairly easy fishing. Johnson has seen anglers catch a hundred trout in a day—an extraordinary catch rate by anyone's standards. You'll find these rainbow around the rocks.

The whole canyon section of the river conforms to the classic riffle-pool-run pattern. As the Smith gains volume with additional water from tributaries such as Rock Creek and Tenderfoot Creek, the riffles and pools become deeper, favoring larger fish. The water flows in more complicated patterns with more eddies and undercut banks. And brown trout make up an increasing percentage of the population. The middle and lower reaches of the canyon call for more skill and sophistication from the angler.

Once the Smith leaves the canyon, the runs lengthen and the gradient begins to flatten. Past the Eden Bridge, the angler begins to run into what Al Wipperman of the Montana Department of Fish, Wildlife and Parks (FWP) describes as "catfish water, with lots of slack water and mud streambed." The Truly Bridge marks the end of significant numbers of trout.

The upper Smith down to Camp Baker once provided lively fishing for the few anglers who tried it. John Bailey, son of the late great angler, Dan Bailey, liked to drive the short distance from Livingston to the expansive hay meadows along this meandering stream. The section from Fort Logan to Sheep Creek was almost devoid of other anglers, but full of cut banks, deep pools, and plenty of trout. But Bailey reports that recent dry years, coupled with two severe winters, devastated the upper Smith. Indeed, many of Montana's smaller, shallow streams froze out during the winter of 1989-90, but fishing appears to be picking up again as fish recruits re-enter these waters. Bailey has high hopes that the upper Smith will soon offer terrific dry fly fishing once again.

When talking with people who have floated the Smith, worries about the future of the river frequently surface. Hank Fischer, who wrote about the Smith in *The Floater's Guide to Montana*, hopes that new cabin subdivisions won't spring up along the banks, ruining the wilderness feeling of the canyon.

Bailey and Wipperman both mention that unhealthy water temperatures due to extensive flood irrigation in the upper basin can be a problem.

But it is Johnson who guards this river most protectively. He worries about both fishing pressure and social pressure. During the prime floating season of late June and early July, floaters descend on the Smith in veritable armadas. The Fourth of July weekend brings out peak numbers. Swifter canoeists annoy the slower rafters. Unoccupied campsites become scarce. Many out-of-state people would still consider the Smith a wilderness experience, but spoiled native Montanans have begun to find it crowded.

Johnson continues with a question: "What if most of those anglers keep a few fish each day they're on the river?" Over the course of a year, the number of trout killed could run into the many thousands. Johnson doesn't begrudge the person who will fry a fish or two for dinner. But he is griped "by the guys with this ego thing who can't release fish even when they know they won't be eaten." These wasted fish end up in the bushes or crystallized in the freezer, never again to reproduce their own kind. Johnson especially mourns the eighteen- to twenty-two-inch prime spawners.

Putting his money where his mouth is, Johnson limits the number of anglers he will guide on the Smith. And he pointedly tells his clients that if they've come to kill fish, they can find another guide to take them.

Then, like the Oregonians who try to discourage everyone from coming to live in Oregon by claiming "the sun never shines in Oregon," and "people don't tan, they rust," Johnson points out some of the dangers and difficulties in floating the Smith. It's unusual not to see a rattler on the trip, for example. And there are so many rocks that the Smith can beat the bottom out of any craft. He also points out the lengthy car shuttle and the long distances to help in case of an accident.

A trip down the Smith River is an unforgetable fishing experience. Michael Sample photo.

Missouri River

Great Falls

Ulm

Truly

15

226

330

Cascade

Eden

Eden Bridge

89

Hound Creek

County Road

Deep Creek

Little Belt Mountains

Tendertoot Creek

Big Belt Mountains

Smith River

Sheep Creek

Camp Baker △

△ Smith River

Fort Logan

North Fork Smith River

Buckingham Bridge

360

Castle Mountains

North Fork Smith River

White Suphur Springs

South Fork Smith River

12

- - - - HIGHWAY
- - - - - COUNTY OR UNPAVED ROAD
△ OFFICIAL PUBLIC ACCESS
▢ RANGER STATION
X BRIDGE
〰 DIVERSION DAM

One inch = approx. 12 miles

SMITH RIVER

Johnson's points do limit floaters to the more adventuresome. And so far, Wipperman's research shows a fishery that is holding its own. The river's protectors would like to keep it that way.

In response to these concerns, FWP has instituted several new regulations. All groups floating the Smith must register at the put-in, and the number of outfitters working the river is now limited. In addition, all parties must declare which campsites they will use during their journey down the Smith. A river ranger ensures compliance with these regulations and offers aid and information to those requesting it. A good river map and detailed information can be found in *Montana Afloat #9, the Smith River*.

When can anglers float and fish the canyon section? Each year's weather pattern differs, but the average peak runoff comes the last week of May. In a year of at least average precipitation, the river is both dangerous and very muddy at the height of runoff. Hank Fischer has had a good trip in April, when he saw black bears and elk on the river banks, but some Aprils in Montana can be miserable for floaters.

Somewhat more predictably, the period of June 20 to July 20 should have mostly clear water at levels neither too high nor too low. Later in the summer the heavy demands of irrigation mean too little water for most crafts to clear the rocks. In some autumns after the irrigation gates close, the Smith has enough water to float it again. The secret here, in John Bailey's experience, is "a slippery bottomed boat."

A heavy thunderstorm in the watershed translates into a rapid rise in the river's level almost immediately, but unlike some rivers, the Smith will usually drop and clear with equal rapidity.

Between the stable banks of the Smith lives a nice range of trout food: mayflies, caddis, a few stoneflies, good numbers of sculpin, and schools of minnows. Combine this food and excellent cover with good water quality, and the result is a fine fishery. Mixing in a spectacular and unspoiled canyon makes a recipe for a float-fishing getaway trip among the best in the west.

Fishing Strategies

Whatever an angler chooses to tie on the end of the fishing line, whether lure or fly, the Smith has the right kinds of water for that choice. Spin anglers will find plenty of deeper riffles and runs as well as the holes to their liking. Cut banks, boulder pockets, and riffles await the fly fisherman. From Rock Creek to Eden Bridge, the Smith is closed to bait fishing to all but children under twelve years, but elsewhere on the river bait anglers enjoy good success.

In the upper river basin from above White Sulphur Springs down to Camp Baker, the Smith meanders through hay meadows and pastureland. A modest-sized stream at this point, the river still provides lots of deep water at the bends. The rainbow and brookies stay in the pools or right up against the bank most of the time, except during the twilight feeding frenzy. Fling your flies and lures at the banks or drift the bait through the holes.

Below Camp Baker, in the bigger river, boulders change the picture somewhat. Holes and banks still hold plenty of promise but rocks provide good cover, too, harboring many a trout.

A skillful nymph angler can really operate if rigged with plenty of weight. In any river, trout spend the vast majority of their time hugging the bottom out of the current's heavy flow. As food tumbles or swims toward the trout, they may move a short distance to seize it. The closer an angler's bait or weighted nymph gets to the bottom where the trout waits, the more likely it will be taken. In the Smith, where holes can be very deep, anglers should load up with plenty of split shot.

Spin anglers happily find the Smith relatively free of serious moss problems. Standard wares such as hammered brass and red-and-whites work well; but if you're floating the canyon, bring a good stock—it's a long way to the nearest tackle shop.

Fly fishermen will not encounter massive hatches of any one bug. Both Bailey and Johnson think it relatively unimportant to match the hatches perfectly. Bailey uses attractor patterns such as Wulffs and Goofus. Hoppers work very well during the grasshopper season and should be fished up against the banks.

Bailey and Johnson also recommend trying any of the standard larger stonefly nymphs, weighted in the pools. Keeping in mind the good population of sculpins, try Muddler Minnows as proven performers, although Johnson confesses he is not convinced trout eat sculpin imitations because they think they are sculpins. And in the autumn, stick a few small streamers in the vest.

Early and late in the fishing season, any time of the day might be good, but when the hot days of mid-summer bear down on the river with their glaring sunlight, fishing is generally best in the mornings or evenings.

Bailey finds that most anglers are not aggressive enough in fishing the Smith. By this he means that anglers will frequently stand in just one spot, fruitlessly whipping the water into a froth without any luck. These anglers assume that if they can't catch fish in the spot they are in, then they can't catch them anywhere in the river. Bailey often finds that, while the first riffle-pool may be dead, the next one might be alive with feeding fish. Keep moving!

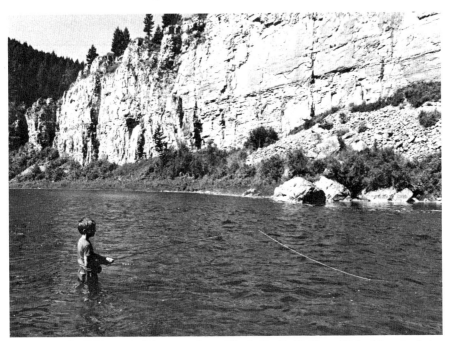

A young angler fishing one of the many deep riffles in the Smith River. Michael Sample photo.

Tributaries

"Some people swear by the North Fork," Bailey reports. Much of the North Fork of the Smith runs through one ranch. Above the fork's reservoir, anglers find a smattering of rainbow mixed in with crowds of brookies. Below the reservoir they find mostly brown trout, which thrive in the warmer waters.

The South Fork of the Smith produces pan-sized brookies by the carload. A small, meandering stream, the South Fork makes a good place to teach youngsters the joys of fishing.

Wipperman singles out three other tributaries of the Smith as good fisheries. The first is Sheep Creek, one of the largest feeder streams and an excellent fishery for rainbow, which is followed by roads much of its length. Second, ten or twelve miles from the Smith, a natural falls interrupts the flow of Tenderfoot Creek. Above the falls swim hybrid rainbow and cutthroat; below, browns and rainbow rule the stream. The third tributary is Rock Creek, which is strong for rainbow and browns.

Access

The Smith has just two developed fishing access sites. The first is at the end of a county road downstream a couple of miles from Fort Logan. FWP does not recommend this spot for putting in to float, but anglers can fish a considerable length of the river up and down from the campground and picnic area and still be within this block of public land.

About six miles downstream from the first access site is Camp Baker, where floaters traditionally put in to run the canyon. While there are no facilities at Camp Baker, FWP has posted a considerable amount of information including an extremely helpful map of the Smith. Floaters must register here. Also, anglers can fish a half-mile or so of the west bank on this smaller parcel of public land.

Other than at a few bridges, no other public access exists. In the upper basin, anglers need to inquire at ranches to reach the river. In the canyon section, several rough roads do reach the cabin communities along the river, but these roads are private and the gates are often padlocked. Below the canyon, the Eden Bridge road provides some casual access, but for most of this section, anglers need to knock on doors for permission.

STILLWATER RIVER

"Stillwater" is a misnomer. One suspects that the early explorer who named this river either looked only at a short section or had a wry sense of humor. The Stillwater has less quiet water proportionally than any river in the state.

Intrepid kayakers love this roly-poly stream. Boulders, many the size of large chest freezers, stud almost the entire length of the river. The melt water from Montana's loftiest mountains courses its way through these boulder fields with plenty of foam and froth. Long after it enters the prairie land of eastern Montana, the Stillwater still looks like a mountain stream.

Surrounded by fabled trout waters such as the Bighorn, Yellowstone, and Madison rivers, the Stillwater receives little national or state attention. Instead, it makes a popular destination for local anglers who know its beauty and excellent fishing. Trout fanciers in any state would love to have the Stillwater nearby.

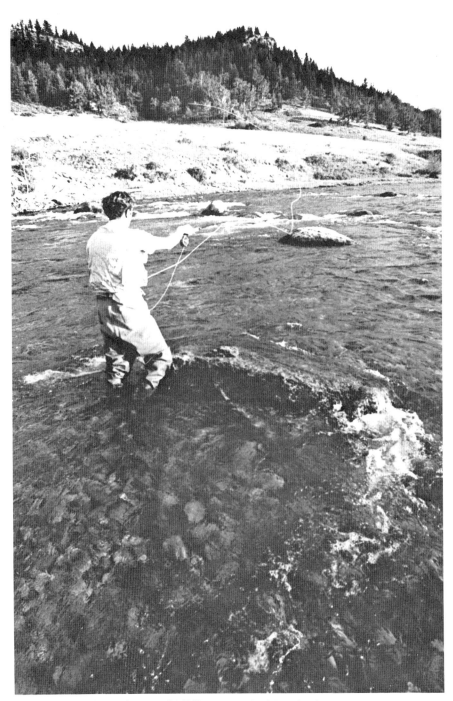

Fishing the boulder pockets on the Stillwater. Michael Sample photo.

A high glacial cirque including Daisy Pass marks the source of the Stillwater. On the edge of this basin stands the remains of mining activity, some of it recent. Water seeping from the mine tailings has a sickening orange color, the telltale of the acid mine drainage which pollutes the first five miles of the river. Below the confluence of Goose Creek the pollution has been almost entirely settled out or diluted.

Despite the tainted beginning, a hallmark of the Stillwater is its clear water, exceptional for rivers east of the Continental Divide. Pat Marcuson, who has spent several years surveying the Beartooth lakes for the Montana Department of Fish, Wildlife and Parks (FWP), thinks the enduring granite rock of the head-waters is responsible for the low dissolved solids of the water. So few electrolytes exist that FWP has trouble during its fish-shocking surveys in the upper reaches and Marcuson has resorted to swimming with a snorkel in the river to count trout.

Below Lake Abundance, the Stillwater cascades out of the high basin and charges through a narrow canyon, pausing only a couple of times in mountain meadows. Wounded Man and Flood creeks add appreciably to the water volume.

Along the popular Woodbine-Stillwater hiking trail, the cascading water slows in pocket pools of deeper water where throngs of pan-sized brookies compete with occasional rainbow and cutthroat. The river widens briefly at Sioux Charley Lake and then plunges by Woodbine Campground and into the prairie.

In the short section between Woodbine and the Mouat mine, the numbers of brookies and cutthroat sharply diminish while rainbow, and increasingly, browns predominate. Near the community of Nye, the West Fork of the Stillwater adds some more water volume. The river warms up and picks up more minerals.

Below Nye, the river no longer stair-steps its way in cascades but continues to act like a mountain stream. The gradient is still steep enough to make a very swift current and, with the constrictions in a riverbed of boulders, rapids, and whitewater as well. Boating in an open canoe between Beehive and Absarokee has been termed suicidal; for the angler wading waist deep, this means continual apprehension about footing and many furtive glances downstream.

Below Cliff Swallow Fishing Access, the velocity slows another notch; the riverbed broadens and braids around islands. Irrigation diversions subtract a considerable portion of the river's water volume, especially in August and September.

At Absarokee, the two Rosebud rivers add their water, but also some silt. The boulders so common to the upper river give way increasingly to smaller cobble. Although more easy-going, the Stillwater continues to feature an occasional swift section, especially a sharp drop-off over a ledge below the White Bird Fishing Access Site (just above the Beartooth Hereford Ranch bridge).

The lower river supports more large fish, due in part to a substantial inter-change with the Yellowstone. Anglers could tie in to brown trout up to six pounds and more between Absarokee and the Yellowstone, while two- to four-pounders make up the vast majority of the top weight class in the river between the Mouat mine and Beehive.

Marcuson finds "pretty good numbers of one- to two-pound resident rainbow" throughout the river from the Mouat mine downstream to the Yellowstone. But from March 20 to May 20, he also finds migrant rainbow surging up the Stillwater from as far away as Big Timber. Why would these fish, some weighing

Legend:
- HIGHWAY
- COUNTY OR UNPAVED ROAD
- △ OFFICIAL PUBLIC ACCESS
- ☐ RANGER STATION
- X BRIDGE
- ⌇⌇⌇ DIVERSION DAM

One inch = approx. 7 miles

Columbus

Yellowstone River

Fireman's Point

△ Swinging Bridge

△ Whitebird

Stillwater River

90

78

Absaroka △

Absarokee

420

Cliffswallow △

East Rosebud River

West Rosebud River

419

Beehive ●
Castle Rock △
Moraine △

Nye ●
△ Buffalo Jump

Mouat Mine ●
△ Woodbine

Stillwater Complex

West Fork Stillwater

Absaroka-Beartooth
Wilderness

STILLWATER RIVER

six pounds and more, travel up to 120 river miles to spawn? Marcuson thinks "the spawning rainbow have a critical need for small gravel, and they can't find enough of these kinds of gravel beds in the Boulder and middle Yellowstone." Fortunately, the river bed between Beehive and the Mouat mine is much more to their liking. Sometimes in just six inches of water, often in the side channels, these wild rainbow start stocking future generations for both the Yellowstone and Stillwater—maybe even some for the Boulder.

In contrast, Marcuson thinks the browns may not move very far to spawn in October and November. "They tend to pick the area behind boulders in two to four feet of water." Such places are widely available in the Stillwater. The browns may move only a few yards or a few miles—the spawning run is plainly not as dramatic as the rainbow.

Fishing for spawning fish is a sensitive subject with anglers and fishing biologists. Marcuson feels spawners are "fair game en route to and from, but I hate to see people fishing for them right on the spawning bed, even though those fish aren't usually biting anyway." Since the river is open to fishing year round, individual anglers will have to deliberate for themselves the wisdom of disturbing and especially keeping broodstock.

Some anglers love whitefish, some hate them, and some just find them a bit of a nuisance. Regardless, the Stillwater has its share. Marcuson notes on the positive side that the river has "some of the best whitefish fishing in the state, in terms of size, around Absarokee." The community of Nye has an annual and popular gathering to catch and smoke whitefish. Yet guide Curt Collins and a chorus of other anglers find the whitefish frustrating and fear they are taking over the river. Collins suggests that trout would be much better off if the whitefish population could be sharply reduced, possibly even commercially harvested for food and fertilizer.

But the Stillwater has more serious problems than too many whitefish. Above Nye, the Benbow and Mouat mines stand as evidence to past mining for chrome in a band of mineralized rock known as the Stillwater Complex. Today, a new, large hardrock mine employing 400 people has revived the threat to the Stillwater's health. Such undertakings involve large scale blastings of tunnels and removal of enormous quantities of ore.

Extra roads, erosion, and potential pollution concern anglers and the FWP. What happens, for example, if an adit hits a column of underground water which gushes down the watershed loaded with nitrates? An extreme case, perhaps, but John Manville already has shut down one adit that flooded. Fortunately, state laws restrict the miners in terms of pollution. FWP has good base-line information on water quality and fish populations; any substantial change could be spotted.

Mike, Steve, and Dewey Mouat, instructors and guides for the Montana School of Fly Fishing located four miles upstream from Nye, point out the larger concern. "The mines bring in lots of people and make them locals. The result is much more fishing pressure." In response, FWP set a two-trout limit, of which only one can measure over thirteen inches.

Marcuson sees the problem a little differently in that he doesn't worry so much about the fishery as he does about the social pressure. "Right now, I don't find that much fishing pressure. You'd think we would have the worst in the state, being this close to Billings, but the hard-core fishermen head west or to the Bighorn." Montanans have a low tolerance for crowding, and crowds would be the result of a large influx of miners and their families.

Deep water pockets near the Stillwater shoreline, great places for trout. Michael Sample photo.

Fast water alternating with deep pools—one reason the Stillwater has good fishing. Michael Sample photo.

Marcuson points out one other potential source of trouble—the possible reopening of the mines in the Lulu and Daisy passes area. Even now, the lingering affects of past mining keeps the Stillwater void of fish down to the Goose Creek confluence.

Perhaps the prices of gold, copper, and platinum will stay low enough to keep these mines too marginal to be feasible. Anglers who love the bright, clean water of the Stillwater certainly hope so.

Fishing Strategies

Wherever found on the Stillwater, the traditional hot spots—logjams, deep banks, the inside of riffle-corners, fast water dumping into slow—will produce fish as they will in any trout stream. But the special feature which the Stillwater displays even more than the Gallatin or Boulder is the boulder-pocket. Like the fellow who orders a hamburger in a restaurant famous for its prime rib, many an angler misses the most exciting part of the Stillwater by dismissing its boulder-pockets.

To the inexperienced eye, whitewater breaking around and over the boulders looks much too fast and shallow to hold trout. Yet, as a wade into the midst of one of these boulder fields will prove, there are many quiet, deep holes, or pockets, behind the current-braking boulders. Trout feel secure beneath the fractured water surface. The aeration of whitewater makes these areas veritable food factories. Once an angler discovers the concentration of trout around these boulders, that person begins to seek this kind of water which so many anglers shun.

The hydrology of these boulder-pockets create problems for spin and bait anglers. The washing machine action of the water behind the boulders wraps the hardware around unseen tree branches or wedges the hooks between rocks. Even though skillful anglers could catch lots of trout in these spots, the bait and spin anglers usually gravitate to the pools where they feel more comfortable.

As a rough generalization, Marcuson points out that the lower river is more suited to bait, the middle section to spinning, and the upper to flies. He finds that the bait usually used is worms, but thinks sculpins might be very effective on the big browns. May and June mark the best months for bait fishing—on all parts of the river. The Mouats suggest using live stonefly nymphs on sharpened eagle claw hooks with lots of weight for the trout nosing against the banks during high water. These stonefly nymphs, or "scratchers," can be caught by screening gravel.

As the water drops and clears enough for trout to see at least a couple of feet, lures come into their own. Mouat recommends Mepps, Thomas Cyclones, and Panther Martins. Red and white lures do not work well. Gold metal brings more fish to the net than does silver or brass. Using a 6.5 to 7.5 foot rod with fourth-ounce lures, Mouat casts upstream and reels back fast or casts downstream with a slow retrieval.

Above Nye during high water, Mouat finds "gaudy streamers are the only flies that work." Anglers should stick to the backwaters, sloughs, and shallows.

Then, in mid-June around Absarokee and ten days later near Nye, a medium size stonefly known in Latin as *doroneuria* emerges and provides some surface action if the water has cleared sufficiently. Several other smaller stonefly hatches come off the water in the next month, occasionally bringing on the spectacle of two-pound brown trout rolling on the river's surface like tarpon.

Small versions (#8) of popular stonefly imitations like the Sofa Pillow and Bird's Stone fished dry or slightly submerged will hook feeding fish.

Marcuson calls the Stillwater "a pretty good stream for caddis hatches in May and on." The rainbow he catches are full of caddis and caddis cases. Mouat likes a light green caddis with an orange head. Or try an elk hair Caddis. And if no hatch is on, Mouat advises using searcher patterns such as #10 Royal Wulffs, Humpies, Adams, and light Cahills.

The Mouats have an unusual tactic for the Stillwater. They float-fish until the water drops too low, around the beginning of August. In this manner, they can avoid the "pounded" public fishing accesses and cover lots of relatively undisturbed water. No one considers the Stillwater a classic float stream, but by picking the best sections, securing permission in advance from the landowners, and carefully guiding their craft so as not to spook the trout, the Mouats have mastered the tactic.

Floating such a turbulent, dangerous stream, especially with waders on, is an invitation to an early grave. Know the troublesome spots in advance, buy good equipment, and know how to use it. But anglers who don't like the sound of these cautionary notes should relax. The Stillwater provides terrific wade fishing from early July throughout the summer. And perhaps the best part, as mentioned before, is wading through the boulder fields.

But where does one cast in the midst of the chaotic currents and boulders? The eddies behind the boulders almost always hold fish. A few fish, including some of the larger ones, will station themselves just in front of the boulders, which bump the flowing water and create an easy place for trout to hover. Watch for the spots where fast, narrow channels deepen and slow—under the tell-tale choppy haystacks wait trout, gulping down the food brought by the conveyor-belt current.

Anglers do best casting just slightly to one side or the other or straight upstream. "Don't cross your pockets," cautions Mouat. Casting into a pocket from the side results in immediate drag on the fly, which does not look natural to trout. Using short casts helps minimize drag as well.

Collins thinks the most common problem fly anglers exhibit is feeling that they must fish with a dry fly. "If they worked with nymphs and streamers they would catch more and larger trout." Mouat recommends gold-ribbed Hares Ear fished near the surface in a free drift. For weighted nymphs fished to bounce along the bottom, Mouat likes a green latex caddis or golden, brown, and black stonefly nymph imitation. Occasionally, he fishes a Bitch Creek nymph like a streamer. For real streamers, he singles out the black Matuka. Anglers familiar with Muddler Minnows will find they work well on the Stillwater.

Streamers come in handy both early and late in the fishing season. For anglers willing to brave the windy and cold early fishing for the spawning rainbow, Mouat advises casting up and a little across, then retrieving with a little tension. He thinks this aggravates the trout, which will strike at the streamer sometimes without intending to eat it. The net result of this is many missed strikes, especially for the inexperienced angler. Practice helps.

Streamers will also catch fish in August and September, especially in the lower half of the river. But this is also the time to use terrestrials. Marcuson calls the Stillwater "a great grasshopper stream." FWP's Clint Bishop recalls seeing numerous black and orange caterpillars as well. Since terrestrials usually fall in along the banks, anglers do best concentrating their efforts along the

Caddis fly hatches such as this can drive trout crazy. Al Troth photo.

edge. Grasshoppers and their imitations will bring fish to the surface, but on bright, sunny days fish will go after the slightly submerged, "drowned" hoppers more often. Black and orange Wooly Worms make excellent representations of the caterpillars.

Tributaries

Of the many streams which combine to make the Stillwater, the three largest deserve mention here. All three drain watersheds in the lofty Beartooth Mountains not far from the main river's drainage.

The West Fork of the Stillwater cascades and pools past Initial Creek Campground at the edge of the Beartooth-Absaroka Wilderness. Skirting Horseman Flats, this medium-sized stream flows through private lands almost all the way to Nye and the main river. Above Initial Creek, the West Fork supports mostly pan-sized brookies; below, some chunky rainbow and browns populate the stream .

Born in the meltwater of Beartooth glaciers, West Rosebud Creek runs through Silver, Island, and Mystic lakes. It furnishes hydroelectric power below Mystic Lake, then provides good fishing through a narrow canyon before running out into the irrigated prairie land for its last twenty-five miles.

Marcuson terms the stream "a good, small fishery," especially between Emerald Lake and the flatlands.

Marcuson rates the East Rosebud as something of a disappointment. The wilderness sections between the lakes furnish some good fishing, but from

East Rosebud Lake down to the confluence with the West Rosebud, fish numbers and sizes are small. FWP has experimented with plantings of different trout, but without marked success. Still, some weekend anglers report fun fishing for pan-sized trout both in the meadows near Black Mountain and below Roscoe along the cottonwoods.

Access

Because of the Stillwater's close proximity to Billings and Yellowstone County, FWP has wisely tried to spread out the angling pressure. Seven FWP accesses, combined with two Forest Service strips of riverbank land plus some casual access, all help anglers reach some of the river, but the large majority of river frontage remains in private hands.

Fireman's Point Fishing Access Site (FAS) provides the first public fishing spot on the drive upstream from Columbus. The next developed access is FWP's White Bird FAS, which, combined with an unmarked access just below White Bird, gives anglers a considerable distance of good riffle water.

Just a mile below Absarokee, Thompson's Bridge crosses the Stillwater. A dirt road to the left runs along the river for quite some distance. Even though the river is so close in places that it could be fished from the car, ask permission.

West of Absarokee, four more FWP accesses allow the angler to reach the middle river. Cliff Swallow FAS features practically every kind of trout water found in Montana. Castle Rock has some shallow riffles and pockets. Moraine has outstanding pocket water. And Buffalo Jump, known locally as Nye Bridge, has some pool, boulder-pocket, and riffle water.

Upstream several miles from Nye and just below the Montana Fly Fishing School lies an unnamed Forest Service access. This strip of land gives a taste of the upper, smaller river with a spectacular mountainous backdrop.

Lastly, the Forest Service's Woodbine Campground and Trailhead stand as the gateway to the upper wilderness section of the Stillwater.

During weekends from mid-April to mid-July, anglers wishing to fish the Stillwater have three choices. The first alternative is to wedge oneself in at one of the established accesses. Watch your backcast, please.

Other anglers may prefer to attempt float-fishing. While opening many miles of otherwise inaccessible river, this alternative nevertheless has several drawbacks. Some sections of the river are too hazardous. On the safer sections, the runoff waters still push downstream at a swift clip, which test the proficiency of even expert casters on occasion. Floating anglers should stay in their boats—easier said than done when a lure-eating log has hold of the hardware.

The third alternative is to seek permission from private landowners, most of whom freely grant it to anglers who will respect their property. Be aware that one bad experience with an angler, whether it be a gate left open, litter, fire, or the like, can close that section of the river to the public for years.

YELLOWSTONE RIVER

Annually, anglers from all over the country and abroad come to the banks of the Yellowstone to pay homage to this revered river. The Yellowstone commands respect and inspires devotion, with a veritable Who's Who of Fishing in its roll call of admirers. Ray Hurley, a fishing guide who moved to Livingston in order to live only a cast away from the river, calls the Yellowstone "the Yankee Stadium of trout fishing."

What makes the Yellowstone so special? For starters, it drains an extraordinary watershed, including some of America's wildest scenery. The river rises just south of incomparable Yellowstone National Park in the Shoshone National Forest of Wyoming. From its beginnings until the river leaves the park at Gardiner, the Yellowstone has a pristine background rivaled by few rivers. Even after it forges its way past Gardiner, the Yellowstone draws added water from the congressionally mandated Absaroka-Beartooth Wilderness. Most trout waters can only wish for such impeccable sources.

Unlike other major rivers, the Yellowstone runs its entire 678-mile course without a major dam. Running free of impounding concrete slabs, the Yellowstone evokes awe in all river lovers who honor things wild. Historically, the U.S. Bureau of Reclamation has not shared this respect for unfettered rivers. In the Yellowstone's case, the Bureau has, for fifty years, proposed a dam at the Allenspur site just south of Livingston. Fortunately, some hitches developed in the plan. Discovery that the damsite lies on a major earthquake faultline made the project unpopular in the downstream communities, especially after Idaho's 1976 Teton Dam disaster. Also, the western side of the dam would abut Wineglass Mountain, known by geologists for its vaulted, and in some areas, hollow rock structure.

But just as serious, the Bureau's proposal runs up against the passionate opposition of trout fanciers from all across the country. If pressed, Yellowstone's fans would wield considerate political clout. Some anglers even vow the dam would be built over their dead bodies. So far, such bravado has not been required, as the proposal gathers dust somewhere in the catacombs of federal government. Meanwhile, just knowing the threat exists makes the faithful that much more attached to the free and wild spirit of the Yellowstone.

In keeping with this wild spirit, the trout that swim in the Yellowstone are the progeny of their wild ancestors. The Yellowstone cutthroat is a true native; the browns, rainbow, and occasional brookies are many generations removed from any hatchery. Although some Montanans don't realize it, anglers from other parts of the country are accustomed to put-and-take operations, even resorting to following hatchery trucks and fishing for just-planted, naive seven-inchers. Moreover, few trout streams have four trout species (although, naturally, a brook trout is a char, not a trout).

Another special attraction of the Yellowstone is the presence of trophy-sized trout. As with most major trout streams in Montana, trout over eighteen inches comprise a small minority of the Yellowstone's population. Fishing guide, Rich Stevenson, formerly a Montana Department of Fish, Wildlife and Parks (FWP) biologist, found that such fish were from less than one to five percent of the trout he sampled, depending on which section he was

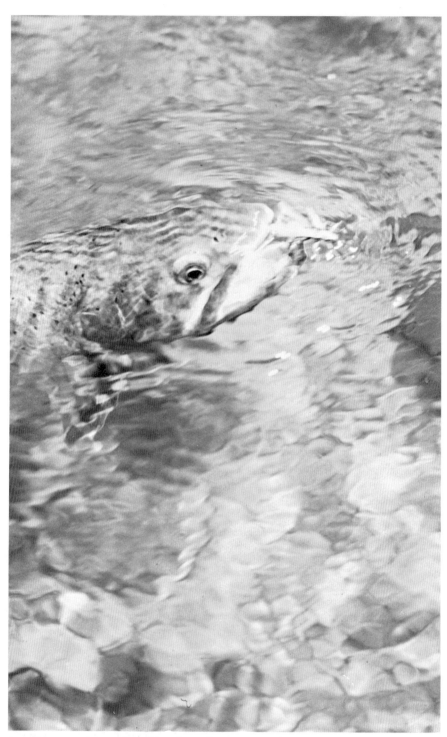

A cutthroat coming up for a big salmon fly. Michael Sample photo.

electrofishing. He also found the growth rate to be unspectacular, even low when compared with tailwater fisheries such as the Beaverhead and Bighorn.

Nevertheless, the Yellowstone does harbor some lunkers. John Bailey, of Dan Bailey's Fly Shop in Livingston, cites the example of a female brown caught on a streamer in April several years ago, which weighed fourteen pounds, fourteen ounces. Stevenson shocked a brown twenty-eight inches long with an incredible twenty-one-inch girth; the fish was too heavy for the scale, but it weighed somewhere between fifteen and twenty pounds.

Then, too, one hears stories of monsters in Yankee Jim Canyon. Richard Parks, proprietor of Parks Fly Shop in Gardiner, tells of local anglers who no longer trust twenty-pound test line. They want "the heavy stuff." And a number of years ago, a crew of fish biologists using a powerful truck-mounted shocking outfit turned up, but couldn't capture a giant fish. Three times the stunned lunker was in clear view, but out of reach of the net. The experienced and perfectly sober biologists estimated the weight somewhere between thirty-five and forty-five pounds. As Parks puts it, "There's always the possibility of running into a trout as big as anyone has ever seen in this country."

Why does this river grow big trout when so many others don't? Several factors come into play here. With only minimal irrigation withdrawals, mining, and timber cutting, the Yellowstone's water quality is superior to most. High water quality results in an abundance of food for trout. In the Yellowstone, this means prodigious numbers of caddis and sculpin. As sculpin are less tolerant of poor water than trout are, the sculpin serves as the canary in the coal mine.

And, as the famous angler Dan Bailey once pointed out, the trout in the Yellowstone have deep pools in which to hide and rest. In the Madison River from Hebgen Dam most of the way to Ennis, trout do not have many of these hideouts and thus remain vulnerable to anglers. Hurley thinks that, in the Yellowstone, fish may die of old age without ever seeing a hook. They simply have a better chance to get big.

It is also possible that wild trout are more intelligent than hatchery fish, and that certain genetically superior trout continue to grow when they become sixteen or eighteen inches by switching their diets increasingly to other fish and not wasting much energy on insect larva. Stevenson once shocked a five-pound brown which had a thirteen-inch whitefish in its stomach. Obviously this fish was well on its way to becoming a trophy.

The Yellowstone has a long fishing season—there's no need to put the fishing equipment in cold storage. The late Joe Halterman, a superb fisherman and powerful friend of the Yellowstone, described the Yellowstone as an "all-season river." Even in January and February, when most western Montana streams are locked up in ice, anglers ply the banks of the Yellowstone on warmer days. Often these hardy anglers find success, even with dry flies.

While to the experienced eye the river looks much the same throughout its length from Gardiner on down, differences between stretches make for some variety. The river comes out of Yellowstone Park at a moderate rush. From Gardiner to the head of the Yankee Jim, the current is mostly strong; the streambed studded with boulders; the riffles and pools very obvious. Anglers find this upper section does not seem as big, even though the river has about the same volume of water here as it does at Livingston. Thanks to appreciable numbers of cutthroat, this upper section has the strongest mix of species.

Sculpins make up a major part of the diet of big trout in western Montana rivers, including the Yellowstone. Al Troth photo.

Despite Yankee Jim Canyon's reputation for wild water, the river actually slows as it narrows. Most of the truly deep water in the Yellowstone occurs in the canyon. Parks recalls reports of a diver who dove to sixty feet. Three or four large rapids break up this otherwise placid stretch of river. Parks rates the canyon generally tough fishing, but with outstanding holding water for some big fish.

Below the canyon, the river spreads out and slows further. A few islands begin to appear as the river moves around the foot of impressive Emigrant Peak. Very stable riverbanks make this a good section for bank-fishing. On the other hand, riffles here are poorly defined and weak for the most part. Few boulders break the smooth water surface of the long pools. Brown trout dominate here, with rainbow and cutthroat in the minority. The scenery alone can keep an angler coming back for years.

Near Mallard's Rest Fishing Access, the streambed tilts downward and the river speeds up. The difference is hardly perceptible from the highway above, but in the river, the change is profound. The floating angler encounters more riffles per mile; these riffles run faster and deeper. The river eats away at the banks much more voraciously. Rainbow now outnumbers browns, and by a wide margin. The trout from Mallard's Rest down to below Livingston are more numerous and bigger fish on the average than in the river above.

Many of the best riffle-pools in this section have reputations and colorful names to match—Weeping Wall, Joe Brooks, Big Armstrong, Warm Springs, Whorehouse, Super, and Pumphouse.

Several miles below Livingston, the river turns its flow from northerly to eastward. In this "Big Bend" section, the river shifts channels from year to year and braids around many islands. The multiple channels create challenging, complex flow patterns and excellent fishing.

Below Springdale, the riffles become farther apart. Angling pressure drops off sharply, but the water quality and trout numbers remain high. Except at the fishing access points, the "middle Yellowstone" from Springdale to Columbus may rank as the most under-utilized fishery of its quality in the state.

From Columbus to Billings, the Yellowstone enters a transition phase to a warm-water fishery. Increasing sediment, turbidity, and water temperatures cut down the number of trout, especially after the Clarks Fork dumps in near Laurel. On an encouraging note, anglers recently have caught more trout in the Billings area than in previous years. But below Billings, the angler's quarries are walleye, sauger, catfish, and even paddlefish. Smallmouth bass have been recently introduced. In the past, Montana anglers have shown little interest in this kind of fishery, but with some encouragement from FWP, this is changing. Tasty, fighting gamefish await the willing angler in the lower, prairie section of the Yellowstone.

FWP's Phil Stewart reports that sauger and walleye are abundant throughout the lower Yellowstone, as are channel catfish. Paddlefish and shovelnose sturgeon are found as far upstream as Forsyth, though the majority are caught at Intake just below Glendive. The smallmouth bass fishery is doing well and attracting a growing number of anglers who enjoy the good fight these fish provide. Some burbot and northern pike round out the list of favored quarry.

Walleye are the prime target here, averaging one to four pounds. Bigger fish are not uncommon, and a walleye weighing over fifteen pounds was recently taken here, setting a new Montana record. Sauger in the one- to two-pound range are common and six-pounders are not unusual. In 1991, the state-record sauger—tipping the scales at just over 7.5 pounds—was pulled from the Yellowstone just above the mouth of the Bighorn. The most popular set-up for these two species is a minnow/bait combination or minnows alone.

Channel catfish run from Huntley downstream, with an abundance of one- to six-pound fish. Ten-pounders are common, and anglers take an occasional fifteen- to twenty-pound catfish. These bottom-feeders go for stink baits and worms.

Angling for paddlefish brings a flurry of activity to the river in late spring. Below Intake, the season opens May 1 and runs through June. Above Intake the fishing begins May 15. Stewart says that "paddlefish are found throughout the lower Yellowstone, but ninety percent of the season's catch occurs at Intake." The fish range from fifteen to seventy pounds, the large spread due in part to a dramatic difference in size between the genders. Says Stewart, "You can usually guess a paddlefish's sex based on its weight. Males run smaller, from fifteen to thirty-five pounds, and females go from forty to seventy pounds." As of 1992, anglers are limited to two paddlefish per season and the fish must be tagged.

Shovelnose sturgeon are also common on the lower Yellowstone, even abundant in the lower Tongue and Powder rivers. Though most anglers don't hit the water in search of sturgeon, quite a number are incidentally snagged at Intake during the paddlefish season. Two- to five-pound shovelnose are typical, but an occasional ten-pounder shows up.

Smallmouth bass are most common from Forsyth to the mouth of the Powder River. Anglers rely on the tried-and-true bass lures and bait. Fish range from .5 to three pounds.

Burbot and northern pike also attract anglers on the Lower Yellowstone. Stewart finds northerns from the mouth of the Bighorn River to Intake and recommends fishing at the mouths of tributaries. "Look in the backwater that usually forms where a stream or river spills into the Yellowstone. If the

Legend:
- **- - - -** HIGHWAY
- ---------- COUNTY OR UNPAVED ROAD
- △ OFFICIAL PUBLIC ACCESS
- □ RANGER STATION
- X BRIDGE
- VVVV DIVERSION DAM

One inch = approx. 29 miles

Yellowstone River

I-94

Hardin

I-90

87

Two Moon Park △ △ Josephine Park

Billings

416

Laurel △ Riverside Park

Clarks Fork of the

Columbus △ Itch-lep-pe

212

191

Indian Fort △ Reedpoint

Greycliff △ Bratten

421

Yellowstone River

72

Big Timber △ Big Timber

Grey Bear △

Stillwater River

Beartooth Range

Springdale

Sheep Mountain △

Boulder River

89

Montana

Wyoming

Livingston

Free River

Carter Bridge △ Mallard's Rest

Absaroka Range

89

Loch Leven △ △ Paradise

Bozeman

Emigrant △ Pray

90

Point of Rocks △ 540 △ △ Queen of the Waters

Carbella Bridge △ Gardiner

Corwin Springs

Gallatin Range

Yellowstone National Park

YELLOWSTONE RIVER (Upper)

Missouri River

Fairview
Diamond Willow
Sidney
Seven Sisters △
Savage △ Elk Island
Intake △

200

Glendive △

200

△ Fallon Bridge

Terry
△ Powder River Depot
Powder River

North Dakota
Montana

253

Big Sheep Mountains

Kinsey Bridge △
△ Roche Jaune
Miles City

22

Yellowstone

Tongue River

Far West
Forsyth
Rosebud
Rosebud East
Rosebud West
Amelia Island

Rosebud Creek

447

Isaac Homestead △
Myers Bridge △
94
△ Manuel Lisa
Custer

Rosebud Mountains

12 Captain Clark △

Pompey's Pillar
Hardin
Bighorn River
Bighorn Mountains

Roundup ●
87
Huntley

94

Pryor Mountains

Billings

HIGHWAY
COUNTY OR UNPAVED ROAD
△ OFFICIAL PUBLIC ACCESS
☐ RANGER STATION
✗ BRIDGE
〰 DIVERSION DAM

One inch = approx. 38 miles

YELLOWSTONE RIVER (Lower)

northerns are running, there'll be a crowd in that quiet water." The best time for northerns comes just after the winter's ice leaves the main stem.

Anglers scheduling their fishing trips should be mindful that the Yellowstone's water clears relatively late. Early fishing, such as in March, is often very good. In May, the river muddies and rises. On the average, runoff peaks around June 18. The record flow of 36,300 cubic feet per second (cfs as measured at Livingston June 17, 1974) was more than sixty times as much water as the record low of 590 cfs in 1940. Individual years vary widely in their snowpack and flow patterns, but the river generally clears by mid-July, barring heavy rains in the wrong places. The Yellowstone often runs dirty even in July and August following major rains in the upper basin. Sometimes these murky flows last for one to two weeks, depending on the severity of the storm. FWP says the culprit is sediment-laden runoff from the sections of Yellowstone National Park that burned during the fires of 1988. As grasses and other plants re-establish themselves in the burns, the clarity of the runoff should improve. But John Bailey contends that these occasional dirty flows pre-date the 1988 fires. He attributes the problem to long-term overgrazing and top soil erosion in the basin below Yellowstone Park. Despite these concerns, the Yellowstone is usually coming into its prime just when many streams are going into hot weather slumps.

For anglers hoping to catch the salmon fly hatch, how the runoff progresses is of paramount importance. Parks has watched the hatch for thirty years. During the hatch he finds the river unfishable below Emigrant except with wet flies. One year in four will be really good from Emigrant up, and one in four will be "rather useless' below Gardiner. The other two years will see a week or two of fishing the salmon fly hatch above Yankee Jim Canyon about the second week of July. It's best to check the river first hand or call someone who knows the hatch and turbidity conditions.

Few rivers have better fishing today than they did fifty years ago—but the Yellowstone does. In those days, the Yellowstone ran heavy with sediment from mining operations around Emigrant and Jardine. Few sculpins and stoneflies lived in the river then, but now they prosper. In fact, the river seems in very good shape now, and most anglers just hope nothing comes along to muck up the river again. As long as the gold dredgers and dam builders and coal miners keep their fingers off the Yellowstone, anglers will continue to honor this giant of a trout stream.

Fishing Strategies

Invariably, the angler's first impression of the Yellowstone is one of bigness. This is no intimate trout stream where the angler can cast or wade from one bank to the other. Small-stream anglers quickly get psyched out looking at this vast expanse of water. And compounding this intimidation is the unmarked, hard-to-read nature of the river. Anglers can't see the familiar nooks and crannies they knew on their streams back in Pennsylvania or New York.

Guides such as Hurley and Parks hear these complaints plenty. Their solution is to quickly cut the river down to size. Hurley wants his clients to fish just "the Triple A water. If you envision this river as a side of beef," he tells them, "we aren't going to take the loin out of it—we're going to take the filet out of the loin and let the rest of it go for someone else."

Where is the filet—the most productive parts of the river? The first part of the strip of water up against either bank, provided the water is eighteen

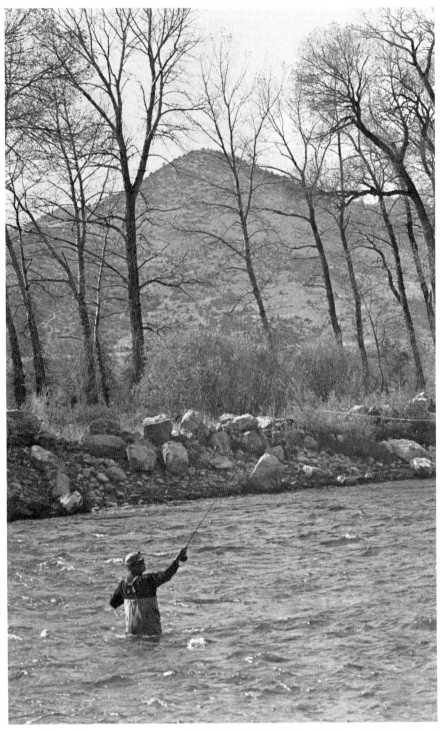

An angler works a streamer across a big riffle in the "Yankee Stadium of trout fishing."
Michael Sample photo.

inches or deeper. Parks describes this strip as roughly five feet wide. Hurley exhorts his clients to cast "two inches from the bank, plus or minus an inch." He scoffs at people who spend hundreds of dollars on their fishing trip, then worry about losing their fly or lure by casting too close. If the bank is shaded by trees or bush, its potential ranks especially high.

Because of the Yellowstone's wandering ways, ranchers with river frontage have often resorted to riprapping to protect their river banks. Usually, riprapped banks make for deep water. And the big chunks of rock used for riprap provide excellent hangouts for trout, some of them big. Anglers should consider these spots as class I water.

Guides call the other most productive parts of the river "riffle-corners," "horns of plenty," or "golden triangles." Whatever the name, these places

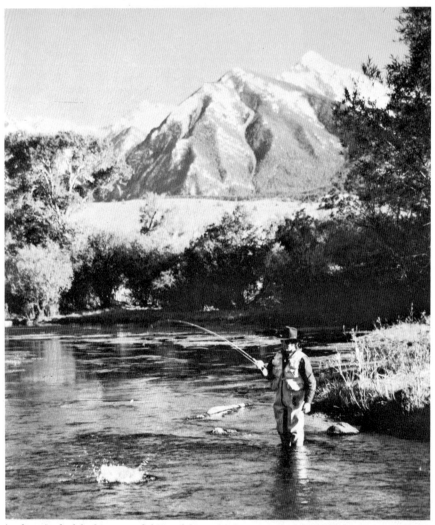

Anglers tired of the big water fishing of the main river can try the Yellowstone's spring creek tributaries, but must have reservations and pay a fee. Michael Sample photo.

occur every time the river bends. When the river sweeps around these bends, it always leaves some quieter water on the inside of the curve. Between the slack water and the heavy, fast water is a zone, an area in the shape of a horn or a triangle, wherein the trout feed. Here the trout can hold their positions against the slower current while still taking advantage of the conveyer belt of food coming toward them.Where the angler finds those familiar nooks and crannies—such as undercut banks, downed trees, boulders, and the lower ends of islands—by all means, they should be fished. And during a spawning season, the tail end of pools and some side channels can provide lively action. Still, probably ninety percent of the river can be skipped. This goes especially for the middle of the river in the slower straight runs. Also, river trout shun slack, dead water.

As Mark Henckel of *The Billings Gazette* puts it, "The truth is that on few other rivers in Montana does the old rule of thumb about ten percent of the fishermen catching ninety percent of the fish hold so true." The number one way that anglers can improve their results is to fish the more productive water. This takes time; the Yellowstone takes a lot of knowing. Those who fish the Yellowstone just once haven't given the river a fair chance.

Anglers who want to know the Yellowstone better would be wise to spend a day with a qualified guide. Arrange a lengthy float trip with the aim of learning some of the best fishing stretches. A good guide will provide a boat transportation, lunch, and a wealth of knowledge—including instructions on how the angler can later return to especially likeable riffles and pools. Most tackle shops, such as Parks', Bailey's, and Anderson's, are happy to help arrange such trips.

Big western rivers like the Yellowstone demand beefier equipment than do Pennsylvania's chalk streams. Generally speaking, the successful ten percent anglers cover far more water than average anglers do. Big water and frequently windy conditions require bigger, stiffer rods and more weight on the end of the line. The Yellowstone is no place for an ultra-light spinning rod or a wishy-washy seven-foot fly rod.

Hurley, for example, often carries two fly rods—an 8.5-foot rod with seven-weight line for fishing dry flies and a 9.5-footer with nine- or ten-weight line for going deep. With these rods, Hurley has mastered long distance casting, sometimes casting as far as 140 feet, which enables him to present his fly to more fish.

Hurley notes that most anglers have only a few hundred good casts in their arms before they "turn to spaghetti." He has one client who prepares for the fishing season by training for a month with a six-pound hammer which he lifts and holds out five hundred times a day. "The Yellowstone is a caster's river," he says, "and this client can fish it for fourteen hours straight."

Most expert anglers do not agree that long-distance casting is necessary. The late Dan Bailey countered that sometimes long-distance casting is "an experience in self-gratification. Some of the most productive fishermen I know," he said, "never cast more than thirty-five feet." But he agreed that many anglers need stronger rods because, in the wind, even short casts must be made with authority.

When the river runs high and muddy in May and June, only bait will catch fish. John Bailey thinks this time of the year marks the peak of fishing pressure on the Yellowstone because so many local people hit the banks. As in almost all trout water, the lowly earthworm catches its share of fish. The smart angler who soaks worms almost anywhere out of the fast main current can catch plenty of whitefish, suckers, and trout with a can of worms.

But in the Yellowstone, the preferred bait is the plentiful sculpin. Those anglers who use sculpin generally net them in shallow water over gravel beds. Carefully hooked, weighted, and allowed to move around in the quieter water of an eddy, next to a bank, or below an island, a sculpin can be deadly bait for big trout—some think too deadly. As with anywhere, check the regulations on the Yellowstone before fishing bait.

Other useful bait includes stonefly nymphs, known as "scratchers," and later in summer, grasshoppers. What about salmon eggs and corn? "They work well on stocked fish, but we don't have any stocked fish in the Yellowstone," says Parks proudly. He continues, "These fish don't recognize them as food— someone lost a garbage truck, big deal."

Once the muddy waters start to settle out and turn greenish blue, the flashy spinning gear becomes effective. Many people with spinning outfits think their only task is to cast as far as possible. Not true, especially during this period of clearing water. The main goal should be getting the lure in front of and close to the fish.

When an angler stands on the bank desperately trying to reach the middle of the river with each cast, then retrieves the lure quickly and perhaps a foot or two below the surface, that angler is bound to be disappointed. Few fish will see the lure. Even if the fish could see it, they probably wouldn't make the effort to come from the bottom into the main force of the current and chase after the fast-moving lure. Lake fish will chase lures long distances; river fish rarely do.

Instead, the spin angler must spot the quieter water and get the lure down to where the fish are holding. And the only way to get a lure down is to allow it to sink before starting the retrieve. A sure prescription for losing lures? Yes, but also the best prescription for catching trout.

The single most popular lure on the Yellowstone, in Parks' estimation, is the Thomas Cyclone. Parks usually recommends brass for ordinary days, but if the water or the weather is dirty, silver seems to work better. John Bailey suggests a lure with a red stripe. If the angler is after whitefish, stock up on Panther Martin Golds.

Spin and bait anglers naturally despise moss. Unfortunately, the green stuff starts showing up on their hooks several weeks after the water clears. August and September usually mark the most bothersome times for moss. The typical hard freeze in early October eliminates most of the problem. Before then, anglers beset by moss will find much less of it above Emigrant, where irrigation returns have not added fertilizer to the water.

A considerable amount of literature in sports magazines and books suggests that anglers must be very particular at choosing their flies, at least on certain trout streams such as the Henry's Fork, Firehole, and the spring creeks. But are the trout in the Yellowstone all that choosey?

"The Yellowstone is not so mysterious," Parks observes. "You don't have to know the Latin names of forty-five bugs. There's so many bugs on the Yellowstone that the fish are looking for everything." The only hatch Parks attempts to match is the salmon fly. Hurley claims that exact imitation of one of the Yellowstone's vast caddis hatches only insures the angler will catch lots of whitefish.

The late Dan Bailey made much of his living tying, selling, even inventing

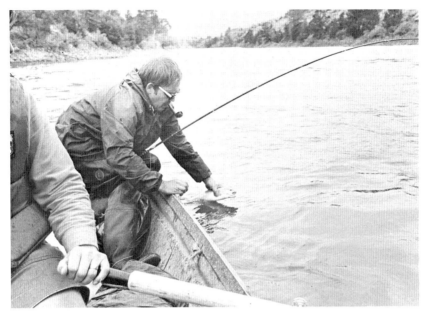

Float fishing can add to success on the Yellowstone, as it does many other large rivers. Mark Henckel photo.

flies. The front counter of his store includes perhaps forty or fifty square feet of tiny boxes with a multitude of different patterns. But, like Parks, he didn't believe in the exact imitation theory. "Human eyes and fish eyes are different." Bailey laughed. "Even on spring creeks, I can do very well with a size 18 Royal Coachman. Tell me what bug a Royal Coachman imitates."

For dry flies, Bailey suggested picking proven patterns that float well and stand up under use. These patterns include the Royal Wulff, the Goofus, the Trude patterns, the Adams, and one of the grasshopper imitations. He added one more to the list: the wet or dry Muddler, "designed to imitate a sculpin but also imitates a hopper...or maybe it just looks good to the fish."

Parks frequently uses a Coachman Trude, a fly which includes some wraps of peacock fuzz. "Peacock does something to fishes' psyche," he theorizes, "it gets into their brains and twists them around until the fish make it what they want it to be." Parks adds that the Coachman Trude works well for beginners who don't quite have the handle on drag. When the fly gets pulled underwater, it acts like a mini-streamer.

If an angler decides to go after the larger trout, then nymphs, wet flies, or streamers are generally the choices. Big trout eat the lion's share of their meals along the bottom, only rarely rising to the surface for dessert. And sometimes, of course, even the smaller trout don't work on surface insects.

Dan Bailey called nymphs "the 'in' thing now—they've almost completely taken over from the old wet flies. But flies like the wooly worm are probably imitating nymphs more than drowned insects, anyway." Parks likes a long-shanked, olive Wooly Worm as the best imitation of a stonefly nymph. With, most likely, a sink tip fly line, nymphing anglers try to achieve a dead drift, then perhaps impart a twitching retrieve toward the bank at the end of the drift. Feeling or seeing the strike is tricky, but the angler who masters nymph fishing is deadly.

Fishing streamers is perhaps the easiest fly fishing technique to master, once the angler has the right equipment. Hurley, who is the most vocal advocate of streamer fishing on the Yellowstone in the fall, uses a super sink, high density shooting head. At the business end of that line he ties a short stout leader. Behind the shooting head, he uses monofilament shooting line such as Amnesia followed by his backing. Whatever streamers he employs, whether it is a Muddler, Spuddler, dark or light Spruce Fly, the streamer has an extra heavy salt water hook on it. This follows his whole aim of getting the streamer down near the bottom quickly.

From September 15th until winter sets in, Hurley takes his streamer outfit to the inside tops of riffles. He is thinking about the big brown trout which at this time of year are establishing their redds. Once in a while, he will pick up a fat rainbow as a bonus. Whether the fish strike at his streamer out of annoyance or hunger or defensive protection is subject to debate, but Hurley wants those strikes, whatever the reason.

The first cast is across and slightly upstream. The current immediately grabs the middle section of his line, but Hurley quickly rolls his rod to mend his line back upstream, which gives his streamer a little more time to sink. The current sweeps line and streamer downstream. As the streamer arcs through the heavy water, Hurley jigs it a few times, then starts stripping in his line in sharp, two-foot jerks. When he has the streamer within thirty feet of his rod tip, he takes a couple of steps downstream and begins to cast again.

In this manner, Hurley works his way through the riffle and the top of the pool. During the middle of a bright fall day, he doesn't bother with the tail of the pool. Instead he moves on to the next riffle, perhaps tying on another streamer pattern.

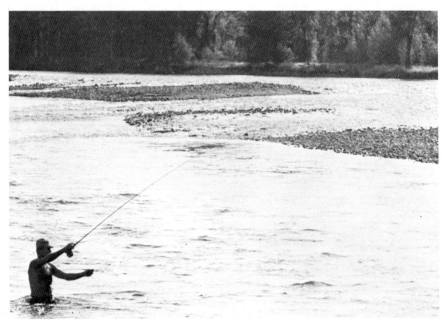

Working the tail end of a big riffle on the Yellowstone. Michael Sample photo.

But later, as the shadows lengthen across the river, Hurley tries the tail of a pool he especially likes. Here, as the streamer starts its arc cross-river and a hundred feet out, he gets a slashing, jarring strike. Hurley strikes back hard. Secure in the knowledge of his strong leader and hook, he applies heavy pressure and soon nets a beautifully colored, three-pound brown. With a few words of admiration to the fish, he unhooks, revives and releases the brown into quiet water. "Just because the Legislature says you can kill five or ten trout doesn't mean you have to do it," he notes. Then he's casting again, hoping the pool holds another fine fish.

The late Joe Halterman had another way of fly fishing the Yellowstone. His method is rarely, if ever, espoused in fishing literature or copied by other anglers, but it worked superbly for Halterman. He used a tall rod, a floating line, and a hair fly known as a Sandy Mite. He had such confidence in this one fly pattern that whole years would go by without his trying any other.

Although Halterman could do well with his technique in almost any kind of water, he especially relished one kind—the places where fast, shallow water piles into a deepening pool of quieter water. Often in such places, little haystack waves ripple the surface. Halterman would wade quietly, sometimes crouching, to a position upstream where he would wait patiently a few minutes in case he had spooked any fish. Then he would cast quartering downstream and, holding his rod high over his head, would drag, skip, and skitter his Sandy Mite across the tops of the haystacks.

He called it "teasing." As with Parks description of the effects of peacock feathers, Halterman thought there must be something about the dancing of that Sandy Mite that intrigued a trout's brain. Some days he found it important to keep the fly on top, while other days it worked better just under the surface. Seeing the strike was important; feeling it was often too late to hook the fish.

Halterman could not explain how his method imitated anything in the natural world of river life. And it goes against conventional wisdom that this teasing would bring big fish up five or six feet through heavy water to the surface. Nevertheless, over the years many lunkers in the three- to six-pound class fell for Halterman's "tease."

On most trout streams, the fishing season dies with the falling of the leaves and the forming of ice along the banks. But locals near the Yellowstone take advantage of warmer periods of weather and sometimes find good fishing. With its stock of 20,000 whitefish per mile, the Yellowstone provides the winter angler an excellent chance to cache a smoked delicacy. Bait and spin anglers can fare well as long as their lines and fingers don't freeze up. Fly fishermen sometime encounter mid-winter hatches of tiny snow midges. And once the spring equinox arrives, the big rainbow are moving into the side channels and over the gravel beds, tempting any sort of angler.

"It's a fascinating river," Hurley muses. "You can catch a whole string of ten-inch fish, then the next one to come up is five pounds." Or maybe, just possible, one bigger than any trout ever caught.

Tributaries

Most rivers offering great trout fishing also have excellent fishing in their tributaries. This self-evident rule has a shining example in the Yellowstone. When the big river is running muddy or when an angler wants a change of pace—a chance to fish smaller, more intimate water—the tributaries of the Yellowstone offer superb alternatives.

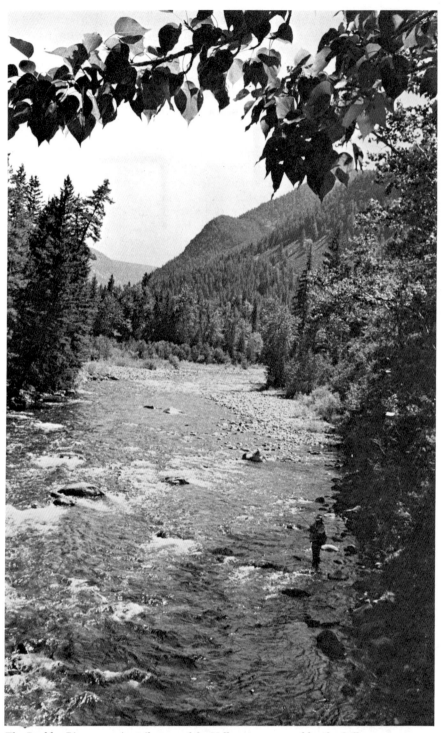

The Boulder River, a major tributary of the Yellowstone, resembles the Stillwater in scenery and fishing potential. Michael Sample photo.

This book covers the Gardner River, a fine trout stream which empties into the Yellowstone at the town of Gardiner, in the Yellowstone Park chapter. The same goes for the Lamar River. The Stillwater and Bighorn rivers, major fishing resources in their own right, are described in their own sections. This section describes the Yellowstone's other major tributaries.

Between Gardiner and Livingston, a number of small streams drain the mountain canyons of the Absaroka and Gallatin ranges. These streams, including Mol Heron, Mill, Tom Miner, Big and Pine creeks, provide the river's cutthroat with spawning water. They also provide fun fishing for mostly pan-sized brookies, rainbow, and cutthroat. Gravel roads make them all accessible. These lightly fished streams are best in July and August.

About eight miles south of Livingston, two short spring creeks flow into the Yellowstone—Nelson's Spring Creek from the east side, and Armstrong and DePuy's Spring Creek from the west. Both are on private land, but anglers can fish them if they make reservations and pay a fee. Local tackle shops such as George Anderson's Yellowstone Angler and Dan Bailey's Fly Shop happily help with the arrangements. The owners allow only fly fishing.

Although the two creeks differ in some respects, especially in the DePuy section, where anglers can fish some dammed-up ponds as well as the main creek, in general the spring creeks are notably similar. Both have some browns and cutthroat, but in each case the star inhabitants are rainbow. Because of the terrific insect life and excellent water conditions, both streams support incredible concentrations of trout, with an impressive number of two- to five-pounders. And both, as George Anderson puts it, "demand the utmost in delicate presentation, fine tippets, and small flies."

By "small flies," Anderson means sizes 16 to 22. Anglers who are not accustomed to working with such microscopic tackle would do well to step into Anderson's shop or to consult another expert before stepping into the spring creeks. Matching the hatches of baetis, mayfly, and midges can make or break the day's experience. Likewise, nymph anglers may want to seek advice on the various mayfly nymphs, midge larva and pupa, scuds, and sowbugs.

Many anglers become a touch uneasy with the special techniques used on spring creeks—"Latinspeak and three weight line," Hurley calls it. And paying for fishing rankles more than a few anglers as well. But the beautiful scenery, water, and trout of these spring creeks do offer a different and exciting experience to the open-minded angler who gives it a try.

The Shields River rises in the Crazy Mountains, flows by the towns of Wilsall and Clyde Park, and dumps into the Yellowstone just east of Livingston. Notorious for its silt problems, the Shields nevertheless deserves a good reputation as a trout stream. Along its cottonwood-lined banks, this small river harbors "more two-pound-and-up brown trout than you might expect," testifies Stevenson, who has run electrofishing surveys in the Shields. The browns hang out in the tree roots, logjams, and deep pools of the lower half of the river. Further up toward the headwaters, anglers catch a mixed bag of rainbow, cutthroat, and brookies. Access is relatively easy.

The Shields suffers from serious dewatering problems and the attendant problem of overheating. Many years ago, Halterman found that the fish in the Shields had one of the fastest growth rates in the state, but increased irrigation has slowed that some. Try this river before the dog days of summer or after the leaves turn color. The river receives only light fishing pressure.

Small flies and light leaders are required for success in fishing spring creeks. Al Troth photo.

The superlative Boulder River bears striking resemblance to its sister stream, just to the east, the Stillwater River. Both feature boulder-pocket fishing in addition to the more familiar riffle-pool type. Both support predominately rainbow and browns, a few of lunker proportions. Both receive an influx of spawning trout from the Yellowstone. And in each case, future mining of the mineral complexes in the Beartooth Mountains may jeopardize the fisheries.

Plans for mining in the Boulder drainage are in the works, and FWP has developed a management plan to cope with the anticipated influx of people. Under the new regulations, anglers on the Boulder and its main tributaries are limited to two trout, only one of which can measure over thirteen inches. From Two-mile Bridge to Natural Bridge, fishing for rainbow and cutthroat is catch-and-release and only artificial flies and lures are allowed. The state will also monitor mining activities and water quality in an effort to protect the fishery.

The Boulder River divides the Beartooths from the Absarokas. Along with its west and east forks, it drains three long, narrow canyons that reach far back into the mountains. The main Boulder runs for many miles through National Forest lands with ample access before emerging from the mountains and dropping as a major waterfall. Thereafter, the river swells substantially with the addition of its forks and continues to rush along its boulder-studded streambed until it joins the Yellowstone near Big Timber.

Above the falls the river has fine fishing, mostly for rainbow in the ten- to fifteen-inch class. But below the falls, where the water has more nutrients, the river harbors both rainbow and browns in the larger weight classes. Fred Terwilliger, who now runs Bud Lilly's Trout Shop in West Yellowstone, recalls a thirteen-pound trout caught in the springtime near McLeod.

But sadly, there is very little public access to this lower, trophy section of the river. FWP maintains three accesses, two of them quite extensive, but still, ninety-nine percent of the river fronts on private, often heavily posted land.

The Boulder has remarkably little cobble and gravel in its streambed. Anglers must therefore wade on what may be the slipperiest boulders in the state. Floating is not a sensible option for most of the river.

Spring runoff in the Boulder comes late and clears quickly, usually by the first week of July. Some of the best fishing takes place before the runoff. Terwilliger enjoys fishing the "tremendous March brown hatch" in April, but notes that most people ignore these early hatches and the super dry fly fishing that comes with them. The Boulder does receive some rainbow spawning from the Yellowstone, although not in such numbers as the Stillwater.

Most of the fishing pressure happens in July and August. Bait and spin anglers have trouble hanging up on the boulders but have some success in the pools. Worms, sculpins, and grasshoppers top the list of bait favorites. Fishing guide Curt Collins advises small lures such as Panther Martins, Roostertails, and gold Kastmasters.

The Boulder has a spotty hatch of smaller stoneflies. For fishing nymphs, Collins selects small golden, early black, and brown stone nymphs. For streamers, he likes olive and black Matukas and small sculpin imitations such as Maribou Muddlers. The four dry flies Collins is sure to have with him include small Adams, Light Cahill, Elk Hair Caddis, and the Joes Hopper. Anderson would add to the list a couple of attractor patterns such as Goofus or one of the Wulff patterns.

Terwilliger observes that most people who are inexperienced at fishing streams like the Boulder, Stillwater, and Madison pass up the swifter sections. The pockets behind the boulders hold lots of fish, and those fish see far fewer hooks than their brethren in the pools.

When the Clarks Fork of the Yellowstone joins the Yellowstone near Laurel, it doesn't look much like a trout stream. The water runs turbid until October,

Pocket water habitat—trout hang out just above and below such submerged boulders. Al Throth photo.

partly from natural causes and partly due to irrigation returns and overgrazing. Former FWP biologist Pat Marcuson terms the Clarks Fork "a sleeping giant," because it would be one of the most productive trout streams in the state if only sediment loads could be cleaned up.

As things now stand, the segment of the river from the state line to Clark has the best trout water and the most diverse fishery. From Clark to Belfry, Marcuson found mostly whitefish interspersed with a few big browns. From Edgar to the mouth, sauger and some huge ling make the river their domain. In 1981, Marcuson weighed one ling, caught by an angler a week before, which scaled just one-tenth of a pound under the state record.

The Clarks Fork has a tributary that has long delighted local anglers from Red Lodge to Billings: Rock Creek comes out of the Beartooths in three forks and a big rush. Below Red Lodge, the combined stream slows and winds its way through wonderful thickets of willow, aspen, and cottonwood. Above Red Lodge a ten-incher would be an extraordinary catch, but from Red Lodge downstream lurk some very respectable trout. The thickets can make casting difficult, but that is where the fish hold out. Avoid the places where bulldozers have moved the streambed; the trout moved out when the cats moved in.

Access *(For information on access to the river within Yellowstone National Park, refer to the chapter on fishing in the park.)*

Anglers wishing either to wade or float from the park down to Livingston have a long list of potential access sites. In view of the size of the river and the distance between riffles, floating makes especially good sense on the Yellowstone. Float trips can take an hour or a day depending on which access sites are chosen, how often the angler stops, and what craft is used. Anyone wishing to float the Yellowstone should pick up a copy of the pamphlet, *Montana Afloat #12, the Yellowstone River.*

Anglers can first reach the river outside the park at the town of Gardiner, where the river splits the town in half. The steep riverbanks prevent launching heavy boats there.

By using the gravel road going northwest from the Roosevelt arch at the park's entrance, anglers can walk to the river across park land for two or three miles below Gardiner.

Off Highway 89, FWP has an access known as "Queen of the Waters" at the upstream end of the Gardiner airport. A better launch site with more river frontage can be had on Forest Service land just downstream. Reach this spot by taking the dirt road right next to mile-marker three from the highway. As with many of these launch sites, anglers with boats on trailers should be very careful how far they back down here, or they may need a tow truck to get back up the bank.

Another two or three miles north on the highway, the roadway comes close to the river by LaDuke Spring. Several turnouts near here provide views of the spectacular Devil's Slide; they also provide parking for foot access to perhaps a mile of Forest Service riverbank and several beautiful riffles.

At Corwin Springs, FWP has an unimproved access where boat launching is possible until the lower water levels of late summer. Anglers would do better by crossing the Corwin Springs bridge and driving about .25 mile upstream to an all-seasons boat ramp on Forest Service and railroad land.

At the head of Yankee Jim Canyon, perhaps 200 yards west of the Joe Brown trailhead, the Forest Service provides a boat launch and take-out spot. The

A nymph, a partially emerged adult, and an adult stonefly (salmon fly). These big insects trigger the appetites of big trout on rivers like the Madison, Big Hole, and Yellowstone. Al Troth photo.

A long-shanked No. 1 hook is necessary to fashion an artificial fly imitating the stonefly (salmon fly) nymph. Al Troth photo.

2.5 miles of canyon downstream is within Forest Service land and is easily accessible from the highway.

A mile or two north of the canyon's mouth, a sign marked "Tom Miner Basin" directs anglers to a substantial BLM access stretching downstream from the Carbella Bridge on the east side of the river. A landowner has allowed boat launching on the west side of the bridge; please respect this kindness.

About four miles north of the Carbella site on Highway 89, you'll find a fork in the highway. To the right, the East River Road closely parallels the river for roughly thirty miles and gives anglers access to the riverbank in several places. Some of these access sites have been developed into campgrounds. If you choose instead to go straight ahead on Highway 89, the roadway will soon cross the Point of Rocks Bridge and parallel the river on the west side.

On this west side, not far downstream from the bridge, anglers can find the FWP Point of Rocks access. This site has a good boat ramp into a fast side channel. Downstream a little further, anglers can use the highway rest area access, although boat launchings involve a fifty-yard carry. Or go a couple of miles farther to an informal boat access by a big bend in the river just opposite Emigrant Peak.

Downstream on the east side, anglers can take advantage of highway right-of-way access above and below Wan-i-gan. McKenzie boat owners will find launching or taking out almost impossible here.

The Emigrant Bridge has a popular FWP access for wading and floating anglers alike. Just north of the town of Emigrant on Highway 89, another FWP access, known as Emigrant North, gives walk-in access over a stile.

At the Pray Bridge, which travelers use to reach the Mill Creek road, a private landowner kindly allows access off the east end of the bridge. Downstream on the east side, FWP maintains the Paradise campground, which includes bank access but no boat ramp. A little farther downstream and still on the east side, FWP's Loch Leven access has a campground, an excellent boat ramp, and substantial bank access.

Downstream on the west side, FWP's frequently photographed Mallard's Rest access has another excellent boat ramp and lots of bank frontage. Perhaps three miles north the Pine Creek Bridge now has a good boat ramp at the west end.

Five miles north, Highway 89 runs right next to a heavily riprapped bank of the river in a place known locally as Bell Crossing. Anglers navigate into the east channel; the west (left) channel has a very dangerous diversion dam for the Livingston ditch.

North of here .25 miles, the East River Road rejoins Highway 89. Driving only a short distance east on the East River Road takes anglers to Carters Bridge, which has a fair boat ramp, although the water is swift here early in the summer. Just downstream of Carters Bridge, FWP's Free River access offers walk-in access by Allenspur.

In Livingston, anglers have a choice of at least four accesses. The 9th Street Island Bridge has a boat launch area on the west, upriver side, but be prepared for some tricky navigating to avoid wrapping around the bridge pillar. Sacajawea Park has foot access for perhaps .75 mile. Mayor's Landing at the old Harvats Bridge has a fair boat ramp. Anglers can also reach the river at the northeast end of town at the pair of bridges by the radio station.

Northeast of Livingston on Interstate 90, Highway 89 branches off to the

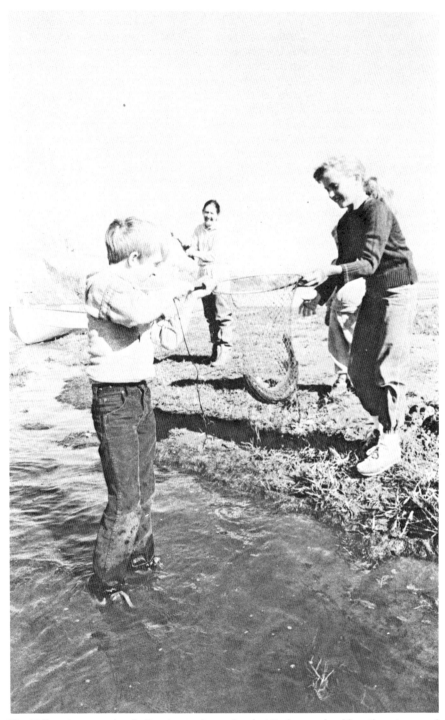

The Yellowstone may be challenging to the angler, but it also can be, like other rivers and fishing in general, a source of family entertainment. Michael Sample photo.

north and shortly crosses the river. A popular, but difficult, launch area is on the south side of the river near the bridge. Or you can continue north over the bridge to a signed gravel road running three bumpy miles downstream to Sheep Mountain Campground, which is equipped with a fair boat ramp. Much easier to reach from Interstate 90, the Springdale Bridge also has a fairly good boat ramp. Grey Bear Fishing Access, reached by turning off at the DeHart exit five miles west of Big Timber, affords anglers a campground, facilities, and another boat ramp.

Between Big Timber and Billings, the access points are farther apart. These four all have boat ramps usable by two-wheeled vehicles—Pelican Fishing Access Site (FAS), a mile northeast of Greycliff; Bratton FAS, sixteen miles east of Big Timber near milepost 381; Indian Fort, a mile north of Reedpoint; and Itch-Iep-pe, just south of Columbus on the road to Absarokee.

Laurel has a park at the south end of the Highway 212 bridge, but it has no boat ramp. Billings has several bridges and, more notably, Riverfront and Coulson parks.

The remaining 361 miles of warm-water fishery is near-wilderness for long stretches. In recent years, FWP has encouraged use of this resource and is actively adding access sites to the lower river. With thirty-five species of fish in the lower Yellowstone, fishing pressure is on the rise, hitting 50,000 angler days per year in 1989.

FWP expects to add more access sites as the lower Yellowstone's popularity grows. For now, most of the access is clustered between the Bighorn and Rosebud Creek and from Glendive to Sidney. The city of Glendive provides an unofficial access with a good boat ramp located between the interstate and city bridges.

ACKELY LAKE

Ackley Lake is a small, 250-acre reservoir on the open plains of central Montana. Located in Judith Basin County, approximately 4.5 miles southwest of Hobson, the reservoir is accessible via a well-traveled county road. A water canal from the Judith River feeds the reservoir; therefore, the bottom is generally quite muddy. Because it is used for irrigation storage, the water level fluctuates somewhat mid- to late summer, depending on the year.

Because Ackley Lake is a multiple-use reservoir, fishing success depends on how severe irrigation draw-down is and when it occurs. FWP has defined the minimum depth to be ten feet, so there should always be some water left in the reservoir. A user fee is now charged at Ackley.

Angling at Ackley is divided between trolling and shore-fishing. If you're trolling, ten to fifteen feet is the best depth for rainbow. FWP currently plants two strains of rainbow, Arlee and Eagle Lake. An occasional brown trout takes a lure too, but kokanee are no longer stocked here. Most anglers stick with standard trolling fare: spoons, spinners, and an occasional bottom bouncer. If you're fishing from shore, the biggest problem you'll have is disposing of all the suckers you catch. The reservoir has been chemically treated in the past to control the sucker population, and according to FWP, this management will continue as needed.

Winter ice-fishing brings lots of anglers out for rainbow. Corn, salmon eggs, or maggots should do the trick. This is fairly open country, and the wind blowing through Judith Gap can get pretty ferocious, so dress accordingly.

Since this reservoir is in open prairie, it is a favorite stopping off place for waterfowl of the Central Flyway in the fall. Canada geese and many varieties of ducks can be seen in the fall, and some shorebirds inhabit the area during the summer. The surrounding coulees and plains host mule deer, pronghorn antelope, and many upland game birds, including sharp-tailed grouse and ring-necked pheasant. Many western Montana bird hunters travel to this part of the state every fall to bag their limit of pheasant. In addition, Ackley Lake provides an opportunity to hunt pheasant in the morning and lazily pick up a nice trout or two in the late afternoon—not bad for a day's work!

ASHLEY LAKE

Ashley Lake, a large, 3,200-acre lake, achieved notoriety a few years ago by yielding the state and world record hybrid cutthroat trout. In May, 1982, Pat Kelly threw an eight-pound test line with a small lure and nightcrawler into the lake. After a forty-five-minute fight he landed the thirty-pound, four-ounce record cutthroat hybrid trout. The fish was 35.75 inches long and 27.5 inches around.

The cutthroat/rainbow hybrid strain was brought up from Georgetown Lake thirty to forty years ago, and though the fish aren't plentiful, conditions are ideal for prolonged life and growth. They do spawn in a few local streams, so anglers can continue to search the lake for these lunkers and hope for another record breaker.

Although big fish have brought Ashley Lake to prominence, there are other unique features that make this lake a popular recreation spot. Located on a county road thirteen miles north of milepost 105 on Highway 2 west of Kalispell, Ashley Lake State Recreation Area offers visitors excellent public facilities. This popular summer resort has well-maintained public toilets, campground, picnic area, and swimming areas.

For the visiting angler, there is good summer troll fishing for cutthroat trout and kokanee salmon. The cutthroat should not be fished too deep (around eight feet is usually sufficient), but if you're after the wily kokanee, be prepared to try several depths—all the way down to 100 to 150 feet deep.

Ashley Lake also has approximately forty acres of shallow areas that are full of water lilies, rushes, and other aquatic plants that can foul a motor or snag your line.

Winter ice-fishing is also very popular at Ashley Lake. Cutthroat, perch, and kokanee all are easily fished through the ice. Standard ice-fishing bait and outfits will work very well.

A good day's catch at Ashley Lake should yield a limit of one eleven-inch kokanee or four to five twelve-inch cutthroat. Winter fishing should yield slightly larger cutthroat than summer fishing, and some nice ten-inch perch. FWP is trying to increase the cutthroat trout population through artificial propagation. The department is also encouraging natural spawning through restriction of fishing on spawning streams and removing beaver dams which block many of the spawning streams. For the latest updates on fishing success, stop in at the Kalispell FWP office or the Snappy Sports Center in Kalispell.

When you're in the area you might observe mule and white-tailed deer, moose, black bears, and the sorrowful loon. Nearby Kuhns State Wildlife Management Area provides excellent white-tailed deer winter range and is

Watching the fly float—a favorite pastime of those who prefer lake fishing. It's very relaxing. Michael Sample photo.

open to public hunting in the fall. Big game hunters should check with a local FWP office for seasons, bag limits, and quotas.

BIGHORN LAKE

Located southeast of Hardin on Highway 313, Bighorn Lake was created by the construction of Yellowtail Dam near Fort Smith in 1965. The seventy-one-mile lake is in a peaceful vista of steep-sided canyons on the Bighorn River. The dam provides electric power, water for irrigation, flood control, and recreation. Fishing, boating, waterskiing, swimming, hiking, and camping are highly popular at this isolated southeastern Montana recreation site. The entire lake is surrounded by the Bighorn Canyon National Recreation Area, which extends into Wyoming.

Bighorn Lake is a long, narrow reservoir, with only two public access sites on the Montana end: the Ok-A-Beh boat launch area located near the Yellowtail Dam and Visitor Center; and Barry's Landing, which includes a public campground. Even though Barry's Landing is located in Montana, it is reached by road only from Wyoming. Due to the steepness of the canyon walls, there are very few places where you can pull a boat up to the bank and fish. However, the scenery in the canyons is spectacular.

According to FWP fisheries biologist Steve Swedberg, Bighorn Lake is primarily a walleye fishery, with some limited rainbow and brown trout, and black crappie fishing. Largemouth bass and channel catfish inhabit the Wyoming end of the lake.

In the spring anglers stick to the "rubble" areas on the points around the lake, mostly still-fishing anchored offshore. Swedberg suggests trying jigs with nightcrawlers attached in about fifteen to twenty feet of water.

For fall fishing, Swedberg suggests trying the brushier areas around the lake edges but cautions that anglers should be prepared to lose a lot of gear. Trolling activity picks up in the fall, and some trollers switch to lures, although the jig-crawler combination is also very popular. The mouths of streams such as Black Canyon, Bull Elk, and Porcupine on the south side of the reservoir are excellent places to try in the fall. Dry Head Creek, on the north side, also is popular in the fall. Swedberg says you might land a lake trout or big brownie in the fall if you troll a little deeper than usual.

A good day's catch at Bighorn Lake should yield your limit of two-pound walleye, with the possibility of hauling in one up to fourteen pounds. In addition, a few rainbow and lake trout might turn up, along with some black crappie.

Maps and information about Bighorn Lake and the Bighorn Canyon National Recreation Area may be picked up at the Yellow tail Dam and Visitor Center near Fort Smith, Montana, and at the National Park Service Visitor Center in Lovell, Wyoming. The Crow Indian Reservation borders the recreation area along most of the east side and surrounds much of the rest of it. Trespassing without permission is forbidden.

BROWNS LAKE

Browns Lake is located in Powell County nine miles from Ovando and about sixty miles northeast of Missoula on Montana Highway 200. This is a shallow lake in an open sagebrush area and therefore unique among western Montana's lakes.

Public camping facilities, including toilets and a boat ramp, are available at the south end of the lake. There is also a small boat launch area on the northwest side of the lake.

In the summer, fishing at the lake is evenly split between trolling and shore-fishing. Trolling is best done using weighted flies such as Wooly Worms and standard spoons and spinners. Shore anglers generally prefer bait such as worms, maggots, marshmallows, and cheese, although some anglers use artificial spinning lures and small spoons. Local anglers report a good summer-time catch averaging three rainbow trout weighing between one and three pounds. Late spring usually produces some nice three- to five-pound rainbow in the twenty-inch range.

Browns Lake really comes alive once the ice forms in winter. It seems to have a special attraction for Missoula anglers. Ice-fishing usually is very good for one- to three-pound rainbows and even an occasional brook or brown trout. Corn, maggots, mealworms, marshmallows, and salmon eggs are the most popular bait. Ice jigs, in light fluorescent colors, also are widely used. More than a few anglers go home at the end of a day with their limit of trout. Because different temperatures and times seem to have a great effect on fishing success, it's important to have a large variety of tricks in your tackle box. Experimentation is the key to success at Browns Lake. Once you find a successful combination, stick with it.

According to local anglers, the south end of the lake is the traditional area for ice-fishing. They recommend fishing close to the bottom. Two to three feet off the bottom is suggested.

FWP, which plans to continue its program of planting rainbow trout in Browns Lake, reports that the lake should continue to provide good fishing.

If you're in Missoula, stop in at Bob Ward's Sporting Goods or Sportsmen's Surplus for the latest conditions and fishing methods. There's always someone around who knows what's happening at Browns Lake.

CANYON FERRY RESERVOIR

Fifteen miles east of the Copper Dome of Montana's capital city lies one of Montana's most popular fishing holes, twenty-five-mile Canyon Ferry Reservoir. Covering 35,300 acres, this Missouri River reservoir has become one of Montana's foremost recreation areas because of its proximity to many of the state's largest urban areas—Helena, Great Falls, Butte, and Bozeman. Residents of both eastern and western Montana often drive over to fish and relax here at one of the many recreation areas scattered around the shoreline.

Attracted by its excellent fishing, sailing and power boating, waterskiing and swimming, clean air and water, and spectacular mountain scenery, recreationists come here to shed the worries and cares of hectic twentieth century America. There's plenty of room to do so at Canyon Ferry, because there are twenty-four FWP-maintained recreation sites around the reservoir. Access to the area is easy from U.S. Highway 12 east of Helena or just north of Townsend.

In the Gold Rush years of the 1860s and 1870s, about 10,000 people mined the gulches around present-day Canyon Ferry. In fact, Confederate Gulch produced the richest gold mine on record in the United States. Names for many of the recreation sites around the reservoir are based on the old mines: Confederate, Whites, Cave, Avalanche, Hellgate, and Magpie all were active mines at one time. Visitors still come to Canyon Ferry seeking buried treasure, but today the treasure is speckled brown and rainbow-colored, and it's not buried in the hills but beneath the surface of the reservoir's clear water.

Rainbow trout, brown trout, whitefish, yellow perch, largemouth bass, and kokanee salmon make up the sport fishing population at Canyon Ferry. The reservoir also has a sizeable nongamefish population which includes carp and suckers.

Fishing activity begins in the spring as soon as the ice goes out of the reservoir. Avid Canyon Ferry angler Jim O'Loughlin of Helena calls it a "license to steal when the ice goes off above the dam along the rocks." The fishing by anyone's standard is excellent for rainbow, occasional browns, and even perch. O'Loughlin suggests using spinning gear with a Thomas Cyclone or Crocodile Mepps lure if you want to fill your creel. In early spring, O'Loughlin says, Confederate Gulch and other nearby bays offer excellent fishing. He suggests trying the channel, using fish eggs or spawn for bait.

Trolling activity begins in earnest in May and continues through June. O'Loughlin suggests keeping boat speed relatively low with no wake. He prefers a spinning rod with monofilament and a sinking Rapala lure. Bob Martinka, another Canyon Ferry regular and the regional supervisor for FWP, prefers using a fat-bodied Rapala with spinning gear. He fishes the area around Cemetery Island during May and June for 1.5-pound rainbow and an occasional two-pounder (when he's lucky). Cemetery Island and the nearby west shore are favorite nesting sites for ospreys. These big white raptors (called fish hawks by some) build their nests, which resemble a bulky mass of sticks, in dead trees, on rock pinnacles, or on the ground.

Almost all local anglers agree that as the water warms up in Canyon Ferry, around June or early July, fishing drops off. Both Martinka and O'Loughlin suggest fishing only in the early mornings, late evenings, and after dark. There is another hazard associated with warm weather fishing: fish spoilage. Martinka suggests keeping a cooler with ice or a bucket with wet rags in your boat or next to your fishing spot on shore to preserve the fish you catch from June on. The bright summer sun and the wide expanse of reflecting water combine to produce sure-fire damage to caught fish.

Fishing in the dark with a lantern in about ten to fifteen feet of water can provide a lot of fun and a creel of trout, according to O'Loughlin. Bait fishing is the rule after dark; worms and marshmallows work well.

Canyon Ferry produces a small mid-summer kokanee salmon fishery, according to Bruce Rehwinkel, fisheries biologist for FWP. So far FWP hasn't been able to get the salmon to spawn in the reservoir or its tributaries, so fish must be stocked. Rehwinkel says FWP is trying to create some spawning habitat and runs so that the population can become self-sustaining. Trolling a large area is necessary to find these fish, but once you get into some, stay with them, because kokanee tend to stay together. Small orange-colored lures on spinning gear seem to work best.

Autumn fishing at Canyon Ferry is excellent by any standards. Martinka likes to troll near the inlet of the Missouri River on the south end of the reservoir. He uses a fifteen-foot boat with a four-horse motor and trolls slowly, creating no wake. He recommends varying the speed and even stopping and casting a bit. Such techniques usually yield ten to fifteen fish in an hour or two. Brown trout begin their spawning runs up the river in the fall. According to Martinka, the real challenge at Canyon Ferry is hooking one of those lunker browns. O'Loughlin says that fall is also a good time for shore-fishing, using marshmallows and worms. For brown trout he uses perch or sucker meat and fishes deep. Fall is also a good time to fish for perch while anchored offshore in ten to fifteen feet of water. O'Loughlin uses perch meat, eyes, or throat for bait. "Perch will pick you to death if you put on worms," he warns.

Winter and cold weather really heat up the fishing action at Canyon Ferry. Ice begins to form in the bays around the reservoir from Thanksgiving on, but the water near the dam usually doesn't freeze until February. The west shore near Beaver Creek Bay is a popular ice-fishing area. Perch and trout are the primary species caught through the ice. O'Loughlin says that ninety percent of the local anglers agree that perch is the best eating there is—all you have to do is fillet them. He uses either maggots or perch meat, eyes, or throat as bait and says that on a good day he wouldn't be satisfied with less than fifty. "There have been a lot of days when I've caught a hundred or more," he adds. O'Loughlin fishes perch fairly deep, usually off the bottom.

Trout fishing in the winter is similar to fishing for perch, except that deep fishing is not the rule. Martinka uses either a rubber-legged jig or maggots through the ice and fishes for trout in about six to ten feet of water. Rainbow trout are the most common in the winter, but Martinka says that browns up to five pounds have been pulled through the ice at Canyon Ferry.

Night ice-fishing with a lantern can be very productive, according to both Martinka and O'Loughlin. However, anglers should make sure the ice is thick enough before they venture out. The FWP office at Canyon Ferry or in Helena can provide information on ice thickness, so don't hesitate to check with them. It can get a little chilly at the reservoir in the winter, and both Martinka and O'Loughlin suggest bringing a thermos of something hot along. Martinka adds that "even a little blackberry brandy isn't too bad."

Public camping facilities maintained by FWP are located all around the reservoir. Near the dam area, camping areas include Jo Bonner, Chinamans, Ponderosa, Court Sheriff, Riverside, and Overlook. On the east shore, campsites are located at Hellgate and Goosebay Marina. On the west shore, campsites are located at White Earth, Silos, and Indian Road. Boat access is available at all of the campsites. A number of additional public boat launch areas are located near the dam on the north end and near Townsend on the south end.

The Big Belt Mountains, which parallel the east shore of the reservoir, offer some of the best mule deer and elk hunting in Montana. Every fall, hunters from both the eastern and western parts of Montana hunt this area. The southwestern end of the reservoir, near Cottonwood, provides excellent habitat for white-tailed deer and ring-necked pheasant. In addition, waterfowl hunters work the area near the Missouri River inlet on the south end of the reservoir early in the season before it freezes over.

Fishing, hunting, boating, waterskiing, swimming, picnicking, and camping all make Canyon Ferry Reservoir what FWP finds to be Montana's most heavily used recreation area. Be sure to stop in at the FWP office at Canyon Ferry Village, near the dam, to pick up maps and information about the public facilities and recreational opportunities available.

Hauser Lake

Closely associated with Canyon Ferry is another Missouri River reservoir, Hauser Lake, located just a few miles downstream. Hauser Lake is easily accessible from Helena via State Highway 280. Bob Martinka likes to fish Hauser almost as much as he does Canyon Ferry. He claims the odds are a little better for hooking a brown trout at Hauser, and there are plenty of rainbow. He uses much the same set-up as he does for Canyon Ferry, and trolls toward the dam in the spring. Rainbow average about a pound in size and browns run two to three pounds.

There are some smallmouth bass and walleye in Hauser. Martinka trolls the shoreline for bass using plugs or poppers and works the area near the causeway for eight- to ten-pound walleye. For the big walleye, he slows his trolling way down and lets his bait bounce along the bottom.

There is some shoreline fishing near the recently completed York Bridge, and it's only a short distance from there up to the York Bar for a big juicy hamburger and a cold beverage.

CASTLE ROCK LAKE

On the north end of the town of Colstrip, Castle Rock Lake offers the perfect family diversion for a summer's evening. This 165-acre lake is owned by the Montana Power Company, but is open to the public for day use year-round. Drive north from Colstrip for .5 mile and turn west on a county road—look for the rod and gun club sign.

Locals fish here regularly, and Castle Rock is gaining regional fame as a largemouth bass and bluegill fishery. The bluegills average about .5 pound and are an easy catch, good fun for even the youngest angler.

The most abundant fish in Castle Rock Lake is largemouth bass, averaging one to two pounds. Northern pike in the same size range are also common, and a good day's catch will include a walleye or two, a channel catfish, and even an occasional burbot. Many anglers are content to fish from the open, gently sloping shoreline, but boaters should be aware that gasoline outboards are prohibited. Bring your electric motor or paddles for this small lake. The Montana Power Company locks the access gate at night and camping is not allowed at Castle Rock.

CLARK CANYON RESERVOIR

Clark Canyon Reservoir, located on Interstate Highway 15 approximately twenty miles south of Dillon in Beaverhead County, produces some great lunker trout. The reservoir is readily accessible from I-15 along the entire length of the east side. Montana Highway 324 on the northwest offers visitors ready access to much of the west side of the reservoir.

This is a large, 6,600-acre reservoir that was created by construction of Clark Canyon Dam on the headwaters of the Beaverhead River. Red Rock River to the southeast and Horse Prairie Creek to the northwest combine to form the waters of the reservoir.

Apart from a couple of rock islands toward the middle of the reservoir on the east side, Clark Canyon is a wide, open foothills reservoir. Fishing access sites and picnic areas are scattered around the northwest and east shores.

Clark Canyon Reservoir is primarily a rainbow trout fishery, although there are sizeable brown trout and burbot or ling populations, and a fair amount of suckers and other nongame species. In 1989, FWP stopped stocking the Arlee rainbow and concentrated instead on two wild strains, the DeSmet and Eagle Lake rainbow. Though slower growing, these strains show better staying power and a stronger proclivity to reproduce in the wild.

Springtime is the most popular time of year for fishing, with spring activity culminating at the Dillon Rotary Club's Fish Derby held on Father's Day. This event attracts out-of-state as well as local anglers. The competition and the fishing are fast and furious.

As soon as the ice comes off the reservoir in March or April, you'll find anglers out on the water. Both brown and rainbow trout are active at this time. In fact, this is the best time of the year for browns, according to Norm Peterson, FWP fisheries biologist. Trolling has long been popular all over the lake, although many anglers concentrate on the east shore from the dam down to the mouth of Red Rock River. And with the DeSmet and Eagle Lake trout, anglers are switching to smaller lures and flies. Some rainbow trout anglers report good success fishing near the mouth of Horse Prairie Creek. Although rainbow trout comprise up to eighty percent of the spring catch, three- to five-pound brown trout are fairly common. Browns up to sixteen pounds and rainbow up to ten pounds have been hauled ashore, evidence that there are some lunkers in this reservoir.

According to Peterson, most trollers use large Daredevle's, sinking Rapala's, and large Thomas Cyclone's on eight-pound monofilament line, usually trolling within eight feet of the surface. Bait anglers generally stick to sucker meat, worms, and marshmallows, using lightweight spin casting gear. Most bait fishing is done from the shore at one of the numerous public access sites. If the traditional gear doesn't do the trick, try smaller flies—and maybe a float tube. Fly fishermen report good success in spring and late summer.

During the summer, fishing pressure increases and the success rate declines. This is the time of year when many visitors from Utah and Idaho make their way north to try their luck in Montana. Peterson advises anglers to troll deep during the summer months to increase their chances of success. Shoreline fishing tends to increase during the warm months.

The southern end of the reservoir, near the mouth of Red Rock River, is the most popular spot for fly fishing. Weighted flies, sometimes including a small bobber attached to the leader, seem to get the best reviews. Late evenings towards sundown is the best time to try using dry flies. Even at that time it gets pretty tricky, and matching the hatch is a must.

In the fall, pressure drops off (it's usually lighter in the fall than the spring), and success picks up; again the emphasis is on trolling with a trend toward smaller hooks.

The reservoir comes alive again in the winter as anglers head out onto the ice. Since this is an open reservoir, with very few natural obstructions to the

Clark Canyon Dam on the Beaverhead near Dillon has some trophy rainbows for lucky anglers. Al Troth photo.

wind, it can get mercilessly cold out on the ice. Ice anglers here fish primarily for burbot; there are comparatively few trout taken. Popular locations include near the dam, the northwest shore, and around the islands on the east side. Most anglers use worms, marshmallows, and corn as bait, but anglers also try cut bait and roe (trout egg sacs). Some open water rainbow fishing takes place in the winter near the Red Rock River inlet, with most anglers using bait.

A good day's catch at Clark Canyon reservoir should yield a dozen two- to four-pound burbot in the winter, your limit of two-pound rainbow, and if you play your cards right perhaps some three- to four-pound (up to ten-pound) browns. Fishing looks good for both the short and long term at Clark Canyon, as FWP has initiated a program to develop a self-sustaining wild trout fishery at the reservoir.

The Bureau of Land Management and the Beaverhead National Forest offices, both in nearby Dillon, have maps available of their respective public lands which border the reservoir. For fishing information, stop in at the Hitching Post Sporting Goods store in Dillon.

COONEY RESERVOIR

Located in Carbon County nine miles west of Boyd on a county road, Cooney Reservoir is a heavily fished state recreation area. There are two public campgrounds at the reservoir, one on the west side and the other on the east. Besides camping facilities, there are public toilets, picnic areas, boat access sites, and beach areas for swimming. Since this reservoir is located near Billings, the largest metropolitan area in Montana, the summer season is fast becoming a potential recreation nightmare because of conflicts between waterskiers, swimmers, and anglers. FWP is working to resolve most of these problems before they reach the critical stage of having to restrict any one activity. Facilities have been expanded and improved in recent years.

Cooney Reservoir was once primarily a rainbow trout fishery, stocked annually by FWP with over 250,000 rainbow. But beginning in 1984, FWP annually introduced walleyes and reduced rainbow plants to 150,000 fish. Biologists hoped to create a two-tiered trout and walleye fishery and at the same time control the burgeoning population of suckers. Although the walleye are not reproducing on their own, some fish from the original stocking have grown to ten pounds. In the meantime, black crappie have been illegally planted in Cooney and are succeeding all too well, posing as a competitive threat to the popular rainbow fishery.

While most nonangling recreationists use the reservoir heavily only during the summer, anglers ply their trade year-round. The best fishing takes place in the early spring as soon as the ice breaks up. At this time, both shore-fishing (where there's open water) and still-fishing while anchored offshore near the ice break-up can be very productive. Bait fishing with worms, grubs, and corn is popular; and lures such as Mepps, Triple Teaser, and Thomas Cyclone seem to work well.

Later in the spring and in the early summer, trollers hit the water before the crush of power boaters and swimmers picks up during the warmer months. Trollers use a single line of eight-pound monofilament, usually on a spinning rod. Daredevles, small sinking Rapalas, and other medium-sized spoons are popular lures for trolling. Cooney Reservoir is not very deep, twenty feet at the deepest, so trollers should stay in the upper eight feet of water. During the summer, angling success drops drastically because of the presence of other recreational users and because of rising summer water temperatures.

When the cooler fall weather begins to move through the area, fishing picks up again; trolling, still-fishing, and bank-fishing all bring out lots of enthusiasts. Anglers use the same methods in the fall as they do in the spring.

Winter ice-fishing at Cooney Reservoir attracts a sizeable group of devoted anglers. Corn, marshmallows, and worms are standard bait choices. Cooney is an open reservoir in prairie and rolling hill country, so bring a good wind-breaker and a bucket of charcoal.

The Big Bear Sporting Goods stores in Billings are good places to stop and get up-to-date information on the conditions at Cooney. In addition, the FWP regional office in Billings has information on fishing, swimming, camping, and boating at Cooney Reservoir.

DEADMANS BASIN RESERVOIR

Located in Wheatland County about fifteen miles east of Harlowton and two miles east of Shawmut on Highway 12, Deadmans Basin Reservoir is a designated state recreation area. It is a 1,900-acre Musselshell River bottom reservoir that reaches a depth of ninety feet at its deepest point. This is a rather bleak spot, but excellent for rainbow and big browns. It is generally a fairly open body of water. Nearby are extensive recreational facilities, including boat access, toilets, campground, picnic area, and shelters. Nonetheless, Deadmans Basin receives only limited use. Because this open reservoir lies in a windswept prairie area, sudden storms do pose a hazard to anglers, swimmers, and boaters, so be watchful.

Deadmans Basin is primarily a trout and kokanee fishery, with rainbow predominating. Some brown trout do migrate from the Musselshell River, so anglers should be able to pick one up every once in a while. FWP has planted rainbow trout for the past eighteen years. In 1972-73, FWP planted some Coho salmon. The rainbow have flourished in the reservoir, but the Coho seem to have disappeared. In 1984, FWP switched to kokanee and still plants about 200,000 each year.

In the summer most anglers fish from the shore, although some extensive trolling occurs in a small area at the upper end of the reservoir about twenty to thirty feet from shore. Rainbow prefer the eight- to ten-foot depth, so trollers should not go too deep. Shore anglers should be careful about bottom fishing, as this reservoir contains its share of suckers. Standard spinners, spoons such as the Thomas Cyclone, and bait work best for rainbow. Please note that use of live minnows is strictly prohibited on this reservoir.

In the fall, browns make their way out of the Musselshell and up to the inlet to Deadmans Basin. Local anglers report that fishing is great for browns between 1.5 and twelve pounds. Wintertime brings out some of central Montana's best ice fisherman, and they hit the ice with a fury. Most of these folks come every year and would be more than happy to help newcomers catch their limit. Corn, mealworms, and marshmallows are standard fare through the ice, but you might have to try several types of bait before hitting on the right one. Bring your long underwear, because the wind really howls along the Musselshell River.

A good day's catch, in the summer, should yield a limit of .75- to 1.25-pound rainbow and an occasional two-pound brown trout. You're probably going to get a few carp and suckers from this reservoir, but you also might pull in a nice two-pound rainbow too. In the winter most anglers are easily able to catch a limit of rainbow, and because most fishing is not on the bottom, anglers usually don't get any rough fish.

Deadmans Basin provides a handy stop-over for migrating waterfowl following the Musselshell River. Ducks, Canada geese, and whistling swans are usually here both in spring and fall. The surrounding countryside provides excellent habitat for mule deer and pronghorn antelope as well as for upland game birds such as pheasants.

Stop in at Ray's Sports and Western in Harlowton to get the latest tips on baits, lures, and places to fish.

FLATHEAD LAKE

All of Montana's other lakes and reservoirs, natural or man-made, pale in comparison to western Montana's famed Flathead Lake, called by many the "jewel of the Northwest." It is the largest natural freshwater lake in the western United States, with over 200 square miles (or 125,250 acres) of surface area and 185 miles of shoreline.

Flathead is renowned for trout (cutthroat, lake, and bull), yellow perch, and lake whitefish fishing; as well as for many other water-based recreational activities such as sailing, power boating, waterskiing, and swimming. The east shore drive along Montana Highway 35, bordered by the magnificent Mission Mountain Range, is thirty-five miles of unexcelled beauty. In summer, roadside stands along the east shore offer a variety of locally grown cherries, apples, plums, and other fruits to delight the palate. The lake is accessible on its west shore along U.S. Highway 93 all the way between Polson and Kalispell.

Wildhorse Island, located along the west shore near the Big Arm, is a 2,165-acre state park. The park, accessible only by boat, hosts bighorn sheep, deer, waterfowl, eagles and falcons, and small mammals such as coyotes and ground squirrels. There are public day use and picnic areas as well as hiking trails and public fishing access sites on the island. You can't camp overnight on the island, but there are plenty of public camping areas on the surrounding mainland shore.

The southern half of Flathead Lake falls within the boundary of the Confederated Salish and Kootenai Tribes Flathead Reservation. All recreationists must purchase a tribal recreation permit for overnight or day use within the reservation boundary. The permits are good for the entire season at a modest cost. You can pick one up at tribal headquarters in Pablo, south of the lake on Highway 93, or at many of the small businesses in Polson, Elmo, Dayton, Rollins, and Bigfork.

FWP maintains thirteen public access sites around Flathead Lake, sites which the State of Montana has acquired over the years by purchase and donation. These sites include Sportsmans Bridge, Somers, Big Fork, and Juniper Beach fishing access sites; Wayfarers, Woods Bay, Yellow Bay, Finley Point, Walstad Memorial, Big Arm, and Elmo state recreation areas, which have toilets, boat launch, camping, swimming, and picnic facilities; and the West Shore State Park, located twenty miles south of Kalispell on Highway 93. With so many sites to choose from, anglers should have no trouble finding a choice spot to fish.

Fishing at Flathead Lake is an angler's dream come true. It offers trolling, bank-fishing; still-fishing; bait, lure, and fly fishing; and a choice of cutthroat, lake, and bull trout; mountain and lake whitefish; largemouth bass; and perch. Both cutthroat and bull trout spawn and rear juveniles in Flathead's remote tributary streams, with some spawning migrations over a hundred miles long. Juveniles then return to the lake to grow and mature. Yellow perch account for about seventy percent of the harvest from Flathead Lake, lake trout twenty percent, lake whitefish ten percent, and cutthroat and bull trout one to two percent.

Spring fishing at Flathead Lake usually begins in April and extends through June. The lake is so large and deep that the water doesn't really warm up until late June and early July. The north half of the lake is the most popular spring fishing area, although there is always some fishing—especially for lake trout— scattered all over the lake. Bull trout tend to concentrate up by the Flathead River inlet. Trolling back and forth in this area should produce some excellent results. Deep trolling (sixty to 100 feet) away from the inlet using steel line, cowbells, and large lures (or even dead fish for bait) works well for both bull and lake trout.

Cutthroat activity in the spring usually is limited to shallow trolling (less than twenty feet deep) and spincasting from shore using monofilament line and a single lure. Shoreline fishing is concentrated in the various bays around the lake and near the north inlet of the Flathead River.

Summer recreational activity at Flathead Lake is extremely heavy, with power boating, waterskiing, and sailing competing with fishing in popularity. Summer is also a great time for lake trout angling. These big fish, many in the twenty-

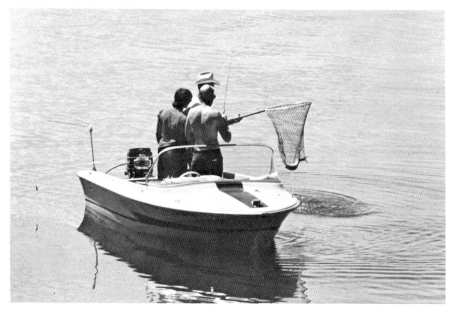

A boat—preferably a large one—makes Flathead Lake fishing more productive and safer.
Michael Sample photo.

to thirty-six-inch range, often concentrate along a line near the center of the lake. Submerged near the centerline is a bar—part of the old Flathead River delta—approximately a hundred feet below the surface, which slopes off to the sides. Fredenberg suggests fishing the edges of the bar for lake trout using down riggers, steel line, and large lures.

Fredenberg notes that cutthroat fishing is almost nonexistent at Flathead. He adds that lake whitefish are an untapped summer resource. "There are tons of whitefish in there, and no one goes after them in the summer," he says. Still-fishing off the bottom, using worms, maggots, or other bait, is one way to reach these nineteen- to twenty-two-inch tasty whitefish. Jim Vashro, FWP biologist, suggests using chartreuse or green jigs (Fuzzy Grubs, Mister Twister, and Foxee) or quarter- or half-ounce spoons in thirty to fifty feet of water off the numerous points along the shore. He says early morning is best and the fastest action comes in July and August and from November through March.

Both largemouth bass and perch fishing are good sport in the Polson Bay area. Bank-fishing or still-fishing from a boat, using bass plugs and poppers for bass and worms or cutbait for perch, are ways of catching these fish. (Even though much of Polson Bay is fairly shallow, it gets a lot of use from power-boaters and waterskiers, so keep an eye out for these folks if you're anchored offshore.) Largemouth bass in Flathead Lake range up to nineteen inches, and perch grow to ten or twelve inches in length.

Cutthroat fishing picks up dramatically in the fall. Shallow trolling and spin-casting from shore using small lures on monofilament line can yield some nice catches. Some anglers prefer shore-fishing for cutthroat from the many docks around the lake, using a bubble or bobber and a Muddler or Wooly Worm fly, while others prefer lures like Mepps or Thomas Cyclone.

Lake trout begin to move into shallower water to spawn in the fall, and anglers follow them. One choice location is around Wildhorse Island, where many anglers concentrate their efforts on the mainland side. A popular local method for catching lake trout is jigging with big jigs or spoons in fifty to 200 feet of water just offshore. In February of 1991, two anglers jigged up ninety-nine lake trout, half of which ranged from eight to thirty pounds. Their one-day catch (all released) weighed an estimated 800 pounds.

Despite the population explosion of smaller lake trout, there are still some lunkers in Flathead. FWP has recovered lake trout up to twenty-five pounds during tagging studies in the fall, and Vashro reports that eight trout ranging from thirty to thirty-six pounds were landed in 1991.

During the winter, anglers must key in on a specific species and choose their fishing location and tackle accordingly. Lake trout fishing really comes into its own during the cold season. Trolling off the underwater bars with cowbells and downriggers should yield a hefty fish and plenty of excitement. Many lake trout anglers put in at Yellow Bay in the winter and fish the area out from the bay.

Whitefish, both mountain and lake, are very popular species in the winter. In fact, winter is the best season for catching these delicious fish. Fish about one foot off the bottom either from a boat or, where the ice is thick enough, through the ice. Maggots and corn are the most popular bait for these species. Flathead anglers also haul cutthroat, bull, and lake trout through the ice, using worms, corn, cut bait, or maggots.

On a good day at Flathead Lake you should be able to catch a few fourteen-inch cutthroat and a bull trout in the twenty-inch range. Around the Polson area, a good day should yield a couple of fourteen-inch largemouth bass and a dozen ten-inch perch. During the winter, it's possible to haul in about fifteen lake whitefish, each nineteen inches long, and five to ten lake trout from twenty-two to twenty-six inches, with an occasional lunker as a bonus.

Flathead Lake certainly deserves the accolades that recreationists heap upon it. Whether you're fishing, boating, swimming, picnicking, or just stopping by in late summer for the cherry harvest, you'll find a myriad of interesting and unique outdoor experiences. There are numerous motels and rental cabins in addition to public campgrounds scattered all around the shoreline. The major population centers around the lake are Kalispell, Bigfork, and Polson, all of which offer a complete variety of groceries, supplies, and information.

FORT PECK RESERVOIR

The waters of eastern Montana are often confounding and mystifying to anglers from other states as well as to native Montanans raised near the crystal clear, cold streams west of the Continental Divide. No stream can lay claim to being at once perplexing and rewarding in quite the same way as the Missouri River once it reaches the Fort Peck Dam southeast of Glasgow and spreads out to become the largest body of water in Montana: Ft. Peck Reservoir. Created by the construction of Fort Peck Dam in 1940, the reservoir extends upstream over 135 miles and has a surface area of over 250,000 acres. Big Dry Arm, near the dam, extends the reservoir's waters another forty miles south up Big Dry Creek.

By the time the Missouri River winds its way past Great Falls and heads through the loose shale country of Fort Benton, it has picked up enough silt and soil to look unfit for fish or fowl. But appearances are deceiving, and even though it has slowed down to a crawl by the time it passes under the Fred Robinson bridge, just west of the defined limit of Fort Peck Reservoir, the Missouri is less like the staid and stolid warm-water fisheries of its midwest cousins than it appears. Beneath the surface of Fort Peck thrives one of the most diverse and challenging fisheries in the northern Great Plains. Northern pike, walleye, lake trout, sauger, channel catfish, paddlefish, burbot, yellow perch, black crappie, white crappie, a few smallmouth bass, and, yes, even an occasional rainbow trout all live here, along with a host of nongame fish such as carp and a variety of suckers. FWP has also started stocking chinook salmon here, and in 1991 Fort Peck produced the state record-breaker at thirty-one pounds, two ounces.

Surrounding this large expanse of water is the Charles M. Russell (CMR) National Wildlife Refuge, managed by the U.S. Fish and Wildlife Service, which provides over one million acres of public land for fishing, hiking, hunting, camping, bird-watching, and almost any other form of outdoor recreation imaginable (excluding golf courses and go-kart tracks). Public access to the reservoir's entire shoreline is restricted only by the dearth of roads, the geography, and weather. If you notice storm clouds approaching from the west and are planning to travel out of the reservoir area on one of the dirt roads, be quick about it. Many an unhappy stranger to this country has gotten stuck on virtually level ground during a rainstorm. Local people refer to the mixture of shale soils and water as "gumbo." It has the capacity to grab hold of two- and four-wheel drive vehicles and render them immobile.

There are three state recreation areas nearby, all located on the south side of the reservoir: Rock Creek, Hell Creek, and James Kipp. There are also four federal public campgrounds: Devil Creek, Turkey Joe, and Nelson Creek on the south side of the reservoir; and the Pines on the north. New fishing access sites, each with a boat ramp, have been added at Duck Creek, Fourchette Bay, and Spillway Bay.

You can reach the CMR Refuge and Fort Peck Reservoir from the west by turning off of U.S. Highway 191 northwest of Lewistown at the Fred Robinson

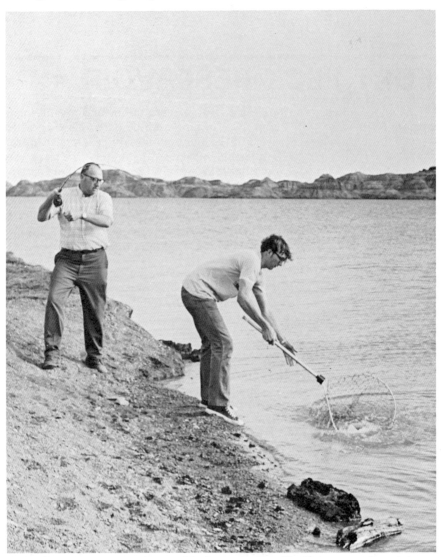

Fort Peck Reservoir is not only one of the largest bodies of fresh water anywhere, it is one of the most productive fisheries in Montana. Frank Martin photo.

Bridge. Travelers from the south can reach it via Montana Highway 200 at Jordan and then north via the county road. The eastern edge of the reservoir is accessible from Montana Highway 24, which parallels the entire length of the Big Dry Arm and passes through the town of Fort Peck and over the dam. The north side of the reservoir is the least accessible from main roads. U.S. Highway 2 between Glasgow and Malta is the closest paved road. There are numerous county roads that take off south from Highway 2 and wind their way toward the reservoir.

First-time anglers often do well by fishing the reservoir from the dam area near the town of Fort Peck. Lake trout, chinook salmon, northern pike, and walleye all frequent this area and provide plenty of excitement. Many anglers begin fishing at the dam and, as they get more familiar with the water and fish, quickly spread out to other areas on the reservoir.

The face of Fort Peck Dam is a very good place to find lake trout. FWP says anglers looking for lake trout concentrate their efforts in May and June, although fall fishing (October through November) is also good. During the warm summer months, lake trout tend to head deep to cooler water, so anglers should shift their depths accordingly. Some anglers spincast with lures from shore, but trolling brings the greatest success. In the spring and fall, trolling between fifteen and twenty feet of depth is adequate, but during the warm summer months it's best to set your line much deeper, eighty to 100 feet, using a down-rigger. Large spoons and lures such as a red and white or pearl-coated Daredevle are very popular. Fast retrieves and fairly fast trolling seem to attract the most fish.

Lake trout populations show a slight upward trend, so they will continue to be a popular sport fish in the coming years. These fish average about eight pounds, but there are some lunkers over twenty pounds in Fort Peck. Lake

Dinner for two—served at lakes all across Montana. Mark Kenckel photo.

trout and some other species have increased in average size in recent years thanks to the introduction of cisco and shiners as a food source.

Northern pike are also popular sport fish in Fort Peck Reservoir. Most northern pike fishing is done by trolling at fairly shallow depths—eight to ten feet—starting near the dam and working around the reservoir. Some summer anglers report success from trolling at greater depths, down to twenty feet. Large spoons and flatfish are the most popular lures for trolling, and some anglers use minnows both for trolling and still fishing. The bays of some of the tributary streams around the reservoir provide excellent northern pike holes, good for either concentrated trolling or still-fishing.

Bear Creek Bay, southeast of the dam, is the first large bay and should provide plenty of fishing challenge. Duck Creek Bay, northwest of the dam, is slightly smaller in size but has numerous shoreline fingers for anglers to work Gilbert Creek Bay further west on the south side is another good place to try. The final south side primary northern pike fishing area is the bay at Hells Creek. Hells Creek is also a state recreation area, with public camping, day use areas, toilets, drinking water, boat ramp, and swimming facilities. You can reach the recreation area either by boat or by road. To get there by road, follow the country road north out of Jordan for twenty-four miles. The bay at Timber Creek is the final north side primary northern pike fishing area. Although most anglers reach these areas by boat from the reservoir, there are roads through the CMR Refuge that will take you to the bays. Be sure to stop somewhere first and pick up a good local map of the area. The Bureau of Land Management publishes several maps that cover the entire area.

Sauger and walleye are different species that look very much alike, behave in much the same manner, and are fished in the same way. Many anglers can't tell the two species apart. Walleye, however, tend to be a bit larger and range up to nine pounds in Fort Peck. These fish will take a variety of lures and bait with medium to large spoons, preferably plugs and minnows. Walleye and sauger are generally taken by trolling; still-fishing; and set-line, or bank-fishing. Trollers should go deeper for these than for northerns, at least twenty to thirty feet deep. In addition, trolling speed should be cut to a slow speed. Unlike northerns, which tend to stay towards the eastern end of the reservoir, walleye spread out all over the reservoir, some even migrating up into the Missouri River. Sauger stay more towards the western end and up into the river. Walleye move into shallower shoreline areas at night, and many anglers do well then.

Some dedicated local walleye anglers maintain that the Big Dry Arm is the best walleye hole in the West. Still others make the same claim for the area between Hells Creek State Recreation Area and west to Fourchette Bay. In either case, there are plenty of walleye for everyone at Fort Peck.

The smallmouth bass population has grown and now attracts a respectable amount of angling pressure.

For some anglers, paddlefish provide the only reason to come to Fort Peck. This abundant, unsightly fish does not bite a baited hook; it obtains its food by straining water through its gill rakers and extracting plankton (small, floating, animal and plant organisms) as it lolls along the bottom. But there is an important snagging fishery for paddlefish in the upper, or western, portion of the reservoir.

Paddlefish taken in Fort Peck and the adjoining Missouri River are larger than those taken anywhere else in the country. Females average eighty pounds and males just under forty. The state record, and possibly the North American sport record, is a 142.5-pounder that was taken in 1973. Most anglers use thirty-pound monofilament line on casting equipment, with three to five treble hooks spaced back from a large sinker on the end. Eighty pounds of paddlefish is a lot of fish, so be sure to use a heavy duty reel and rod. Anglers snag both from boats and from the shoreline. From the end of March through June is the prime snagging season, while these huge fish move up the Missouri to spawn. The area from just west of the reservoir up to Fred Robinson Bridge on the Missouri River is the most popular snagging area. New regulations limit anglers to two paddlefish per season and each fish must be tagged.

The bottom of Fort Peck is also home to channel catfish, which spawn in the Musselshell and upper Missouri rivers. Catfish up to thirty pounds have been pulled out of the reservoir. They are attracted by many natural and artificial kinds of bait; generally, the smellier the better. The primary fishing area for catfish is the mouth of the Musselshell and the entire UL Bend area. Some channel catfish anglers swear that the upper Big Dry Arm is just as good as the western portions of Fort Peck. Most fish are taken by set-line or bank-fishing, usually in June when the water warms up to sixty degrees.

Another fine sport fish in Fort Peck is yellow perch, prized for its delicious taste. Even though it's not a large fish, a pan full of perch fillets is pretty hard to beat. There is no limit on perch, and they will take worms, maggots, and the flesh of any fish. Perch are fished year-round, including through the ice in winter, and they are found throughout the reservoir. Most perch weigh less than a pound, and catch rates are down for this species so it may take some work to pull in enough fish for the table.

Burbot, or ling, at Fort Peck are mostly caught by ice-fishing in the winter. This is one of the reservoir's most popular fish, though no one bothers them much from spring through fall. Spearfishing from dark houses on the ice furnishes excellent wintertime recreation. Rock Creek Bay and the upper Big Dry Arm are the most popular burbot fishing areas. Winter ice-fishing is popular not only for burbot, but also for lake trout, northern pike, walleye, sauger, and perch. Besides spearfishing, many winter anglers use tip-ups and lightweight spinning gear. Maggots, worms, cutbait, and corn are widely used for ice-fishing.

A good day's catch at Fort Peck should yield about three northern pike in the one- to thirty-pound range, your limit of four- to five-pound (up to twenty-pound) lake trout, four to five channel catfish averaging about five pounds, five walleye or sauger averaging one to two pounds, and a number of perch. In the winter you should be able to haul a few perch and burbot through the ice. Ten-pound lake trout are becoming more common.

Clearly, Fort Peck is one of Montana's prime fishing locations. It is awe-inspiring in its size, rewarding in its catches, and truly unique in the diversity of species which thrive in its waters. The surrounding CMR Wildlife Refuge and the picturesque Missouri River Breaks provide a thrilling backdrop for a quality fishing experience.

FRESNO RESERVOIR

As a part of the Milk River system, Fresno Reservoir provides irrigation storage for nearby farmers and recreational opportunities for anglers. Located approximately twelve miles west of Havre in Hill County, the reservoir has easy access two miles north of Highway 2. Canadian visitors can reach Fresno Reservoir by crossing the border at Port Willow Creek and heading south on Highway 232.

Surface area of this northern prairie reservoir is approximately 5,700 acres. Its depth averages around ten to twenty feet, reaching about thirty feet at the south end near the dam. Because this reservoir is heavily used for irrigation, it suffers severe fluctuations in water level during the summer and has been almost completely drawn down at times. Besides irrigation draw-down, future problems for fish include the possibility of hydro-power development at the dam.

Local anglers who hang out at Masters Sports in Havre report that the reservoir yields good early summer and spring fishing for northern pike, walleye, and perch. A good day's catch according to these folks is a freezer full of 1.5-pound to 2.5-pound northerns or a limit of 1.5-pound walleye. In the past FWP has planted smallmouth bass, rainbow trout, and perch, and northern pike were apparently planted illegally. So far, very few trout and bass have turned up in anglers' creels; no one has pulled a trout from these waters since 1974. But be prepared for them just in case they are still in there.

Trolling is the preferred method of fishing in spring and summer. Most anglers use spinners, spoons, or lures such as Rapala. Some anglers prefer bottom bouncers with a night-crawler attached. Trolling depth should be set between eight and twenty feet. Of course, if you want to try for bass, any of the standard bass plugs or flies can be used. Please remember that use of live minnows for bait is strictly prohibited on this reservoir; FWP is trying to keep the Milk River drainage from becoming saturated with the small fish.

Winter ice-fishing for northerns and walleye, using tip-ups baited with grocery store smelt, is good to excellent. Local anglers report catches of nineteen- to twenty-four-inch northerns and fifteen- to twenty-inch walleye. If you're trying for perch, any fleshy bait, or even corn, should yield a nice catch. This reservoir is located on the windy Hi-Line, so bring a good wind-proof parka along and a bucket of charcoal to help keep you warm.

GEORGETOWN LAKE

Easily accessible by State Highway 1 approximately eighteen miles west of Anaconda, Georgetown Lake ranks as one of western Montana's most popular fishing spots. In fact, this lake receives more fishing pressure per acre than any other lake in the state. The surrounding mountains, the Flint Creek Range to the north and the Pintlers to the south, also see their fair share of recreationists during backpacking season and the fall big game season.

Georgetown Lake is a large (3,000-acre), high (over 6,000 feet) mountain lake that tends to be a bit shallow. It is a very productive lake, as evidenced by the extensive weedbeds and by the excellent fishery.

Kokanee salmon, the most sought-after species in the lake, make up over fifty percent of the summer angler harvest. Rainbow trout rank a close second in popularity, with brook trout and a few bull trout somewhat down the scale. Both the salmon and brook trout populations are self-sustaining, while rainbow are planted annually by FWP. The average size of rainbow has been increasing recently, and four-pound 'bows are not uncommon. FWP also reports a few lake trout are being taken, including a fifteen-pounder in the summer of 1991. As with most lakes, Georgetown seems to have its share of nongame fish, such as suckers.

Georgetown has four public boat ramps, and fishing from boats—either trolling or still-fishing—is extremely popular at the lake. Trolling is best done in the spring, early summer, and fall, because weeds really proliferate during the warm months. Jim Vashro, FWP fisheries biologist, suggests that summer trolling success can best be achieved by staying above the weeds, in less than eight feet of water. Shore-fishing picks up during the summer months because of the trolling problems.

Most anglers use medium to small lures—Thomas Cyclones, Mepps, Triple Teasers—and Wooly Worms while trolling; and worms, corn, and marshmallows for bank-fishing or still-fishing. Local anglers report some success in late August and September using a jig and maggots for kokanee, concentrating their activity in the Pump House region of the lake. Jericho Bay and Piney Point are popular rainbow trout summer hangouts and are best fished by trolling in the weedless areas.

Georgetown Lake is also a popular place for fly anglers to try their luck. Float tubes, waders, and even plain old bank-fishing all get a good workout from fly anglers. The west end of the lake provides a challenge to fly anglers who want to fish by drifting over the weedbeds in either a boat or a float tube. For the nonpurists, a popular method of catching trout is to use a small bobber attached about four feet above a wet fly or Wooly Worm, using a slow, twitching retrieve. Dry fly aficionados will have their work cut out for them at Georgetown. Lighter shades of Wulff patterns, including Royals, are a good starting point.

In late fall, salmon snagging becomes the most popular activity at Georgetown. Treble hooks, pencil lead, and twenty-pound line are the standard tools of the snagging trade. Kokanee salmon spawn at various sites around the lake, including Stuart Mill Bay, Pump House, and Dentons Point. They generally move into these areas from middle to late October, and spawning takes place November through December. Both still-fishing and bank-fishing can be very effective for snagging—it all depends on where the salmon are on any given day. If you hit a school, you're likely to bring in sixty to seventy salmon! Conditions change daily, so you may have to move around some.

Winter ice-fishing produces over a quarter of the annual angling harvest at Georgetown. Bait fishing using maggots, worms, marshmallows, and corn is the predominate method, but some anglers trying for salmon use a jig or Glo Hook in combination with bait. Rainbow are generally spread out all over the lake in the winter, while kokanee tend to congregate in localized areas. Depending on which species you're after, you may have to try a number of different ice-holes. According to Vashro, the fish don't go too deep here in the winter, therefore he recommends setting your depth at no more than eight feet.

A good day's catch at Georgetown should yield your limit of twelve- to fourteen-inch rainbow, or three or four twelve- to fourteen-inch brookies. During snagging season in the fall, an average kokanee daily catch should number between sixty and seventy fish; but watch out, because some anglers have reported hauling in 100 kokanee!

Georgetown Lake affords the angler breathtaking views of the Pintler Mountains; excellent fishing any season of the year; and a chance to observe many species of waterfowl, including shorebirds; along with a sizeable white-tailed deer population in the Flint Creek drainage. The lake acts as a wild-life crossroads between the surrounding mountain ranges, and it's not uncommon to see an occasional bear doing a little fishing.

There is a Deerlodge National Forest ranger station north of Georgetown Lake, just a few miles south of Philipsburg. There, you can get maps and information on the Anaconda-Pintler Wilderness Area and the Flint Creek Mountains. James Stuart, at Stuart's Landing on State Highway 1 near the lake, can answer most of your questions about daily conditions.

HEBGEN LAKE

Hebgen Lake, gateway to Yellowstone Park, is fast becoming one of Montana's prized fishing and recreation areas. Located along Highway 287 eight miles north of West Yellowstone in Gallatin County, this beautiful Madison River Canyon lake was severely battered during the Montana-Yellowstone earthquake of 1959. Near Hebgen Dam, which separates Quake and Hebgen lakes, is a Forest Service Visitor Center commemorating the event and explaining the geological activity. It's well worth a visit when you're in the area.

Since the earthquake, Hebgen Lake has thrived as a prime recreation area. It's a summer tourist haven for sailing, waterskiing, picnicking, and camping, in addition to fishing. Even though it receives heavy use, Hebgen is increasing in fishing potential, according to FWP's regional fisheries biologist Dick Vincent, who says, "The long-term outlook is up; fishing should continue to get better year-round." The fact that this lake continues to improve even under heavy pressure is excellent testimony to FWP's successful management efforts.

Hebgen Lake is a rather elongated, sixteen-mile by three-mile liver-shaped body of water surrounded by the timbered mountains of the Madison Range to the northeast and the Continental Divide to the southwest. Access is relatively easy because of numerous roads which outline most of the lake, including Horse Butte peninsula on the east, which separates the Madison and Grayling arms of the lake.

Browns, rainbow, and mountain whitefish make up the active sport fishery at Hebgen. Early spring as soon as the ice comes off (through May and June) is the best time of the year for catching brown trout. Still-fishing from a boat positioned slightly offshore (as the ice break-up permits) is the ideal approach. Most anglers use worms or marshmallows to entice the hungry browns. There is some rainbow activity during the spring, which usually picks up as the water warms.

While rainbow fishing picks up in the summer, the success ratio for browns declines. Trolling eight to ten feet down for rainbow (deeper for browns) is the most popular summer angling technique. Medium-sized spoons and lures such as Thomas, Mepps, and Rapala all seem to work well. Bank-fishing for trout is also very popular in the summer. There are plenty of public access areas from which to choose. Spincasting, with either lures or bait, is popular with bank anglers. Jerry Cobb of West Yellowstone designs and makes what local anglers call a "killer" lure: a two-color spin-jig. Stop in and see him and give it a try—the results may be terrific.

Bait anglers also do well from a boat anchored about 200 yards offshore, fishing deep—just off the bottom. During the summer months, brown trout head down to the cool deeper reaches and loll around near the bottom. A nice two- to four-pound brown could be your reward for patience.

During the warmer months, the Madison Arm and the bay area near the mouth of the South Fork of the Madison host numerous fly anglers. Anglers employ float tubes, wading, and still-fishing to get the "gulpers" on the surface. In the fall, when the browns begin migrating, both the Madison and Grayling arms see plenty of activity. In the Grayling Arm, near the mouth of Duck Creek and on up into the streams itself, migrating browns provide fly anglers with plenty of action. Both wet and dry flies seem to work well during the fall, depending on time of day and temperature.

In the fall, fishing for rainbow increases, with most anglers fishing with bait from the shore. The scenery in the Madison Canyon during this time of the year is absolutely spectacular, so pop an extra roll of film into your fishing vest. Also, be on the lookout for early snowstorms in the fall. Fishing and driving can both get pretty nasty when it's cold and wet outside.

Winter ice-fishing has been slow in the past, but it has improved recently because of management efforts of FWP. If you do plan a winter visit, be prepared to shovel snow off the ice. The most popular area for ice-fishing is near the dam on the north end of the lake. Mountain whitefish, rainbow, and a very few browns make up the winter harvest. Maggots, grubs, marshmallows, worms, and corn are the preferred bait for dropping through the ice.

During the winter, don't forget to bring your cross-country skis. Neighboring Yellowstone Park and the surrounding mountains offer some of the most spectacular skiing in all of Montana.

Besides being an angler's dream come true, Hebgen Lake provides visitors with an excellent opportunity to observe many different species of wildlife.

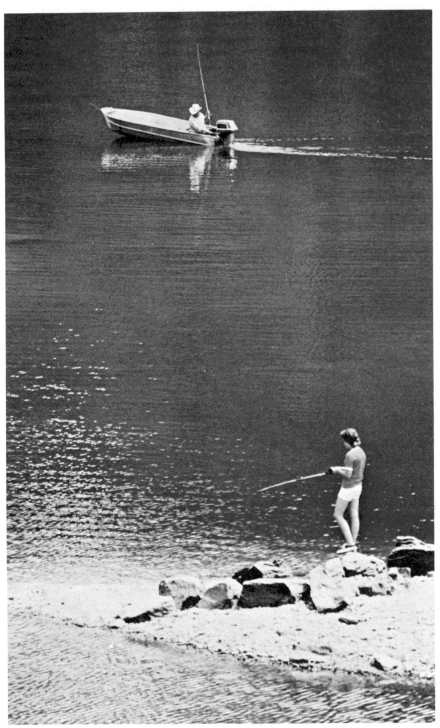

Each lake has its own fishing patterns, and learning those patterns is part of the fun. Michael
Sample photo.

Black and grizzly bears have been sighted around the lake, sometimes even sneaking into a campground looking for handouts. (Remember—all bears are dangerous and should be treated with healthy respect and left alone.) In addition, it is not uncommon to see moose feeding at stream inlets early in the morning and late in the evening. Deer and elk abound practically everywhere. Waterfowl, including pelicans, are common; and both bald and golden eagles are frequent visitors. Osprey show the human anglers what fishing is all about.

The Forest Service's Hebgen Lake ranger station, located just north of West Yellowstone on Highway 287, has maps available for visitors. The ranger on duty also can help provide information on camping sites and boat access sites.

HUNGRY HORSE RESERVOIR

Hungry Horse Reservoir is one of the few large Bureau of Reclamation reservoirs that boasts a naturally reproducing trout population; in fact, it produces some of the best "lake" fishing in Montana. Located just off U.S. Highway 2 south of Glacier Park near the towns of Hungry Horse and Martin City, this excellent cutthroat trout fishery was created on the South Fork of the Flathead River with the construction of Hungry Horse Dam. When the dam was completed in 1953, Hungry Horse was the fourth largest and highest dam in the world. Electric power generated at the dam is fed into the Bonneville Power Administration's Northwest Power Grid and shipped throughout western Montana, Washington, Oregon, and Idaho.

Surface area of this thirty-four-mile by 3.5-mile reservoir is approximately 22,000 acres. It has a maximum depth of 500 feet when full. Since it is located in a river valley, numerous tributary streams flow into the reservoir. These small tributary streams, along with the South Fork and Spotted Bear rivers, provide the habitat and conditions that make natural trout reproduction possible and that set Hungry Horse Reservoir apart from most other reservoirs in Montana.

Situated in one of the most picturesque wildland areas of Montana, Hungry Horse Reservoir is bounded by Glacier Park on the north, the Great Bear Wilderness on the northeast, and the Bob Marshall Wilderness just ten miles south. These unique wildland areas provide anglers and other visitors with breathtaking scenery, exciting backcountry challenges, and some of the best fishing in Montana. The surrounding mountains and hills are home to deer, moose, elk, bighorn sheep, black bears, and even the threatened grizzly bear. Glacier Park was once the focus of an annual bald eagle migration every fall, but with the collapse of the kokanee fishery in the Flathead most of the eagles have moved on to other feeding sites. Nonetheless, the entire Flathead area, including Hungry Horse, supports a healthy resident population of these majestic birds—apt testimony to the excellent fishery located here.

Most fishing activity doesn't really get started until the middle of June, when the reservoir nears full capacity, but from then on it continues full steam throughout the summer and on into the fall. Unfortunately, there is virtually no winter fishing because of the extreme draw-down for power generation. But once moderating weather starts to move through in late spring, local anglers get itchy feet and head for the reservoir.

Overall, this is a good to excellent trout fishery, with cutthroat predominating.

Most cutthroat anglers try the bay areas near the tributary streams and, because of the steep banks, tend to favor using boats anchored offshore. There is little shoreline fishing. The most popular bay areas tend to be on the north end of the reservoir near the dam; but the bays near Emery, Riverside, and Quintonkon creeks on the east side and Doris, Lost Johnny, Wounded Buck, Jones, and Forest creeks on the west side also see their share of eager anglers.

Light spincasting gear is favored by many anglers, with small Daredevles, Kamloops, Mepps, and Thomas Cyclones being the most popular cutthroat lures. Trolling is one of the most popular methods for fishing this large reservoir. Anglers trolling for cutthroat favor using a single line with small Rapalas, Triple Teasers, Swedish Pimples, and Mepps lures, usually working these lures ten to twenty feet down. A good day's catch should yield your limit of twelve-to sixteen-inch cutthroat.

According to Bob Schumacher, retired FWP regional fisheries manager, Hungry Horse Reservoir also supports an excellent bull trout fishery. The south end of the reservoir near the mouth of the South Fork and its tributary, the Spotted Bear River, are the most popular bull trout fishing areas. Schumacher cautions anglers not to neglect the mouths of some of the smaller tributary streams on the south end of the reservoir, as they can be very productive.

Most bull trout anglers use large wooden plugs or large heavy Daredevle type lures. Medium to heavy duty spinning gear should be used, because there are some large fish in the reservoir. Local anglers are fond of reciting this little line: "There are some lunkers in Hungry Horse; all it takes is the time to get them." A good day's catch should yield your limit of two- to ten-pound bull trout. Remember to stay alert, because a ten-pound fish can turn a lazy summer afternoon into a fantastically exciting day.

Fall at Hungry Horse is one of the most visually spectacular and colorful seasons of the year. The surrounding fir and larch forests become a checkerboard of dark green and bright yellow colors as the larch needles die in preparation for winter. But spectacular vistas are not the only reasons to head to this reservoir in October. Schumacher says that this is prime mountain whitefish angling time—a time that allows whitefish anglers a chance to show the rest of us what fishing is all about. Popular tackle includes light spincasting gear or a fly rod using maggots and grubs on very small hooks, sometimes attached to a small fly with red webbing on it. A good day's catch should yield a limit (100 fish) of nine- to ten-inch whitefish, so don't forget to bring a bucket or bag to haul yours home.

Fly fishing aficionados shouldn't stay away from this reservoir because of a dislike for impounded water. Purists may so choose, but if you like to fly fish and want an interesting and challenging piece of water located in a beautiful setting, then try it out. Hungry Horse is mostly a dry fly area, the most popular patterns being Wulff, Mosquito, grey or yellow Bi-visible, and (heaven forbid) a Wooly Worm-bobber combination. Again, most fly anglers stick to the bay areas near stream mouths.

Not only is the fishing at Hungry Horse great from mid-July through August, but the surrounding mountains conceal some of the most prolific and abundant huckleberry bushes in the state. Nothing tops a day of berry picking like a late afternoon expedition to the reservoir for some fresh trout. Steamed or fried trout sprinkled with lemon juice and green onions, baked potatoes and sour cream, and a fresh-baked huckleberry pie—now that's a menu that can't be beat!

If you're planning a trip to this truly spectacular area, stop in at the Snappy Sports Center or The Sportsman in Kalispell for some tips from local anglers on the latest conditions at the reservoir. In addition, the Forest Service's Hungry Horse Ranger Station also has information on camping, fishing, and boating conditions. Both locations should have maps available of the reservoir and the surrounding mountains.

LAKE KOOCANUSA

Northwestern Montana contains some of this nation's most magnificent scenery, ranging from the frosty, snow-laden peaks of the Cabinet Mountains—which contain several species of pine and fir trees, abundant larch, and the only grove of western red cedar in the state—to the floor of the Kootenai River Valley and some of Montana's most productive trout waters. The whole area teems with big game, birds, fish, and other wildlife. Bighorn sheep, moose, elk, and deer are all found in abundance; along with a large bald eagle population, the state's only harlequin ducks, and many other species of birds.

Not only are there natural wonders to explore in this region of the state, but man-made wonders as well. Lake Koocanusa, located in Lincoln County approximately seventeen miles northeast of the town of Libby on State Highway 37, is one of the largest man-made, mud-lined reservoirs in Montana. The reservoir, which extends forty-eight miles north to the Canadian border, was created when the United States Army Corps of Engineers completed construction of Libby Dam in 1972.

Before further describing the Lake Koocanusa fishery, it is appropriate to mention something about the "good old days" on the Kootenai River prior to construction of Libby Dam. FWP issued a report in 1975 assessing both the fishery in the dam project area prior to impoundment and the fishing potential after impoundment:

"Prior to impoundment, the Kootenai River was in a near natural state. Access to the river and its tributaries was good. . . .

"The Kootenai River prior to impoundment, because of its large size, good access, and excellent fish population was considered to be capable of sustaining harvests far in excess of present day demands. . . ."

After impoundment by Libby Dam, FWP had this to say about Lake Koocanusa:

"The reservoir is bordered by conifer covered mountains having steep slopes. Access to the reservoir is poor, a direct result of the steep slopes, reservoir fluctuations, and absence of roads to the immediate shoreline. Few adequate boat launching sites are present. Construction of Libby Reservoir (Lake Koocanusa) has adversely affected fishery resources. The dam has blocked upstream and downstream spawning migrations and recruitment of game species to both the river below and the reservoir above the dam." (Montana Department of Fish, Wildlife and Parks, Libby Dam Project, Kootenai River, Montana, April 4, 1974, Joe E. Huston.)

In order to create a recreational fishery of equal or better value in Lake Koocanusa, FWP instituted an extensive program of cutthroat trout planting, which consisted of dumping literally millions of cutthroat trout into the reser—

voir. In 1973 alone, approximately one million fingerlings were planted. Since that time FWP has stabilized its plantings to an annual total of approximately 100,000.

Besides the planted cutthroat trout, the reservoir now contains virtually all of the fish that inhabited the Kootenai River prior to impoundment by Libby Dam. In fact, kokanee salmon that migrated from British Columbia down to the reservoir made up over forty percent of the game fish caught in Lake Koocanusa by September 1981. In addition to cutthroat trout and kokanee salmon, the reservoir now contains rainbow and bull trout, mountain whitefish, burbot (or ling), suckers, peamouth, and squawfish. British Columbia began planting Kamloops rainbow in the reservoir in 1985 and FWP followed suit in 1988. The nongame fish population has dramatically increased in the reservoir, so anglers should not be surprised to hook a few.

Lake Koocanusa is open for fishing year-round, but most active fishing takes place in the spring, summer, and fall. Like most reservoirs used for hydroelectric production, it suffers from daily fluctuations of surface elevation, as water is released for power generation, and therefore it never freezes over in the winter. The daily and seasonal water fluctuations also wreak havoc on shoreline access sites. Under severe draw-down, most boat launching facilities are left high and dry.

Since the reservoir extends forty-eight miles through a narrow valley, almost all fishing activity, be it trolling, still-fishing, or shore-fishing, takes place along the north-south shorelines, and all access sites are located on either the east or west side of the reservoir. On the west side, beginning at Libby Dam and following Forest Service Road 228, recreation and access sites include the Souse Gulch Picnic Areas (Army Corps of Engineers), McGillivray Campground, and Barren Creek Boat Ramp (Forest Service). On the east side, starting at Libby Dam and following State Highway 37, recreation and access sites include the Cripple Horse Marina (private), Peck Gulch Boat Ramp, Camp 32 on Pinkham Creek, and Rexford Boat Ramp, all maintained by the Forest Service. Since there are only four developed recreation or access sites on each side of the reservoir, most anglers stick to fishing the mouths of tributary streams, either shore-fishing, still-fishing from a boat anchored offshore, or trolling parallel to the shore when reservoir levels allow boat access. Although much of the shoreline is steep and inaccessible, adventuresome anglers do hike to undeveloped areas, almost all of which are legally accessible because the reservoir is completely surrounded by public lands of the Kootenai National Forest.

Bob Schumacher, retired FWP regional fisheries manager, describes Lake Koocanusa as a "half and half cutthroat-rainbow trout fishery, although salmon fishing has a strong attraction for many anglers, especially in the spring." Schumacher suggests March through April as the prime time for anglers to try for salmon. Catch rates for kokanee are good and the fish average a plump eleven to twelve inches. Trolling works well and locally popular lures include cowbells, wedding rings, and kokanee killers. Needlefish and maggots also get the job done.

Trout anglers should do well with spincasting gear, fishing either from shore or from a boat anchored just offshore, using light hardware tackle, spinners and spoons such as small Mepps or Thomas Cyclones. Schumacher reports good success on a lazy day by using a wooly worm type fly set about four feet below a bobber on lightweight spincasting gear. Such techniques should yield your limit of fourteen-inch rainbow or cutthroat trout on a good day.

By switching over to heavier gear and using medium to large plugs and red or green Daredevles, you should be able to haul in a few bull trout, especially toward the north end of the reservoir. Schumacher says a lot of anglers try their luck fishing right around the mouth of the Tobacco River near Rexford, some even working their way up into the river for bull trout.

Trolling in Lake Koocanusa can also be a fairly productive way to fish, provided you can get your boat to the water. Once on the lake, trollers do have an advantage over bank anglers, because they can move into areas nearly impossible to reach from the steep side slopes of the shoreline. Depending on water temperature, most anglers troll about eight to twenty-four feet deep, using small to medium size lures. Kamloops, red/green Daredevles, Triple Teasers, and Martin Radiants all get heavy use, although experimenting with any heavy-bodied trout lure may produce some nice fish. Rainbow, cutthroat, and kokanee are all fished by trolling. Schumacher reports that many kokanee anglers "flavor" their lures with some type of bait—a piece of corn, maggots, or a bit of worm—but he adds, "I'm not convinced it's necessary."

Mountain whitefish are making a comeback at Lake Koocanusa, and anglers using light spinning gear with small hooks and maggots should be able to haul in some nice fourteen-inch fish. Local anglers report some success using standard store-bought whitefish flies either on light spinning tackle or on fly rods.

Lake Koocanusa also hosts one of Montana's most interesting (some say ugly) fish: the burbot, or ling. This strange-looking fish has a single chin barbell, or whisker (unlike catfish, which have two), and an elongated, eel-like body with long dorsal and anal fins. Burbot are freshwater codfish that usually grow to twenty or thirty inches long. Many anglers consider them a gourmet delicacy. These fish prefer large rivers and cold, deep lakes and seem to be doing well in the reservoir. The most likely spots to find these strange fish are in the northern third of the reservoir near Rexford. Burbot weighing around seven pounds have been taken from Lake Koocanusa in the past few years.

Schumacher suggests fishing for burbot in twenty to forty feet of water, just off the bottom. Still-fishing from a boat is about the only way to reach these fish. Many anglers prefer to hang near the mouth of the Tobacco River. According to Schumacher, "a gob of nightcrawlers or a piece of fish is all you need for bait."

Lake Koocanusa is so large that it helps to get some local advice if you're planning your first fishing trip to Lincoln County. If you approach the reservoir from the south end, stop in at the Sport Shop in Libby to find out what's happening on the lake. If you are coming from the north, the FWP fish hatchery at Eureka is a good place to stop and ask for advice. Any of the Forest Service ranger stations in the area should have maps of the Kootenai National Forest available. These maps cover Lake Koocanusa and the surrounding area. Canoe Gulch Ranger Station is located just a few miles downstream from Libby Dam on State Highway 37.

For the past few years, Libby area residents have been fighting attempts by the Corps of Engineers to build a re-regulating dam below the big dam. So far such citizen involvement has paid off, and Congress has refused to authorize construction of that facility. But there is another threat to the remaining free-flowing Kootenai River about thirty miles below Libby Dam at Kootenai Falls—the proposed Kootenai Falls Dam. Kootenai Falls is one of northwest America's last great waterfalls, so if you get a chance (it might be your last), drive over on U.S. Highway 2 and take a look at this spectacular natural wonder. There are picnic facilities available, and the fishing is great above the falls.

A seven-pound rainbow from a small central Montana reservoir. (It's a secret place.) Frank Martin photo.

LAKE MARY RONAN

Lake Mary Ronan, located in Lake County eight miles northwest of Dayton at milepost eighty-three on Highway 93, is one of the few lakes in Montana not open to year-round fishing. The fishing season on this 1,500-acre lake is closed from March 15 through the third Saturday in May in order to allow undisturbed spawning for the lake's self-sustaining rainbow trout population.

This lovely lake, located in rolling timbered hills and mountains, has become a popular summertime recreation spot for anglers, boaters, waterskiers, and picnickers. There are a number of private cottages and cabins situated around the shoreline. The cast side of the lake houses the Lambeth State Recreation Area. Lambeth provides public camping, boat access, toilets, and a picnic area.

Lake Mary Ronan is a highly popular fishery June through February for rainbow and cutthroat trout, kokanee salmon, and largemouth bass. With that array of fish from which to choose, the lake is an angler's smorgasbord, although most anglers who visit the area seem to concentrate their efforts on bringing home a creel of salmon. But the lake does have its dedicated trout anglers and hardcore bass fanatics.

The lake has a tendency to get a bit muddy from time to time, but it still provides an easy opportunity for most anglers to catch their limits, according to Bob Schumacher, retired FWP regional fisheries manager. Schumacher suggests trolling fairly deep for salmon, using either Triple Teaser, Swedish Pimple, or Mepps lures, almost anywhere in the open water region of the lake. If bait is your preference, then try using maggots and fish in thirty to forty feet of water. Weigh anchor and jig with Glo Hooks and Swedish Pimples.

Salmon snagging in the fall still attracts a fair number of anglers. The key is finding where the salmon are concentrating. Standard snagging gear is the rule: treble hooks, pencil lead, and twenty-pound test line. (The wind can really pick up during the fall months, so bring some warm clothing for snagging.)

Winter really brings out the crowds at the lake, so pack your long johns, grubs or maggots, corn and marshmallows, and head on out. A popular method of pulling fish through the ice involves using a jig sweetened with bait. Kokanee, rainbow, and cutthroat all succumb to the jig and bait combination. Twenty-inch, four-pound rainbow trout have been taken in February, so be on the watch for one of those big rainbow.

Local anglers describe the lake as a three-story affair in the summer, with kokanee found in deep water, rainbow and cutthroat mid-way down or just off the weedbeds, and bass in the shallower shoreline areas. Fly fishing is best during spring and summer using mayflies, caddis, and damselflies. Ten- to eighteen-inch cutthroat and feisty rainbow up to twenty-two inches provide some great fishing.

The weedbeds in the shoreline areas are prime largemouth bass hangouts and provide a lot of exciting fishing during the summer months. Although a wide variety of bass plugs and poppers is necessary for spincasting gear, some anglers report success fly fishing using frog and mouse imitations.

A good day's catch here should yield your limit of fourteen-inch salmon or trout; bass anglers should be able to bring home a few two- to five-pound bass.

In the fall, winter, and spring, visitors are likely to see deer near the lake and may even get a chance to see a moose wade out into the water. The warble of a loon can often be heard, and ducks and geese stop during the spring and fall migrations.

Local angling conditions and information can be obtained at either the FWP office in Kalispell or at Camp Tuffett in Proctor on the way to the lake.

LINDBERGH LAKE

Located in the northwest corner of Missoula County, Lindbergh Lake is a rather narrow, long, summer resort lake. A county road sixteen miles north of the town of Seeley Lake on Highway 83 provides easy access. Lindbergh Lake, located near the divide between the Swan and Clearwater drainages, is an excellent jumping-off point for nearby high mountain lakes. Crystal, Turquoise, and Glacier lakes are all within an easy day's hike from Lindbergh Lake.

Because of limited spawning areas and low basic productivity due to low temperatures and lack of food sources, this is not an outstanding angling location, but it is still a very scenic and remote spot. FWP annually plants the lake with 30,000 four- to six-inch cutthroat trout and about 100,000 kokanee salmon, but there just isn't enough food to sustain a large fish population, and the lake is too remote for more intensive management.

All that aside, the lake does provide good summer fishing for twelve-inch cutthroat trout, and you may be able to land a decent sized bull trout. In addition, kokanee salmon provide plenty of challenge to any angler. Thomas Cyclones and Mepps spinners do well, along with other artificial lures, when trolled about eight to twenty feet deep. There is virtually no winter fishery here because of the lake's severely low temperatures and remoteness. FWP says that the lake is holding its own as a fishery. The department will continue its present stocking rate and schedule.

Lindbergh Lake is remote enough that your chances of seeing some big game and other species of wildlife is good. Moose, mule deer, white-tailed deer, elk, and black bears frequent the area and usually can be seen early in the morning and late in the evening. There is a Forest Service campground at the north end of the lake, and anglers report waking in the morning and watching a moose gently wade along the shallower edges. And, of course, the late evening lullaby of the loon has put many a weary camper to sleep.

Stop in at the Forest Service Condon Ranger Station, located on Highway 83, for backcountry maps and information on fishing conditions at the lake.

MARTINSDALE RESERVOIR

Martinsdale Reservoir sits on the county line between Meagher and Wheatland counties. It is located just outside the town of Martinsdale off Highway 294, two miles from the Highway 12 junction. The reservoir was created by the building of a Works Progress Administration (WPA) dam in the 1930s for the multiple uses of fishing, waterfowl hunting, and irrigation storage. Unlike many irrigation storage reservoirs, Martinsdale is not hampered by severe draw-down and water fluctuations; consequently, fishing is good almost year-round.

Martinsdale is holding its own as a rainbow and brown trout fishery, though it receives heavy fishing pressure all year. FWP has also begun planting Yellowstone cutthroat trout. Trolling and shore-fishing are both popular here, but most anglers use boats, as Martinsdale is a fairly large body of water—1,000 acres. Trollers report good success between ten and fifteen feet deep using standard spoons and artificial lures, although cowbells and worms yield fish too. Local anglers suggest that you should easily catch your limit of twelve- to sixteen-inch rainbows and brown. If you shore-fish and let your bait sit on the bottom too long, you are liable to hook a sucker or two, but currently such rough fish pose no threat to the overall health of the reservoir.

Winter-ice fishing at the reservoir attracts many visitors from Billings, Roundup, and Bozeman. Standard ice-fishing bait such as corn, salmon eggs, mealworms, and marshmallows should do nicely. Most anglers fish fairly close to the surface, no deeper than ten feet. In general, larger trout are taken from Martinsdale during the winter months than at other times of the year.

Martinsdale offers better fishing for rainbow and browns year-round than do most irrigation reservoirs. FWP plans to continue planting approximately 100,000 rainbow fry per year, so this reservoir should continue to produce exciting trout fishing for the foreseeable future.

There are good public camping facilities around the shore, and boats are easily launched from the rocky shoreline. If you are in a boat, watch the weather, because sudden, furious winds can make it dangerous to be out on the water.

Besides recreational fishing, waterfowl hunting on the reservoir and the nearby canal enjoy a good deal of popularity. Duck hunters can easily bag their limit in the fall by jump-shooting along the canal or by setting out some decoys on the reservoir.

McGREGOR LAKE

Just west of Marion in Flathead County, approximately thirty miles west of Kalispell on Highway 2, lies McGregor Lake. This large (approximately 1,500 acres), picturesque, timbered lake probably fits everybody's dream of a scenic postcard lake. Towering fir and pine trees grow right to the water's edge, and at dusk the cry of the loon lingers hauntingly over the water. Bears, deer, and moose frequent the lake in the early mornings and late evenings. Bald eagles often stop over on their circular peregrinations over northwestern Montana.

The best angling at McGregor Lake occurs in spring, early summer, and through the ice in winter. The lake has a good self-sustaining population of lake trout and is stocked by FWP with rainbow trout. In addition, the lake sustains viable brook trout and yellow perch populations. Most anglers concentrate on the lake trout because of their size, fishing for them at depths of ninety to 130 feet.

A mid-lake bar splits McGregor Lake in half; many anglers successfully fish along both sides of the bar. On a good day you should expect to catch your limit of two- to four-pound lake trout. Some good-sized lake trout, thirty-six inches or longer, have been pulled through the ice in mid-winter. Rainbows in the three- to five-pound range can be caught along the shore.

During the spring and summer, most anglers troll or still-fish from boats using spoons, spinners, and cowbells with worms. When fishing deep for lake trout, many anglers use depth-marked line, which makes it easier to judge how deep you're fishing. Since lake trout are very sensitive to temperature, it is important to find the right temperature regime and depth. If you have a water thermometer, be sure to use it, because in winter and early spring the forty- to fifty-degree temperature regime preferred by lake trout may be fairly close to the surface. By summer, however, that same ideal temperature may be 100 or more feet below the surface.

McGregor Lake also offers backpacking anglers a beautiful trailhead for a backcountry trek. Nearby Lolo and Kootenai national forests provide a number of developed public campgrounds, and Logan State Recreational Area has toilets, drinking water, and camping and picnic areas. If you plan to do any backcountry hiking in the area, pick up either a Lolo or Kootenai national forest map before heading out. And check with local rangers about bear activities. This is grizzly country, even though they are rare. Take all bear country precautions.

MEDICINE LAKE

Medicine Lake, an 8,000-acre reservoir in the northeast corner of the state, once hosted an exceptional northern pike fishery. The original edition of *The Angler's Guide to Montana* reported northerns in the eight- to nine-pound range. But recent years of drought—particularly several winters of low snowpack— have allowed the lake to freeze solid, wiping out any sport fishery. The U.S. Fish and Wildlife Service, which manages Medicine Lake as part of a National Wildlife Refuge, reports that fish won't be restocked until water volume in the lake returns to a suitable level.

NELSON RESERVOIR

Located in Phillips County approximately fifteen miles east of Malta on Highway 2, Nelson Reservoir provides northern border anglers with ample opportunity to ply their trade. In addition, nearby Hewitt Lake and Lake Bowdoin national wildlife refuges provide spectacular waterfowl observation sites. Canada geese are a common sight on Nelson Reservoir as well as at the nearby refuges. Pronghorn antelope and mule deer abound in the surrounding glaciated plains, and upland game birds such as ring-necked pheasant and sharp-tailed grouse are common in nearby grain fields.

The surface area of Nelson Reservoir is approximately 4,500 acres. The reservoir is easily accessible by paved road one mile north of Highway 2. The Bureau of Reclamation maintains a rather nice campground here, and there are plenty of sandy beaches and shallow shorelines for family water sports.

Fishing for northern pike, walleye, and yellow perch is best April through November, with prime time coming early in spring when the ice breaks up. Late in the fall, just before freeze-up, fishing activity picks up again. In the

Ice fishing on Nelson Reservoir—as always, hoping for a big one. Frank Martin photo.

warm open-water months, most fishing is done by trolling off the bottom over the bars. You may use live minnows as bait, and many anglers report good success with live bait. Of course, some anglers prefer common pike lures.

You should be prepared for good-sized northerns in the three- to four-pound range and large perch up to two pounds. In past years, a forty-one-inch, fifteen-pound northern was taken in July, and a thirty-four-inch, seven-pound northern was taken during September. According to FWP biologists, Nelson Reservoir holds northerns up to twenty pounds, so be prepared for a lunker to hit. Local anglers report a good day's catch to be seven to eight game fish.

Winter ice-fishing on this northern border lake can be fast and heavy, but button up, because the winds get pretty strong along the Hi-Line. Perch and walleye far outnumber the number of northerns hauled through the ice. Fleshy bait, corn, and marshmallows are used for ice-fishing. Some anglers prefer spearing for northerns and find that this method works best right after freeze-up.

Before heading out to Nelson Reservoir, it's a good idea to stop at a sporting goods store in Malta to see what local anglers are using (nightcrawlers and spinners frequent the list) and what fish are hitting.

Nelson Reseervoir, one of the most popular fishing holes in Montana. Mark Henckel photo.

The walleye, definitely a big warm-water drawing card in a state full of trout fanciers. Mark Henckel photo.

NILAN RESERVOIR

Located approximately eight miles west of Augusta in Lewis and Clark County, Nilan Reservoir is a highly popular year-round fishing hole for refugees from nearby Great Falls and Helena. This 500-acre prairie reservoir, which is reached by county road, provides not only recreation opportunities but also irrigation storage for neighboring farms. Because of this multiple use, recreationists should be prepared for late summer draw-down and resulting loss of fishing and other recreational opportunities. Because Nilan is a prairie reservoir like its neighbor, Pishkun Reservoir, it also serves as a stop-over site for migrating waterfowl of the Central Flyway.

In addition to the spectacular scenery of the Rocky Mountain Front, the nearby Lewis and Clark National Forest also provides something more immediate for visitors: public campgrounds. Another public campground is located about eight miles north of the reservoir.

Boat launch facilities at Nilan are adequate until mid-summer, when trailer launching becomes a chore. Later on in the summer, when severe draw-down occurs, trailer launching becomes impossible.

Nilan Reservoir is best known as a rainbow trout fishery, though an occasional cutthroat makes it into an angler's creel. Like many man-made reservoirs with severe water-level fluctuations and subsequent warmer water temperatures, Nilan Reservoir also hosts a significant sucker population.

Most anglers prefer trolling for rainbow, but some also bank-fish, especially during lazy summer days. Local anglers suggest trolling about ten to fifteen feet deep using small spoons, spinners, or cowbells and worms. On a good day, you should be able to catch your limit of ten- to twelve-inch rainbow, with some anglers hauling in an occasional five-plus-pounder.

As with any prairie reservoir, watch the weather to the west for signs of a summer storm moving in. This is not an extremely large body of water, so there is no major hazard, but the quickness of their approach makes prairie storms unsettling and uncomfortable.

Winter ice-fishing draws enthusiastic crowds here. Normal ice-fishing bait—corn, marshmallows, trout eggs, and mealworms—are all popular at Nilan. Experimentation is the only way to select proper bait. Be sure to bring a good windbreaker, because the wind sweeps down from the Rocky Mountain Front and really rages once it hits the flatland.

FWP reports that Nilan Reservoir is doing well under heavy fishing pressure and future management depends on the severity of water level fluctuations due to irrigation demand.

Paul Mihalovich, a retired game warden from Augusta, is a knowledgeable local angler; look him up if you'd like to ask about fishing conditions at Nilan.

PISHKUN RESERVOIR

Situated approximately ten miles east of the Rocky Mountain Front in open prairie, Pishkun Reservoir is unique among prairie lakes because of its crystal clear water. This record salmon-producing reservoir also provides ample stopover space for migratory waterfowl of the Central Flyway. Pishkun is located in Teton County approximately twenty miles southwest of Choteau, and several other reservoirs—Nilan, Willow Creek, and Gibson—all lie within thirty miles.

A public campground with boat launch facilities is located at the reservoir. Boat users should be aware that a dangerous whirlpool lurks at the outlet. It should be avoided at all cost.

Pishkun ranges in depth from thirty feet on its western end to a maximum of eighty-one feet near the eastern end, and it's a good prairie fishery because of its high water quality. Northern pike, rainbow trout, and yellow perch all provide the most sophisticated angler with plenty of excitement. At one time, Pishkun held a thriving kokanee fishery—in fact, Montana's record kokanee salmon weighing five pounds, fifteen ounces, was taken out of Pishkun in 1976. But the salmon have declined in recent years and kokanee stocking may be discontinued.

Northern pike are active both summer and winter at Pishkun. In warm water, still-fishing from a boat around the brushy areas using spoons, large flies, and grocery store smelt is a good bet. In winter, a tip-up baited with grocery store smelt is very effective.

Rainbow trout are most active in spring and summer, with limited activity in winter. In the spring, try fishing around the reservoir inlet and work the area well, using a number of different baits and lures. Local anglers suggest using trout eggs in spring. During the summer, most people troll for trout at depths between ten and fifteen feet using spoons or cowbells and worms.

A good day's catch at Pishkun should yield three northerns in the three-pound range with an occasional five- to ten-pounder thrown in, or a couple of four-pound rainbow trout. Recent lunkers caught at Pishkun included a six-pound, twenty-two-inch rainbow caught in August 1982 and a thirty-two-inch, eight-pound northern hauled through the ice in December 1982.

As with any reservoir that has fluctuating water levels, recreational fishing at Pishkun is always subject to change depending on the irrigation demand in any one year. Spring and fall usually provide a spectacular show of many different kinds of geese and ducks. Canada, Ross', and snow geese have all been known to sojourn here, along with hundreds of ducks. Mule deer and upland game birds inhabit the surrounding coulees and plains, so keep your eyes open as you drive in and out of the reservoir.

RAINBOW LAKE

Rainbow Lake, or Dog Lake, as it is known locally, is located on the western boundary of the Flathead Indian Reservation along Highway 28, equidistant between the towns of Plains and Hot Springs in Sanders County. It is situated on a ridge that divides the Clark Fork and Flathead river drainages, surrounded by pine and fir forests.

Facilities at the lake include toilets, campgrounds, picnic areas, and boat access. These facilities are maintained by both the Hot Springs Lions club and the Confederated Salish and Kootenai Tribes.

Many species of big game can be seen around the lake and the surrounding forest. Moose, mule deer, bears, and even elk frequent the area. In addition, ducks and geese migrate through in the spring and fall, and whistling swans often stop off here. Beaver, muskrat, and other furbearers also abound. Nearby springs have attracted wild turkeys and many species of nongame wildlife.

Anglers and hunters should note that a tribal recreation permit is required for all fishing. Hunting of big game and other native wildlife is strictly prohibited. Tribal recreation permits are readily available in Plains or Hot Springs and at tribal headquarters in Pablo. The Flathead Indians welcome nontribal people to their reservation to camp, fish, and picnic but have reserved big game for the preservation of their traditional ways.

Rainbow Lake was once a 100 percent rainbow trout fishery, with a handful of sunfish in the lake, but trout fishing dropped off after northern pike were illegally introduced in the mid-1980s. The northerns reach ten to eighteen pounds, but heavy fishing pressure is levelling off their size and numbers.

Still-fishing from boats is the preferred method for trout, although both trolling and shore-fishing will yield some nice fish. Rainbow Lake still produces good numbers of five-to ten-pound rainbow.

In winter, many anglers enjoy Rainbow's excellent ice-fishing. Corn, worms, maggots, and marshmallows all seem to work fine, although corn is definitely preferred. You should be able to catch your limit and have a great time doing it. Since it can get rather chilly, bring a bucket with charcoal or something comparable to keep your hands warm.

If you are able to get to Rainbow Lake in the spring, be sure to scout the surrounding forest for edible mushrooms. Local anglers tell tales of secret morel stashes hidden along the nearby bogs. Be sure to consult a good identification book before eating any wild plants to prevent eating potentially fatal poisonous plants.

SEELEY LAKE

Thirteen-hundred-acre Seeley Lake is another of western Montana's prized recreation spots. Located just fifty-five miles northeast of Missoula on Highway 83, near the confluence of the Clearwater and Blackfoot rivers, this heavily used summer resort is surrounded with cabins, beaches, and picnic and camping areas.

The lake sits in a beautiful setting of larch, fir, and pine forests with vegetation reaching right down to the water's edge. It is a rather long, narrow lake with little shoal area and a fairly rapid drop-off. The bottom plunges to 110 feet within a few feet of the shore. As the lake sits at approximately a 4,000-foot elevation, the nights cool down quite rapidly in the summer, and the water in the lake stays cool all summer.

Cool temperatures don't deter recreational activities, however, and it's likely you'll see plenty of waterskiers on the lake, especially on the weekends. There are occasional conflicts between young ski enthusiasts and anglers, so be prepared to assert your right to fish. Usually a word of caution or warning will suffice, and most skiers will leave you undisturbed.

Fishing at Seeley Lake is usually good. The lake contains kokanee salmon; largemouth bass; cutthroat, rainbow, and bull trout; and a few perch. Because of its sizeable bass population, Seeley Lake is one of Montana's most popular bass fishing spots. Most anglers use normal bass gear—rubber worms and surface plugs—but some very ardent bass anglers have tried their luck at fly fishing and have even landed a few. The best fishing for bass is at the lake outlet and shoal areas, and from the numerous docks around the shoreline. Spring and mid-summer are the best time to fish for bass, with most anglers concentrating their effort on dusk or nighttime.

Salmon-snagging off the docks in the fall is a popular way of hauling in a bunch of nice, mature fish. Snaggers use large treble hooks with two to three inches of pencil lead wrapped around the top and a twenty-pound test line. The technique is pretty simple; success depends entirely on finding a school of fish. You just toss the hook twenty feet or so out and retrieve it by a series of quick, hard jerks, hopefully snagging a salmon in the process.

In the summer, anglers troll deep for kokanee salmon, using cowbells, spinners, and spoons. If you want to try for trout, don't troll as deep, only about ten to fifteen feet, and use similar spoons or spinners. There is some still-fishing for trout using worms, but keep an eye out for waterskiers.

A good day's catch at Seeley Lake should yield around five to ten nine- or ten-inch salmon or two or three eight- to ten-inch trout with an occasional four-pound rainbow turning up.

Seeley Lake also provides ample opportunity for young anglers to test their luck. Kids will get a thrill out of fishing for perch from any of the many shoreline docks. Salmon eggs or other fleshy bait works well. Some people claim that there is no finer eating than fillet of perch.

Winter ice-fishing, primarily for perch and rainbow, is fair to good at Seeley Lake. Although you might hook some cutthroat and kokanee, they usually are too small in the winter to be of much use. This is another mountain lake, and winter temperatures dip pretty low, so bring your longjohns if you plan to be out on the ice.

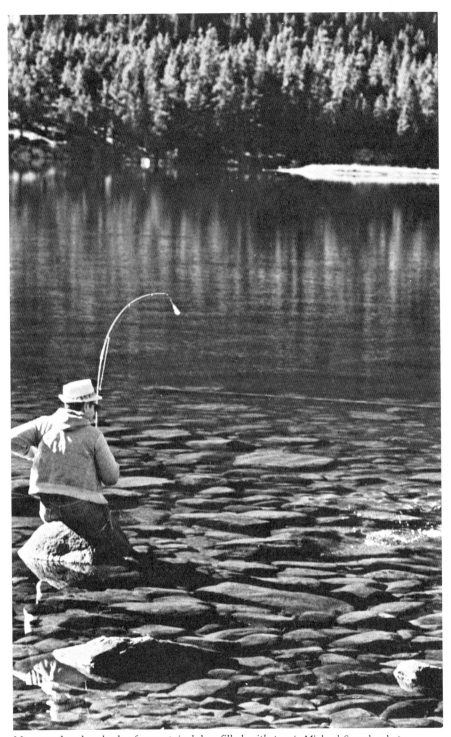

Montana has hundreds of mountain lakes filled with trout. Michael Sample photo.

FWP and the Forest Service are cooperating to install some sunken shelter for bass, which should improve bass fishing. Also, FWP is planning to continue planting cutthroat trout, so there should be some improvement in the cutthroat fishery as well.

If you want some local advice on fishing, stop in at Dan's Sporting Goods in Seeley Lake and talk to Dan Cainin. If he can't answer your questions, he'll know somebody who can.

SOUTH SANDSTONE RESERVOIR

South Sandstone Reservoir is located seven miles south of Plevna in Fallon County. The town of Baker is only twelve miles to the west via Highway 12. The dam and reservoir, built in 1975, are fairly recent additions to the Montana State Recreation System. Facilities at the site include boat access, toilets, drinking water, camping and picnic areas, and shelters.

Since 1975 FWP has planted northern pike, walleye, and perch in the reservoir, and they appear to be doing well. Local anglers report catching some black bullheads in addition to the species that were planted. Highest fishing success is reported in the spring and fall. Trolling and bank-fishing are both popular at this eastern Montana water hole. If you have a boat and want to troll, don't go too deep, because all you'll get is the bottom. Live bait, worms, and minnows are used extensively as well as standard pike lures, spoons, Rapalas, and jigs.

FWP also planted largemouth and smallmouth bass, and crappie, here, and the largemouth population has fared well, producing good numbers of one- to two-pound bass. The smallmouth bass and crappie are less abundant.

A good day's catch in the spring and fall should yield three or four two- to five-pound northerns and two or three two- to four-pound walleye. Winter ice-fishing is reported to be mediocre at the present time, but that could change as the reservoir matures.

South Sandstone Reservoir is welcome relief from the dry surrounding countryside. But just because the area is dry does not mean there's no wildlife. Visitors should expect to see mule deer and pronghorn antelope as well as upland game birds on the surrounding native grasslands. Waterfowl use the reservoir in the spring and fall as a stop-over during their annual migrations. Nearby in the Long Pines area, wild turkey hunting is an annual event. Nongame wildlife such as turtles (including snapping turtles) inhabit the reservoir.

This reservoir is one of Montana's most recent recreational additions and shouldn't be missed if you're traveling across eastern Montana. It is a splendid example of a prairie ecosystem, and the fishing is good.

SPAR LAKE

Lincoln County is blessed with many excellent trout streams and lakes, but none is prettier than Spar Lake. Situated in the Cabinet Mountains south of Troy, west of Montana Highway 56 on the Lake Creek road, Spar Lake ranks as one of western Montana's most picturesque mountain lakes.

Spar Lake is primarily a summer trolling fishery for cutthroat, lake, and brook trout and kokanee salmon. Anglers should be able to catch some three- to ten-pound lake trout here. Thirteen- to fifteen-inch brookies have been pulled out of the lake, also. FWP has been stocking the lake heavily with kokanee salmon for the past few years, and Spar now produces some of the largest salmon in the area, ranging from sixteen to eighteen inches.

As Spar is a 400-acre, cold, clear, deep mountain lake, fish productivity is not exceptional. However, the surrounding terrain and the nearby Cabinet Wilderness Area provide ample incentive for anyone seeking spectacular scenery and peace and quiet.

The Kootenai National Forest maintains camping facilities at the west end of the lake, and there are marked trailheads for backcountry enthusiasts. The ranger station in Troy can provide you with maps of the lake area and the designated wilderness area. The area is full of wildlife, including mule deer, elk, moose, and black bears, along with a few grizzly bears. Since this is bear country, please take precautions in storing and disposing of foodstuffs and fish remains.

SWAN LAKE

Swan Lake, located in Lake County right on Highway 83 near the town of Swan Lake, is one of northwestern Montana's crown jewels. The lake provides a quality fishing experience worthy of acclaim, even though it may not make the list of Montana's blue-ribbon hot-spots.

Swan Lake is one of the midway stops on the annual 250-mile Tour of the Swan River Valley (TOSRV) bicycle trip. This trek, which attracts riders from all over the world, starts in Missoula and follows a loop trail through the Swan River Valley and back down the Mission Mountain Valley to Missoula. There really isn't time during the tour to throw a line into Swan Lake, but many riders return later in the spring and summer to camp and fish at this scenic lake.

The Swan Mountains to the northeast and Mission Mountains to the southwest surround this picturesque lake. This is a fairly large lake, about ten miles long and one mile wide, with a surface area of about 2,680 acres.

There is a Forest Service campground at the lake's north end and a water-fowl refuge on the south end. Scattered around the lake shore are a number of private summer homes and several private resorts.

Currently, FWP is trying to establish some cutthroat trout spawning runs in the lake's tributaries, and so far they have been moderately successful. The lake is home to rainbow and cutthroat trout, kokanee salmon, yellow perch, northern pike, sunfish, and bull trout. The pike have largely wiped out a once resident bass population. Besides these game fish, the lake supports an abundant northern squawfish and peamouth population.

Anglers do well trolling for salmon and trout in the summer using Mepps spinners or Thomas Cyclone spoons. There is some nightcrawler use in conjunction with a bottom bouncer. Shoreline and tributary inlet areas are good for rainbow and cutthroat during spring and fall. Summertime plugging for northern pike, using standard plugs and flatfish or Rapala lures, should yield a limit of four- to eighteen-pound northerns.

Fly anglers should not neglect this beautiful lake. Beginners should stick to either the north or south end at the river's inlet and outlet, using Wooly Worms or nymphs. In late summer, Joe's Hopper works well on the river stretches. There is some dry fly fishing on the lake itself, but it is not easy, and matching the hatch is a must. Try a very small caddis fly imitation in one of the lighter shades.

Winter ice-fishing often yields bull, cutthroat, and rainbow trout, kokanee, plus a smattering of perch. Fleshy bait is more often used, but corn and marshmallows should also be tried. January ice-fishing has produced seven- to ten-pound bull trout. This is a precious native fish, so the limit is one bull trout per day.

Local anglers tend to hang out at the Elm Court and Swan Village Market in Swan Lake, so stop in and get the lowdown on how to fish this lake.

In the spring and fall Swan Lake attracts abundant waterfowl, including a lot of Canada geese. During the evenings, loons break the mountain quiet with their eerie call. Bald eagles and osprey make the rounds of this fishing hole just as much as human anglers. Mule deer, elk, bears, and many species of nongame wildlife abound in the surrounding forests. In fact, wintertime driving near the lake on Highway 83 can be hazardous because of the many deer crossings.

For anglers who also like to backpack, Swan Lake is a perfect jumping off point for either the Bob Marshall Wilderness to the northeast or the Mission Mountain Wilderness to the southwest. Bears—both black and grizzly—live in both wilderness areas, so take necessary precautions by hanging your food away from your tent and by thoroughly cleaning your utensils and your campsite. Check in with the Forest Service ranger stations at Seeley Lake and Bigfork for fishing and backcountry hiking information.

TONGUE RIVER RESERVOIR

In the heart of the northern plains coal country is one of southeast Montana's finest recreational jewels, the Tongue River Reservoir, a state record-winning fishery. Because this reservoir is located a few miles north of the town of Decker in Big Horn County and five miles north of the Wyoming state line, it is heavily used by citizens of both states.

Tongue River Reservoir, a prairie fishery widely used by boaters, swimmers, picnickers, and anglers, is a long narrow channel, approximately five miles by one-eighth mile. Although this is a prairie reservoir, there are a few trees around the shoreline. The reservoir was created on the Tongue River when the State of Montana built an irrigation storage dam. In recent years, high water has done serious damage to the dam. The Montana Department of

Natural Resources and Conservation (DNRC) reports that the dam is in such poor condition that it could collapse during a major flood. As of this writing the DNRC, Bureau of Reclamation, Bureau of Indian Affairs, and the Northern Cheyenne Tribe are conducting a feasibility study to determine what should be done to repair or replace the project. Estimates for repair or replacement of the existing dam range from fifty million to 120 million dollars.

Because of its location as a part of the Tongue River system, the reservoir supports a large diversity of fish species. Walleye, sauger, crappie (black and white), perch, and smallmouth bass are all found here. The walleye have become abundant thanks to an annual planting program begun in 1986. Channel catfish are also quite common. Although the northern pike population has declined, anglers can always hope for the rare lunker. FWP calls it the best warm-water fishery south of Fork Peck.

Walleye seem to respond most in early summer, around June. Die-hard northern pike anglers can test their patience in early spring and late fall. Both species are best fished by trolling with standard pike lures, flatfish, Rapalas, or big spoons. (When you troll, don't go too deep—ten feet at most—as much of the reservoir is twenty feet deep or less.) Live bait, especially minnows, works well for still-fishing during the warm weather months. Winter ice-fishing for walleye is generally good; local anglers prefer live minnows for bait.

Tongue River Reservoir provides excellent crappie fishing for bait anglers from mid-May through mid-June and into early August. Feathered and plastic lead-head jigs are popular patterns. Mealworms, angleworms, corn, and small spinners also work well against these feisty fish.

Smallmouth bass attract as many anglers as almost all the other species combined. Along with the anglers come the gourmets, most of whom claim there is no finer eating in the world than fillet of smallmouth bass. Sharpen your knives and your patience and head for the Tongue River. Fishing is good from late June throughout the summer. Most anglers fish by casting out and then bouncing the lure or bait along the bottom. Bottom bouncers work well, but some people prefer to do it naturally.

A good day's catch on the Tongue River Reservoir should yield four to five walleye around three pounds, but an occasional lunker in the nine- to twelve-pound range does turn up. The Montana state record northern pike was taken from the reservoir in 1972—it weighed 37.5 pounds—but few of these big fish remain. If you spend any time fishing the bottom, you probably will turn up some channel catfish around eighteen to twenty-two inches long. If you concentrate on the smaller fish, you'll probably get a bonanza of thirty to forty ten-ounce crappie. Smallmouth bass are plentiful; you should be able to bring home about ten fish if you are conscientious.

The nearby Tongue River Breaks offer some spectacular prairie scenery and provide habitat for many species of wildlife. Mule and white-tailed deer, pronghorn antelope, and many species of migrating waterfowl and shorebirds frequent the area. Human anglers are not the only ones to flock here: white pelicans are a common sight on the river.

If you look closely at the soil in the Breaks you should be able to spot a dark, black layer or seam running through the soil. It's coal, and it's both a bane and a boon to the region. Nearby strip-mining of coal poses a constant threat to wildlife, fish, groundwater, and the Tongue River itself. In addition, there is renewed interest in coal slurry pipelines to ship the black gold out of the region. Opponents to slurry pipelines argue that they would deplete

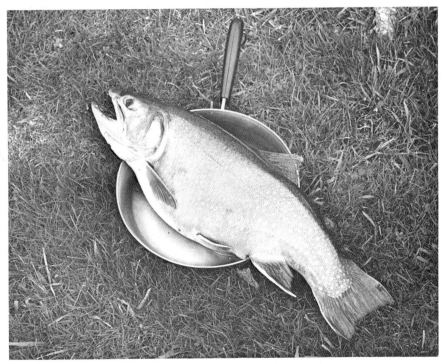

One of the famous Montana pan-sized trout. Mark Henckel photo.

the region's precious supply of clean water and wreak havoc on the state's major industry, agriculture. Needless to say, the export of water from the Tongue River would have a devastating impact on the fisheries both in the reservoir and in the mainstream of the river.

The State of Montana has not released any of the bonds posted by coal companies for reclamation of strip-mined coal fields, because standards have not been met. However, there are some hopeful signs. Cooperation between the Decker Coal Company and FWP has increased, and Decker now maintains adequate water levels in a northern pike rearing marsh for young fish. The marsh is stocked with 500,000 to 800,000 northern pike fry each year. The fry are allowed to grow unmolested, and the fingerlings are then placed in the Tongue River Reservoir for future recreational fishing.

Alpine Lake Fisheries

Even more so than the blue-ribbon rivers and broad valley lakes, Montana's alpine lakes offer an angling experience unique to the Big Sky. Regardless of which high-country fishing hole you choose for a particular trip, spectacular scenery is guaranteed. Most of Montana's mountains also provide good opportunities for solitude, wildlife watching, and a wide palette of colorful fish—rainbow, browns, goldens, lake trout, cutthroat, brookies, and grayling.

For all that, fishing mountain lakes can be unpredictable, uncomfortable, and even hazardous. Winter freeze-outs may wipe out a lake's fishery until new recruits move in or are planted. Stocking cycles also change, an important factor in determining the number and size of fish in lakes that cannot support a permanent, self-sustaining fishery. And even lakes with thriving fisheries run hot and cold—one day the trout hit on every cast, and the next day brings nary a nibble.

Mountain weather can be even more fickle than fish, changing from sun to rain to sleet or snow and back to sun within an afternoon. Snow can fall any day of the year at higher elevations. Always be prepared for wet weather and colder temperatures—ideal conditions for inducing hypothermia (low body temperature). Loss of body heat is as potentially lethal in July as it is in January. Remember that many alpine areas are remote and little-traveled; help may be days away.

The best safeguards for mountain travel are planning, common sense, and experience. If you're new to backcountry expeditions, go with a group of experienced friends or hire an outfitter. You'll have more time to enjoy the fishing and plenty of chances to gain valuable skills and knowledge.

Many of the lakes listed in this section are in designated wilderness areas and are accessible only on foot or horseback. Always check with the local Forest Service or Montana Fish, Wildlife and Parks office before hitting the trail. Ask about trail conditions, stocking schedules, and special regulations governing fishing, camping, or livestock use.

District and wilderness area maps are available at Forest Service offices. Maps in the wilderness series are particularly useful, showing elevational contours, forest coverage, property ownership, access roads, trails, and detailed physical features.

To protect fragile shoreline soils and vegetation, pitch your tent at least 200 feet from the water's edge and picket livestock on higher, well-drained ground. Practice no-impact camping—use a campstove instead of an open fire, bury human waste far from any water source, and pack out all garbage. A clean camp is particularly important in bear country.

Most important of all, fish gently. Growth rates are slow in these high-country lakes, and trout work harder to survive here than in more hospitable waters. Some tarns hold the last remaining pure strains of native grayling and westslope cutthroat. You can help preserve this precious resource by practicing catch-and-release, using barbless hooks, and working your catch quickly so as not to exhaust the fish. For eating, keep only as many fish as you need for the next meal, and take only small fish. Two nine-inchers are as filling as one lunker, and probably tastier.

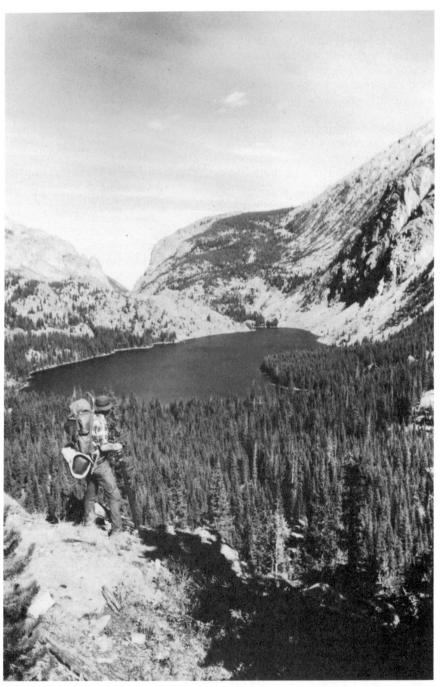

The Absaroka-Beartooth Wilderness contains hundreds of backcountry lakes, including Rainbow Lake in the East Rosebud drainage, shown here. Chris Cauble photo.

A number of Montana's mountain ranges and lakes are missing from the following list. Many of these are already heavily visited and could not bear increased use. A handful are still well-kept secrets, pristine and wild. Let's keep them that way.

ABSAROKA-BEARTOOTH WILDERNESS

Montana's highest mountains rise in a vast complex of peaks, plateaus, and lake-studded stream drainages along the northeast border of Yellowstone National Park. This windy, rugged landscape contains more than 1,000 lakes, 435 of them harboring fish. A trip in the Beartooths offers outstanding scenery and solitude, a genuine wilderness experience, and excellent alpine fishing. A select handful of lakes are described here, and anglers wanting more comprehensive information on the Beartooths should pick up a copy of *The Beartooth Fishing Guide* by Pat Marcuson. It describes more than 1,000 lakes and streams in the Beartooth Plateau, detailing the location and size of each lake, access, stocking frequency, and successful fishing strategies.

Beginning on the western end of this area, the Absaroka Mountains dominate the skyline above the upper Yellowstone River and Paradise Valley. Access to lakes in the Absarokas is more limited than in other regions of the Beartooths, primarily because private lands run much of the way between Highway 540 and the national forest land. Use one of four trailheads on the Yellowstone side of the range—up Mill, Emigrant, Sixmile, or Bear creeks—or the Davis Creek trail from the West Boulder River side.

Pine Creek Lake offers ready access to good cutthroat fishing; even "skunked" anglers come home happy after a day of watching fifteen-inch cutts hide behind watery reflections of the surrounding peaks. The trail to Pine Creek Lake is steep but less than four miles long. Cutthroat also swim in many of the lakes feeding into Mill Creek, all at least a day's backpack from the trailhead. Near the head of Bear Creek, Knox Lake is noted for pan-sized brook trout and Fish Lake offers cutthroat. Both make for a good overnight trip, about eight miles one-way from the trailhead in Jardine.

Moving eastward, some thirty-seven lakes in the Boulder River drainage harbor trout, with most of the fishable lakes concentrated on the Lake Plateau and at the heads of Fourmile and Speculator creeks. The Boulder Road provides good access, though it can test the stoutest shocks on any car.

The Lake Plateau offers cutthroat and rainbow; the set of six Rainbow Lakes is a popular destination for hikers and horsepackers. Also drop a line in Horseshoe, Fish, Mirror, and Blue lakes. At the head of Fourmile and Speculator creeks—or just over the ridge—try for rainbow in Silver Lake and cutthroat in Speculator, West Boulder, and Kaufman lakes. Trail distances and hiking times to these lakes vary depending on which approach you use, but each basin warrants at least an overnight stay. Remember too that your pace may be slowed by the steep gradient and thin air common to these high-elevation trails.

Bridge Lake, at the base of Crow Mountain, boasts some of the biggest cutthroats in the Beartooths; it's well worth the eight-mile uphill climb.

Most of the fishable lakes in the upper Stillwater drainage are clustered around Flood Creek and the Middle and North forks of Wounded Man Creek. Goose Lake and other lakes at the head of the Stillwater are more easily reached from the Cooke City area. Anglers will find every variety of trout except browns, and no grayling dwell here.

The West Rosebud is not known for its fisheries, although Mystic Lake garners some attention from local anglers. But the East Rosebud headwaters include some thirty-five lakes with trout. A tour of these lakes would produce a wide variety of trout—brookies, rainbow, cutthroat, and golden. East Rosebud lake also hides some big brown trout. Six miles upstream, Rainbow Lake holds golden-rainbow hybrids, and Lake At Falls produced a record-breaking 20.5-inch golden in 1981. At the head of East Rosebud Creek, nearly fourteen miles from the trailhead, Fossil Lake regularly wows anglers with big cutts, and anglers shouldn't neglect the many off-trail lakes along the upper Rosebud's tributaries.

Forty-three fishable lakes are found in the Rock Creek drainage. Twenty-three of these hold brook trout, and cutthroat swim in thirteen others. The remainder house a mixture of brookies and cutts or rainbow. Good access to the main lake basins is provided by the West Fork Rock Creek Road, Lake Fork trail, and the old Hell Roaring Creek Road. Hot spots include Black Canyon Lake about five miles up the Lake Fork trail, Sliderock Lake and the Hell Roaring Chain within half a day's hike from the Hell Roaring Creek Road, and Moon Lake, a worthwhile side trip 2.5 miles north of Glacier Lake at the end of the Rock Creek Road far below Beartooth Pass.

The Forest Service has special regulations on party size and livestock use within the Absaroka-Beartooth Wilderness—check at the ranger districts in Gardiner, Livingston, Big Timber, and Red Lodge for more information.

ANACONDA-PINTLER WILDERNESS

With Georgetown Lake to the north and the famed Big Hole River to the south, the Pintler Mountains serve as a spectacular backdrop to many a successful fishing trip. The Anaconda-Pintler Wilderness, locally known as the "A-P," follows the Continental Divide here, helping to protect the headwaters of three of western Montana's premier trout streams: Rock Creek, and the Bitterroot and Big Hole rivers. The wilderness area also boasts a number of respectable fishing holes in its own right.

The highest fishing pressure in the A-P is found at the northside lakes ringing the base of Warren Peak. Carpp and Lower Carpp lakes hold cutthroat and rainbow trout, and Upper Carpp Lake hosts a fine population of rainbow. Tamarack and Edith lakes have good fishing for cutts. To the southwest, Johnson Lake offers up pan-sized rainbow and a good base camp for hiking to a handful of smaller lakes including Martin, Rainbow (aptly named), and Phyllis. Trailheads to these lakes are found at the ends of the Moose Lake Road (Forest Service Road 5106) and Meadow Creek Road (Forest Service 5141), both of which fork south from Montana 38 just west of Georgetown Lake. Hiking distances range from three to twelve miles—many backpacking anglers like to set up base camp at Edith Lake and then day hike to the other lake basins.

At the headwaters of the East Fork of the Bitterroot lie Ripple, Kelly, and Hidden lakes. No lunkers here, but no crowds either. Go prepared for an eleven-mile march from the East Fork ranger station east of Sula—a tedious walk, more enjoyable from the back of a horse.

South of the Divide and buried in dense lodgepole are Mystic, Crystal, and Lion lakes. All three hold feisty eight- to ten-inch rainbow trout, though Crystal is shallow and usually unrewarding. From the gate on the Howell Creek Road, follow trail #369 six miles to Mystic Lake. Lion Lake is reached by walking 1.5 miles past the gate on the road, then climbing five miles along the East Fork of Thompson Creek on trail #7.

Mussigbrod Lake is a 200-acre reservoir northwest of Wisdom just outside the wilderness boundary. You can drive to the campground at the lake but the access road requires high clearance and may be impassable when wet. Brookies and grayling here provide good fishing.

The road to Pintler Lake and campground is wide and well-graveled, reflecting the heavier use this lake receives. Look for brook, cutthroat, and rainbow trout. As with other lakes on the Big Hole side of the Divide, mosquitos here are legion and voracious through July.

Three miles north of Highway 43 on Highway 274 (the road to Anaconda), Forest Service Road 934 heads northwest to Lower Seymour Lake and campground just south of the wilderness boundary. Brook trout are the catch of the day here, while cutthroat and rainbow swim in Upper Seymour Lake, about six miles by trail from the end of the road.

BEAVERHEAD RANGE
(West Big Hole)

The mountains of the West Big Hole, known locally as the Beaverheads, trap moisture from passing fronts, supplying water to a spectacular constellation of alpine and subalpine lakes above the Big Hole Valley. Although the trout here rarely measure more than eleven inches (even smaller in the higher lakes), fishing action can be fast and fun, particularly during early summer.

Driving south from Wisdom on Highway 278, turn west on Forest Service Road 945 to reach Twin Lakes and the Twin Lakes campground. Boat fishing for brookies, rainbow, grayling, and lake trout is popular here. Continue south on Road 945 to Forest Service Road 625 and the trailhead to Slag-a-melt Lakes for brookies and cutthroat, Lena Lakes for cutts and rainbow, and Ajax Lake for rainbow. Expect a five- to seven-mile hike to any of these higher lakes, depending on road conditions and your choice of trails.

From Jackson on Highway 278, follow Forest Service Road 182 eleven miles to the Miner Lake campground and Lower Miner Lakes. Anglers choose from a smorgasbord of cutts, rainbow, brookies, grayling, and mountain whitefish. If the fishing is lukewarm here, hike up to the forks of Miner Creek and choose either Upper Miner Lakes (brook and cutthroat trout), Ridge Lake (cutthroat), or Rock Island Lakes (cutts and rainbow). All three can be done as day hikes; strong hikers could fish the lakes above both forks in one long day.

An exposed lake in the Bob Marshall Wilderness. Darrin Schreder photo.

Also from Highway 278 at Jackson, Forest Service Road 181 wends south to Van Houten Lake and twin campgrounds near the head of the Big Hole River. Van Houten produces some nice brookies and rainbow. Berry and Timberline lakes, up trail #468 to the northwest of Van Houten, provide good cutthroat fishing in a spectacular set of alpine meadows. Just south from Timberline, Skytop Lake holds golden trout, and Pioneer Lake supports a good population of cutthroat. Plan at least an overnight to comfortably hike the round-trip distance. Continue south on Road 181 to Reservoir Lake and campground, actually in the Bloody Dick and Horse Prairie creeks watershed. Anglers here vie for brook and cutthroat trout.

Other high-alpine lakes in the Beaverheads offer decent trout fishing, but access may be limited. Ask landowners for permission before crossing private land. Also check at the Forest Service district office in Wisdom for up-to-date trail information.

BOB MARSHALL WILDERNESS COMPLEX

The Great Bear, Bob Marshall, and Scapegoat wilderness areas together comprise one of the largest remaining expanses of roadless land in the contiguous United States. From the southern boundary of Glacier National Park to Highway 200, the Bob Marshall complex runs along both sides of the Continental Divide, unbroken by roads and crossed only by horse and foot trails. Most of the fishing concentrates around the lakes and streams of the Sun River drainage and the Middle and South Forks of the Flathead River basins.

The South Fork offers the best variety of fishable lakes. Sunburst and Olor lakes contain cutthroat trout, with Sunburst offering the better fishing of the two. These lakes require a minimum of a three-day trip, and can be reached from trailheads at the end of the South Fork Road above Spotted Bear Ranger Station or at the end of the Soup Creek Road east of Highway 83.

A number of fishable lakes are tucked within the wilderness boundary east of the Holland Lake basin off of Highway 83. All require at least an overnight trip, although strong hikers could do the upper Necklace Lakes as a long day hike. The three Necklace Lakes hold rainbow up to a foot long. To the north, Woodward Lake contains rainbow and cutts, but is not served by an official trail.

Lena Lake, some fourteen miles from the Holland Lake trailhead, lies at the northern foot of Shaw Mountain. Lena holds cutthroat and some rainbow-cutt hybrids. To the southwest, Lick, Koessler, and Doctor lakes each nestle at the head of their respective drainages. Lick Lake, home to a naturally reproducing population of stout Yellowstone cutts, is best reached cross-country from trail 35 over Gordon Pass. Trail 291 leads to Doctor Lake from the main trail north of the Shaw Creek backcountry ranger cabin. An angler's trail branches north from Doctor Lake to Koessler; both lakes hold twelve-inch westslope cutthroats.

The trail to George Lake forks from trail 35 at the Shaw Creek cabin for a total distance of about sixteen miles from Holland Lake Lodge. Expect good fishing here for native and planted cutts.

Pyramid Lake is one of the more accessible lakes in the southern reach of the Bob Marshall and offers fifteen-inch cutthroat trout and rugged scenery. Take Forest Service Road 477 north from Seeley Lake and hike about five miles over Pyramid Pass on trail 416.

The largest lake in the Bob is Big Salmon Lake, west of the upper reaches of the South Fork and on a line with the town of Condon to the west on Highway 83. Big Salmon harbors native westslope cutts and rainbows ranging from ten to sixteen inches. Serious anglers should pack in a float tube and plan a week-long stay. The closest trailheads are nearly twenty miles distant, either at Holland Lake or the end of the road above the Spotted Bear ranger station.

In the watershed of the Middle Fork of the Flathead River, several lakes in the Great Bear Wilderness are within a few hours walk of Highway 2. Stanton Lake is only two miles by trail and holds cutts, rainbow, and mountain whitefish. Look for the pull out and trailhead about 6.5 miles east of Nyack on Highway 2.

Dickey and Almeda lakes are half-day hikes from Forest Service Road 1639, which leaves Highway 2 about one mile northwest of Essex. Both lakes contain westslope cutts. Marion Lake harbors twelve-inch cutthroats and is an easy three-mile walk from the Izaak Walton Inn at Essex.

To better experience the wilderness qualities of the Great Bear, take a long weekend trip into the Tranquil Lakes basin and hook into a twenty-inch native cutthroat. Look for the trailhead about .5 mile east of where the Middle Fork of the Flathead drops south and leaves the side of Highway 2. Trail 155 follows the river's east bank to a junction with trail 489 to the flanks of Mount Furlong. Continue east to the two Tranquil Lakes and angler's heaven.

Three lakes in the heart of the Great Bear Wilderness offer good fishing for westslope cutthroats in one of the wildest and most remote settings imaginable. Castle Lake is reached by packbridge across the Middle Fork about one mile west of the Granite patrol cabin. Scott Lake and its larger neighbor, Flotilla Lake, both boast naturally reproducing cutts and plenty of solitude. Count on at least two days of travel from the trailheads at Spotted Bear or along Highway 2.

On the east front of the Rockies, the Sun River drains a drier corner of the Bob Marshall Wilderness. Lakes are fewer in number here, but so are the anglers. Bear Lake is the most accessible of the backcountry fishing holes, about eight miles west of Gibson Reservoir on trail 222. Cutthroat here range up to fifteen inches. Three other lakes abut the Continental Divide and require longer forays into the wilderness. To the north, Lake Levale lies off trail about three miles below Switchback Pass. Fishing action is good, but the cutts here are small. Continuing south on trail 175, Sock Lake is also found off trail about 1.5 miles west of Lookout Mountain.

Unnamed Lake lies about ten miles west of the Gates Airstrip at the head of a tributary to Rock Creek. Cutts swim here, including a rare lunker in the eighteen-inch class.

CRAZY MOUNTAINS

The Crazy Mountains were named, so one story goes, after a lost pioneer woman wandered out of them alone and half-crazed. Cross-country hikers can easily experience the poor woman's plight in the Crazies' compact jumble of peaks and canyons, but well-beaten trails lead to the best fishing lakes in this range.

Rock and Smeller lakes, just west of the Crazie's divide below Iddings Peak, both hold Yellowstone cutthroat. Take the country road (which becomes Forest Service Road 199) directly east from Clyde Park and hike in five miles on Trail #270. Roughly one mile from the trailhead, trail #200 forks east and climbs three miles to Smeller Lake. To the north, Cottonwood Lake heads the creek of the same name and harbors some foot-long cutts. Drive to the gate at the end of Forest Service Road 6620 and follow the old grade and then trail #197 for 5.5 miles to reach the lake.

The Cottonwood Creek trailhead also provides the most popular access to Campfire and Moose lakes, which drain into the Middle Fork of Sweetgrass Creek to the east. About one mile from the gate at the end of the road, turn left onto trail #268 along Trespass Creek. The trail climbs steadily for five miles to the divide and then drops down to Campfire Lake, with cutthroats, and Moose Lake, home to rainbow.

On the windy east side, Granite, Thunder, and Blue lakes receive heavy use due in part to the ease of access. Drive north from Big Timber on U.S. 191, then west on Forest Service Road 197 to the Half Moon campground and trailhead. The lakes are clustered below 11,214-foot Crazy Peak about six miles from the trailhead. You'll catch rainbow here, and more of them from Blue Lake than its neighbors. If the wind abates, climb the rough-and-tumble headwall above Blue Lake and drop a line in Pear or Druckmiller lakes for more rainbow, ranging up to eighteen inches long.

The Half Moon trailhead also leads to Twin Lakes, about four miles from the end of the road. A long history of stocking began with brook trout in 1936.

Rainbow, and more recently grayling, were also added to the lake, and a recent study by FWP suggests that rainbow are the likely catch here.

Swamp Lake harbors good numbers of brookies, but fishing here can be less than rewarding. Though close to Big Timber—turn west on the dirt ranch road just three miles north of town on U.S. 191—access is sometimes limited by landowners whose ranches straddle the sole dirt road leading to the Swamp Creek trailhead. Call ahead to obtain permission, or stop in at the Forest Service office in Big Timber. If you do manage to get to the lake (after a six-mile hike), don't be surprised if the wind follows you. John Bailey, of Dan Bailey's Fly Shop in Livingston, had long heard "rumors of good fishing," but came away disappointed. "We couldn't cast. The wind blew our lines—weighted sinking lines—out of the water." Bailey still remembers Swamp Lake as "a beautiful spot;" he'll try it again when the skies are clear and quiet.

Forest Lake, in the northern foothills, offers car camping and some lively rainbow. From Martinsdale, drive west on Highway 294 and turn south on Forest Service Road 66.

EAST AND WEST PIONEERS

Nearly encircled by the renowned Big Hole River, it should come as no surprise that the Pioneer Mountains contain more than their share of fine trout fishing. After all, a riverine trout fishery lives and dies on the quality of the surrounding watershed. Fully thirty-three percent of the Pioneer's lakes hold trout, the highest occupancy rate of any mountain range in southwest Montana. Thanks to good road access and a well-developed trail system, most of these lakes are comparatively easy to get to.

At the northern end of the West Pioneers, take the Bryant Creek Road from Highway 43 and hike over Foolhen Ridge or follow trail #8 five miles up Alder Creek to reach Ferguson and Foolhen lakes, both home to cutthroat and rainbow. Further south, along the popular Pioneer Loop Trail, Sand and the two Stone lakes hold cutts, rainbow, and a hybrid of the two. Baldy Lake, just one mile south of Sand Lake, is one of the deepest holes in this range at eighty-five feet and has a host of rainbow trout. Sand and Baldy lakes are an easy day-hike's distance from the trailhead at the end of the Steel Creek Road, which joins Highway 43 at Wisdom. The Steel Creek trail also provides quick access to Lily Lake, home to cutts and rainbow.

East from Steel Creek and in the heart of the West Pioneers, Lake of the Woods and Odell Lake offer good campsites and a chance to climb 9,446-foot Odell Mountain. Cutthroat swim in both lakes, and Odell Lake supports some beautiful grayling. Hikers can reach these lakes from either Steel Creek or the Wise River Road (Forest Service 484) in an easy day, and the area is heavily used. Pitch your tent at least 200 feet from the water's edge and practice no-impact camping. The three Bobcat lakes are also in this corner of the West Pioneers, with rainbow and grayling rising to flies.

In the East Pioneers, try Estler Lake for cutthroat/rainbow hybrids and the trio of Pear, Boot, and Anchor lakes for cutthroat. Hike in from the east from trailheads on Forest Service Road 192. Estler Lake is less than three miles from the end of the road, and the Pear Lake basin lies some six miles above the Dinner Station campground.

Brownes Lake, about eight miles up the Rock Creek Road from Interstate 15, has a drive-in campground and good fishing for brook, cutthroat, and rainbow trout. Follow trail #122 from the campground one mile to Lake Agnes for grayling and another two miles to Rainbow Lake for cutthroat. From the end of the road above Brownes Lake, trail #2 follows Rock Creek for five-plus miles to Waukena and Tahepia lakes, holding cutthroat and rainbow respectively.

North of Waukena Lake, and accessible from the Canyon Creek Road out of Melrose, anglers have their choice of Crescent, Grayling, Lion, and Canyon lakes, and Lake Abundance. All of these are stocked with cutts and rainbow and can be reached in half a day from the car campground at Canyon Creek.

The list of fisheries in the Pioneers goes on: golden trout in Hidden and Sawtooth lakes; rainbow in Schulz, Lower Boatman, and Grouse Creek lakes; cutts in Lower Elkhorn and Gorge lakes. There's just not enough room to list the remaining fifty-plus fishable lakes dotting the Pioneers, but then half the fun of planning a fishing trip is poring over maps in search of new waters.

GALLATIN RANGE

When the Gallatin and Madison rivers are swarming with the latest hatch of drift boats and hip waders, Bozeman anglers head for the hills, to the lakes of the Gallatin Range.

Hyalite Reservoir, eighteen miles south of Bozeman, tops the list of multiple-use recreation areas in the Gallatins. Most anglers prefer boat fishing on the reservoir, launching from the ramp at Hood Creek campground. The main quarry here is Yellowstone cutthroat, with some brook trout and grayling. Ice-fishing is also popular through December and January.

Hyalite Lake, a three-acre tarn some seven miles by trail from the reservoir, holds cutthroat. Emerald and Heather lakes, six miles up trail #434 along the East Fork of Hyalite Creek, harbor cutthroat and grayling.

The remaining alpine lakes in the Gallatins are best reached from Forest Service roads and trailheads branching from U.S. 191 along the Gallatin River. Rat Lake and its adjoining campground are accessible to cars by driving five miles up Squaw Creek Road to the forks, then 2.5 miles further on the south fork of the road.

Also from U.S. 191, take the Portal Creek Road east to find Hidden Lakes and the trio of Golden Trout Lakes. Only five of the eight Hidden Lakes hold trout—rainbow and goldens—but the basin is an easy three-mile hike from the road and fishing action is generally good. Golden Trout Lakes are nestled on the northern slopes of Eaglehead Mountain, about three miles by trail from the end of the Portal Creek Road. Two lakes of this trio are barren, but the first holds golden trout and some cutthroat.

Ramshorn Lake is possibly the most scenic lake along the Gallatin Divide, couched below Ramshorn Peak and Fortress Mountain. Cutthroat provide the sport here. The hike into Ramshorn is also one of the prettiest in the Gallatins, following the meanders and meadows of Buffalo Horn Creek. From U.S. 191, turn east on the two-mile dirt road that cuts through the 320 Ranch. Follow trails #1 and #160 to cover the seven miles into the lake.

MADISON RANGE

Most of the alpine lakes in the Madison Range are clustered in two areas—the Spanish Peaks unit to the north, and the Taylor-Hilgard unit to the south. Unfortunately, both areas have received heavy fishing pressure for decades and many lakes are scarred by innumerable campsites, trees hacked for firewood, and trampled, devegetated shorelines. When the Spanish Peaks and Taylor-Hilgard units were added to the national wilderness system in the mid 1980s, word of their natural beauty and resources spread, attracting even more visitors.

Conscientious anglers can avoid these high-use basins and still enjoy good fishing (and solitude) at a handful of lakes scattered among the Madison's rugged peaks. Cutts and rainbow are the rule here, and many populations have hybridized over the years.

Lake Cameron is a good five-mile hike above the North Fork of Bear Creek on the west slope. Cameron has long been popular with the locals for both rainbow and cutts. To the south, a full day's hike from either the Bear Creek or Indian Creek trailhead, No Man Lake harbors cutthroats. The No Man Creek trail (329) receives only sporadic maintenance from the Forest Service, and heavy downfall in the lower timbered section may hinder packstock.

From the Jack Creek Road east of Ennis, trails 317 and 319 lead some six miles to Lost Lake and Shadow Lake. Lost is barren, but Shadow holds some nice cutts, rainbows, and hybrids. Both lakes are on Plum Creek Company land, so check ahead about logging activity in the area.

On the east side of the range, Albino Lake is a shallow reservoir best reached from the Taylor Creek Road on trail 33. It's an easy three-mile walk into the lake, home of rainbow and cutthroat.

MISSION MOUNTAIN WILDERNESS

Just west of Highway 83 between Seeley Lake and Swan Lake, the Mission Mountains rise as a wall of soaring peaks, shining glaciers, and dense forests. The Missions are studded with clear, cold lakes, many of which harbor good-sized trout. Most of the range is designated as wilderness, and the west slope lies within the Flathead Indian Reservation. The public is welcome on these tribal lands, but all visitors must first obtain a permit available at most sporting foods stores in Polson, Pablo, or Ronan. All of the lakes described here lie on the east slope, within the wilderness boundary, and are the best accessed from Highway 83.

Near the north end of the wilderness area, Cedar Lake holds small but feisty cutthroats. After driving up Forest Service Road 888F, the lake is a four-mile hike in on trail 690. Another four miles south on trail 690 is Piper Lake, which can also be accessed by trail from Forest Service Road 966 about 2.5 miles north of Salmon Prairie on Highway 83. Piper harbors cutts in the eight-to-fourteen-inch range, but fishing is spotty at best.

Moving south, Upper and Lower Cold lakes lie directly west of Condon on Forest Service Road 903. Follow Cold Creek along Road 9599 to the gate near the wilderness boundary. Lower Cold Lake is two miles in and the upper lake is nestled just .5 mile above. Both offer good fishing for cutthroats up to fifteen inches; not surprisingly, Cold Lakes receive fairly heavy fishing pressure.

The Crescent Lake basin lies snug against the base of Point St. Charles at the head of Glacier Creek. The four largest lakes in the basin—Crescent, Glacier, Heart, and Island—all are fished heavily for small cutts. A number of smaller tarns in the area also offer good fishing and a chance for solitude. From Highway 83, follow Forest Service Road 561 west to the end of the road. Crescent Lake is about three miles in.

For sporadic cutthroat fishing but outstanding scenery and good opportunities for solitude, try Gray Wolf Lake near the southern boundary. At best, the lake is a stiff eight-mile hike from the nearest trailhead on Forest Service Road 906, but the route provides good views much of the way in. Because the trail briefly crosses tribal lands, all travelers should carry a tribal permit. The main trail can also be accessed from several trailheads along Lindbergh Lake.

TOBACCO ROOT RANGE

Though scarred from heavy mining activity for more than 100 years, the Tobacco Roots still offer good trout fishing. More than thirty-seven lakes contain fish—brookies, cutthroat, rainbow, and a scattering of grayling. But with the exception of Branham lakes and Noble Lake on the west, angling here is often an exercise in perseverance.

From Pony, park at the end of the North Fork of Willow Creek Road and follow the old mining roads west toward the 10,604-foot landmark, Hollowtop Mountain. Three paternoster lakes—Hollowtop, Deep, and Skytop—nestle below the peak's east face, about five miles from the end of the road. All three hold rainbow but most anglers content themselves with the scenery and a few nibbles from the trout in Deep Lake. Albro Lake, directly south on trail 365, holds a particularly shy strain of cutthroat.

On the Willow Creek Road west of the Potosi campground, follow trail 305 three-miles-plus to Bell Lake for cutthroat and vistas of 10,000-foot peaks on three sides.

Twin lakes, at the foot of Lady of the Lake Peak, host a healthy population of brook and lake trout. The lakes are accessible by car from either Pony or McAllister by driving the year-round Willow Creek or North Fork Meadow Creek roads. Turn southwest on Forest Service Road 338 toward Kid Mountain. Also at the end of this road, a short hike to the south, lie Cliff, Lupine, Alpine, and Lily lakes. Only the first two harbor fish, brook and rainbow respectively.

Branham lakes and campground are possibly the most popular destination in the Tobacco Roots, rewarding anglers with hungry, pan-sized brook trout. The lakes and campground are nestled below the peaks at 8,800 feet but are readily accessible by car. Follow Mill Creek Road directly east from Sheridan for about fourteen miles. Noble Lake, a half-day hike from the head of the Noble Creek Road north of Sheridan, holds cutthroat, rainbow, and hybrids.

77 Other Montana Lake Fisheries

As a bonus feature, we have included in the following table seventy-seven more outstanding or very popular lakes, ranked in order by their sizes.

The codes used in the last column of this table are as follws: A—abundant, B—abundant with a porportion of large fish, C—common, D—declining, E—presence expected, R—rare, U—uncommon, V—uncommon with large fish, and Z—abundance unknown.

Lake	Drainage	County	Size (Acres)	Depth (Ft)	Species	Abundance
1. Lake Elwell	Marias River	Liberty	17,000	150	rainbow	U
					perch	C
					pike	C
					walleye	A
					burbot	U
2. Noxon Rapids Reservoir	Clark Fork	Sanders	8,800	250	cutthroat	V
					rainbow	V
					whitefish	V
					brown	V
					bull trout	V
					perch	A
					largemouth bass	A
					smallmouth bass	A
					pike	R
3. Lima Reservoir	Red Rock River	Beaverhead	7,413	32.8	burbot	C
4. Lake Francis	Dry Fork, Marias	Pondera	5,536	45	northern pike	C
					rainbow	R
					walleye	A
					perch	C
					burbot	U
5. Bynum Reservoir	Miller Creek	Teton	4,120	25	walleye	C
					perch	A
6. Cabinet Gorge Reservoir	Clark Fork River	Sanders	3,800	220	rainbow	U
					cutthroat	U
					brown	U
					northern pike	U
					whitefish	U
					bull	U
					largemouth bass	U
					perch	A
					smallmouth bass	R
7. Ennis	Madison River	Madison	3,780	18	rainbow	A
					brown	A
					grayling	C
8. Little Bitterroot	Bitterroot Creek	Flathead	2,925	260	kokanee	A
					cutthroat	C
					rainbow	V
					perch	C

Lake	Drainage	County	Size (Acres)	Depth (Ft)	Species	Abundance
9. Upper Red Rock	Red Rock River	Beaverhead	2,206	6	grayling	D
					cutthroat	V
					burbot	C
					brook	V
10. Lake Helena	Missouri River	Lewis & Clark	2,100	14	brown	R
					perch	V
					rainbow	U
					largemouth bass	U
11. Pablo Reservoir	Flathead River	Lake	2,040	39	largemouth bass	A
					perch	A
					rainbow	C
12. Ninepipe Reservoir	Flathead River	Lake	1,852	27	largemouth bass	A
					perch	A
13. Duck	Milk River	Glacier	1,398	60	rainbow	B
14. Tally	Logan Creek	Flathead	1,326	250	kokanee	A
					bull	C
					rainbow	C
					cutthroat	C
					lake	U
					pike	C
15. Gibson Reservoir	Sun River	Lewis & Clark Teton	1,282	90	rainbow	U
					cutthroat	R
					brook	R
16. Bull	Lake Creek	Lincoln	1,249	64	cutthroat	C
					kokanee	U
					largemouth bass	C
					rainbow	V
					brook	U
					perch	A
					bull	C
					northern pike	Z
17. Placid	Swan River	Missoula	1,110	90	perch	A
					rainbow	U
					largemouth bass	U
					cutthroat	C
					brook	R
					kokanee	C
					brown	R
					bull	R
18. Warhourse	Buffalo Creek	Petroleum	1,000	12	largemouth bass	R
19. Ruby Reservoir	Ruby River	Madison	970	66	brown	U
					cutthroat	Z
					rainbow	U
20. Willow Creek (Harrison Res.)	Willow Creek	Madison	868	74	rainbow	C
					brown	C
21. Painted Rocks Reservoir	Bitterroot	Ravalli	803	180	cutthroat	C
					rainbow	C
					bull	R
					brook	R

Lake	Drainage	County	Size (Acres)	Depth (Ft)	Species	Abundance
22. Kicking Horse Reservoir	Flathead River	Lake	800	28	largemouth bass	A
					perch	A
					rainbow	V
23. Frenchman Reservoir	Frenchman Creek	Phillips	790	23	perch	C
24. Lower Glass Lindsey	Sweetgrass Creek	Sweetgrass	768	22	perch	A
					rainbow	C
					brown	C
25. Como	Bitterroot Rvier	Ravalli	753	100	rainbow	C
					cutthroat	U
26. Willow Creek	Lodgegrass Creek	Big Horn	750	95	rainbow	A
					brown	A
27. Gaffrey	Lake Creek	Sheridan	637	15	northern pike	Z
					largemouth bass	Z
28. Upper Stillwater	Stillwater River	Flathead	630	74	rainbow	V
					cutthroat	D
					northern pike	A
					brook	V
					perch	A
					largemouth bass	E
29. Cliff	Madison River	Madison	620	125	rainbow	C
30. Hyalite Reservoir	Hyalite Creek	Gallatin	618	125	cutthroat	A
					grayling	A
					brook	Z
31. Salmon	Clearwater River	Missoula	613	70	rainbow	C
					bull	R
					cutthroat	C
					kokanee	A
					brown	U
					perch	A
32. Middle Thompson	Thompson River	Lincoln	601	160	rainbow	V
					kokanee	C
					brook	U
					largemouth bass	B
					cutthroat	A
					lake	V
33. Quake	Madison	Gallatin	600	80	rainbow	Z
					brown	Z
					cutthroat	Z
34. Dickey	Kootenai River	Lincoln	579	74	kokanee	C
					brook	V
					cutthroat	V
					northern pike	V
					rainbow	V

Lake	Drainage	County	Size (Acres)	Depth (Ft)	Species	Abundance
35. Echo	Flathead River	Flathead	546	70	whitefish	V
					northern pike	A
					brook	V
					perch	A
					largemouth bass	B
36. Petrolia Reservoir	Flatwillow Creek	Petroleum	514	42	perch	U
					burbot	R
					walleye	C
					pike	U
37. Helena Regulating Reservoir	Missouri River	Lewis & Clark	499	67	kokanee	C
					perch	U
38. Swift Reservoir	Birch Creek	Pondera	498	60	rainbow	U
39. Hubbard Reservoir	Little Bitterroot & Flathead rivers	Flathead	483	62	rainbow	A
					brook	U
					salmon	E
40. Lake 12	Lake Creek	Sheridan	474	12	northern pike	V
41. Smith	Ashley Creek	Flathead	443	13	perch	B
					cutthroat	V
					brook	V
					rainbow	C
42. Holland	Holland Creek	Missoula	427	155	bull	V
					kokanee	V
					cutthroat	V
					rainbow	V
					perch	C
43. Eureka Reservoir	Teton River	Teton	400	25	rainbow	C
					brook	Z
					brown	Z
44. Silver	Storm Lake Creek	Deer Lodge	394	72	bull	V
					lake	R
					rainbow	V
					kokanee	C
					cutthroat	R
45. Blaine	Flathead River	Flathead	372	140	brook	U
					northern pike	C
					cutthroat	C
					lake	V
					largemouth bass	C
					whitefish	V
					kokanee	C
					perch	A
46. Glen	Glen Creek	Lincoln	340	38	bull	D
					kokanee	A
					rainbow	A
					brook	V
					whitefish	A
47. Grey Wolf	Swan River	Missoula	228	200	cutthroat	A
48. Smith River Reservoir	Smith River	Meagher	327	60	rainbow	C
					brook	U
					burbot	C

Lake	Drainage	County	Size (Acres)	Depth (Ft)	Species	Abundance
49. Lebo	Spring Creek and Big Elk Creek	Wheatland	314	14	rainbow brown tigermuskie	C C U
50. Morony	Missouri River	Cascade	300	60	rainbow brown perch walleye	U U C U
51. Alva	Clearwater River	Missoula	292	95	cutthroat bull perch kokanee	C V A C
52. Upper Aero	Skytop Creek	Park	291	95	cutthroat	C
53. Mission Reservoir	Mission Creek	Lake	289	70	cutthroat	A
54. Inez	Clearwater River	Missoula	286	69	cutthroat bull kokanee perch	C U U C
55. Newlan Creek Reservoir	Newlan Creek	Meagher	280	100	rainbow brook cutthroat	U U U
56. St. Mary	Dry Creek	Lake	272	272	cutthroat brook rainbow	A C C
57. Coopers	Blackfoot River	Powell	274	55	cutthroat brook rainbow bull	C U U V
58. Bair Reservoir	Mussellshell River	Meagher	271	60	rainbow brook	C C
59. Foy	Ashley Creek	Flathead	270	133	rainbow	A
60. Big Creek 1 & 2	Big Creek	Ravalli	269	140	rainbow	C
61. Egan Slough	Flathead River	Flathead	266	27	northern pike perch	A A
62. Lower Stillwater	Stillwater	Flathead	248	52	northern pike rainbow perch cutthroat bull	A V A V U
63. Loon	Kootenai River	Lincoln	238	115	rainbow cutthroat brook largemouth bass smallmouth bass	C V V A C
64. Rogers	Sickler Creek	Flathead	237	19	perch	C
65. Elk Lake	Elk Spring Creek	Beaverhead	235	66	grayling burbot cutthroat lake	D U C C

231

Lake	Drainage	County	Size (Acres)	Depth (Ft)	Species	Abundance
66. Granite	Lake Creek	Carbon	238	125	rainbow	C
					brook	U
67. Sophie	Kootenai River	Lincoln	214	60	bull	V ·
					largemouth	
					bass	A
					cutthroat	C
					rainbow	V
					perch	A
68. Bean	Dearborn River	Lewis & Clark	206	30	rainbow	C
69. Island	Pleasant Valley Creek	Lincoln	205	55	largemouth	
					bass	A
					cutthroat	E
					brook	E
70. Church Slough	Flathead River	Flathead	205	35	largemouth	
					bass	C
					perch	A
					northern	
					pike	C
					whitefish	U
71. Fennon Slough	Flathead River	Flathead	200	20	largemouth	
					bass	C
					perch	C
					northern	
					pike	C
72. Yellowtail Afterbay	Bighorn River	Bighorn	200	25	rainbow	C
					brown	U
73. McDonald	Post Creek	Lake	188	106	rainbow	U
					brook	U
					cutthroat	C
					bull	D
74. Crystal	Swan River	Missoula	174	66	cutthroat	A
75. Hidden	Madison	Madison	156	50	rainbow	C
					brown	C
76. Lake Five	Mud Creek	Flathead	156	62	largemouth	
					bass	C
					cutthroat	E
					brook	U
					perch	U
77. Blanchard	Flathead River	Flathead	147	32	perch	A
					northern	
					pike	A
					largemouth	
					bass	A

GLACIER NATIONAL PARK

Glacier National Park is best known for its spectacular scenery, wildlife, and backcountry hiking opportunities. Nearly 1.5 million visitors come to the park each year to experience its grandeur. Straddling the Continental Divide in northwestern Montana along the Canadian border, Glacier Park features rugged mountain peaks and some fifty glaciers. Wildflowers blanket the high mountain valleys and grassy meadows. Wildlife abounds—mountain goats, bighorn sheep, elk, moose, deer, black bears, and, most notably, grizzly bears. Glacier Park is one of the grizzly's few remaining strongholds in the lower U.S.

Thus, for most people, fishing is a secondary attraction to Glacier Park. But the park offers good fishing opportunities, highlighted by the chance to catch a variety of native species from Glacier's pristine waters. In many sections of the park, fish are small due to cold and nutrient-poor waters that limit insect populations and fish growth. However, some lakes provide anglers a chance to catch trophy fish. And almost anywhere anglers go in Glacier, they'll be surrounded by extraordinary beauty.

Waters from the park flow into three oceans. The west side of the park drains into the north and middle forks of the Flathead River, eventually reaching the Pacific Ocean. East of the Continental Divide, park waters drain north into the St. Mary River and south via the Missouri River, eventually reaching the Arctic and Atlantic oceans, respectively.

Fish management in Glacier Park has changed during the last fifteen years. Emphasis has shifted away from consumptive fishing for stocked fish to sport fishing for native species. Creel limits have been reduced for native species; and several streams, particularly along the Middle Fork of the Flathead, have been closed to fishing to protect important cutthroat and bull trout spawning waters. Lakes and streams are no longer stocked because introduced species proved detrimental to native species. Park management efforts are now directed at preserving natural aquatic systems.

Native species of concern to park management programs include the westslope cutthroat trout, bull trout, and lake trout. Historically, westslope cutthroat trout were found throughout the waters of the Columbia River system, but they were eliminated in many areas. Populations remain strong in Glacier Park, however, providing the main catch for anglers today.

Lake trout, native only to lakes east of the Divide, were introduced into several lakes on the west side of the park. These fish get very large, often exceeding fifteen pounds in some park lakes.

Bull trout are native to the Columbia and Saskatchewan river drainages of Glacier Park. They grow to remarkable sizes; fish over two feet long have been taken from some park waters. Bull trout are known for their remarkable spawning runs, and many "park" fish are spawners from Flathead Lake, more than thirty miles to the south.

Kokanee salmon were introduced throughout Glacier Park during the early 1930s and continue to thrive in several park lakes. Kokanee from Flathead Lake once spawned in large numbers in lower McDonald Creek each fall, attracting a spectacular concentration of bald eagles. But this kokanee population collapsed and now the eagles gather in lesser numbers at Lake Koocanusa and along the upper Missouri River.

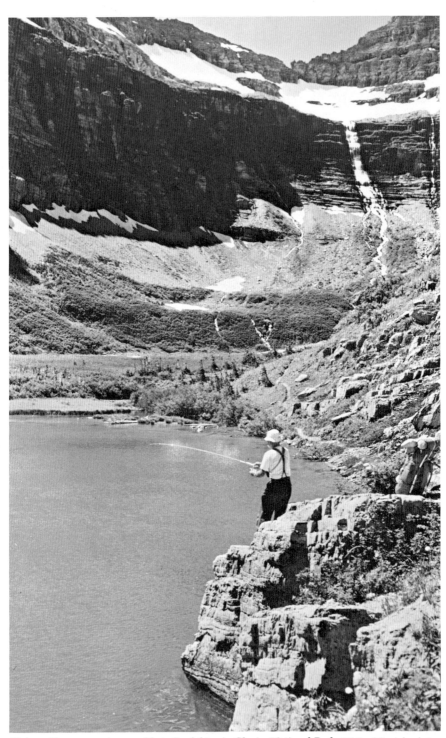

Unbeatable scenery always adds to the fishing in Glacier National Park. Michael Sample photo.

Grayling is another introduced species that now receives special management consideration. The grayling survives only in a few isolated waters in Montana and is considered in need of special support. Experts believe Glacier is within the grayling's historic range, and the park provides needed grayling habitat today.

Bears also have an interest in the fish of Glacier. They are attracted by fishy odors and may potentially cause trouble for a careless angler. Park regulations concerning the handling of fish in the backcountry are designed to minimize these encounters and should be judiciously heeded. Occasionally, authorities must close an area to fishing to avoid conflicts between humans and bears.

Anglers should pick up a copy of Glacier's fishing regulations before wetting a line. Available at ranger stations and visitor's centers, the regulations detail various seasons, closed waters, and limits.

Fishing pressure in Glacier Park is light compared to Yellowstone National Park. Approximately ten percent of park visitors fish, and few of them spend more than a couple of hours at it.

The main threats to the park fishery are from activities outside the park boundaries. Extensive clear-cutting on forested lands outside of the park may cause sedimentation problems for bull trout and cutthroat trout in the Flathead River System. Similarly, a proposed open-pit coal mine just north of the park in Canada could result in deterioration of water quality in the North Fork of the Flathead River and reduce native fish populations. For now, these mining plans have been tabled.

Even more threatening is the potential for acid rain in the park's mountain lakes. With little buffering capacity, these lakes could easily acidify, eliminating aquatic insects and other fish food sources. Ultimately this could impact fish populations through productive failure and/or starvation. Friends of the park will need to raise their voices in the coming years.

Fishing Strategies

In Glacier, almost all of the fishing action takes place in the fifty or sixty lakes that support fish. As in most high mountain lakes, the fishing in Glacier can be very temperamental—dead at some times, fast and furious at others.

What makes for hot or cold fishing has puzzled anglers for years, but two factors seem relatively clear. First, low light levels make fish feel safer from their predators, and therefore fish tend to be more active in the early morning and late evening hours. Heavily overcast or stormy times also seem better. Secondly, hatches of insects on a lake's surface often galvanize the fish into action. Once one fish begins to feed on the bugs, the others are likely to join in and dimple the lake's surface with their rises.

Don Alley, who operates the Big Sky Fly and Tackle Shop in Kalispell, advises that the best fishing, in general, occurs in lakes not accessible by roads. For example, McDonald Lake and St. Mary Lake are two of the most accessible in the park. Alley describes them as beautiful to look at, but disappointing to fish. He finds much more satisfying results in some of the backcountry lakes.

When anglers arrive at a lake ready to fish, they should look the lake over for special features where fish tend to congregate. Inlets and outlets are often hot spots. Alley also mentions checking out promontories, fallen trees, steep dropoffs, and shoals. He emphasizes that anglers should approach lakes carefully to avoid spooking fish along the edge. Most of the insect life is along the shoreline, which brings cruising trout in to feed. The first casts should be in close; later the angler can work further out in the lake. And generally speaking, anglers do better when they move away from the most heavily used and easily accessible part of the shoreline.

Flies, lures, and bait all catch fish in Glacier. In fact, some of the fish are so hungry and unsophisticated that they will "grab anything that looks remotely edible," as Alley puts it. At other times, the fish seem much more choosey about what they ingest. Fish in certain lakes—such as Hidden and Oldman—have reputations for being quite discerning.

Whether cast with a fly rod or with a bubble on spinning gear, flies often prove most effective at catching fish. Gary Sakahare, who works at The Sportsman in Kalispell, recommends long leaders and small flies. When the fish are rising to the surface, he uses dry flies; if there is no surface action, he ties on a small nymph, such as a hare's ear.

Alley agrees with this strategy. He finds sizes 16 to 20 dry flies work better than the larger sizes. Three patterns he especially likes are the black gnat, mosquito, and Adams. He prefers larger flies when fishing wet, such as #6-10 Wooly Worms, #8-10 damselfly nymphs, #6 leech patterns, and #6-8 Careys Special. If fishing for bull trout, he ties on one of the larger nymphs or a Maribou Muddler. When fishing wet, anglers should slowly retrieve their nymphs. With a streamer, the retrieve should be faster, perhaps eighteen inches at a time.

For spinning lures, the Thomas Cyclone probably ranks as the most popular hardware. Alley suspects the original red and white Daredevle catches more than its share. Also, the various types of Mepps and Panther Martins fool plenty of fish. Tom Shepherd, who works with Sakahare at The Sportsman, especially likes to do his spinning with an ultra-light rod, which makes great sport out of fighting even a ten-inch brook trout.

The three most widely used baits include salmon eggs, sucker meat, and nightcrawlers (which cannot be dug up in the park), but some anglers prefer marshmallows, cheese, or maggots. The regulations strictly prohibit the use of live fish for bait as well as the use of set lines.

Fishing for lake trout generally requires special techniques. Having the use of a boat is usually an advantage, because lake trout summer in the deep parts of lakes. Bank anglers have their best chance at a lake trout either in spring, just as the ice comes off; or in late fall, when lake trout come into the shallows to spawn. Early season anglers may have trouble gaining access to a particular lake due to snow on the trail. In some places, the trails do not clear until July.

Fishing Waters

Following is an alphabetical list of fishing waters in Glacier, with a brief description of the angling possibilities. Anglers headed into the backcountry must have a camping permit. All anglers must obtain a nonfee daily permit to fish anywhere in Glacier.

Akokola Lake offers good fishing for small cutthroat plus a few bull trout. Easily fished from shore and about twenty-three acres in size, Akokola is a six-mile hike from Bowman Lake.

Arrow Lake is a steep, 6.5-mile hike from Lake McDonald into dense bear habitat. Also easily fished from the shore, this sixty-acre lake grants excellent fishing for some nice cutthroat and small bull trout. Check for special restrictions.

Canada
Montana

KINTLA LAKE

WATERTON LAKE

BOWMAN LAKE

COSLEY LAKE

GLENNS LAKE

ELIZABETH LAKE

QUARTZ LAKE

Many Glacier

LOWER ST. MARY

SWIFTCURRENT LAKE

SHERBURNE LAKE

LOGGING LAKE

North Fork Road

TROUT LAKE

ST. MARY

Going-to-the-Sun Road

HIDDEN LAKE

LAKE McDONALD

RED EAGLE LAKE

Highway 89

HARRISON LAKE

UPPER TWO MEDICINE LAKE

West Glacier

TWO MEDICINE LAKE

LOWER TWO MEDICINE LAKE

East Glacier

Glacier National

Park

to Kalispell

N

Highway 2

GLACIER NATIONAL PARK

HIGHWAY
COUNTY OR UNPAVED ROAD
△ OFFICIAL PUBLIC ACCESS
□ RANGER STATION
X BRIDGE
〜〜 DIVERSION DAM

five miles

GLACIER NATIONAL PARK

Avalanche Lake is an easy two-mile hike from the Avalanche Creek Campground and subsequently gets fairly heavy fishing pressure. A lovely, small cirque lake lying below several waterfalls, Avalanche has a good population of eight- to ten-inch cutthroat. Fly anglers may wish to take their waders with them to reach the deeper water for unhindered backcasts. The water is extremely cold.

The Belly River is one of the best streams in the park. Accessible by trail from the Chief Mountain Customs Station, the stream holds seven- to ten-inch rainbow as well as some grayling close to either end of Elizabeth Lake.

Bowman Lake has cutthroat trout, kokanee, and some bull trout, but it requires skill and knowledge to fish for them successfully. A boat helps, although the north shore has some good bank-fishing. Bowman has road access.

Bullhead Lake, a fairly level, four-mile hike from Many Glacier Hotel or Swiftcurrent Motel, has good fishing for eight- to twelve-inch brook trout.

Camas Creek has some good cutthroat fishing in places. The whole drainage of this creek has restrictions on tackle.

Camas Lake offers very good fishing for cutthroat, but requires a ten-mile hike from Lake McDonald and is subject to special fishing restrictions.

Cerulean Lake has no trail or road leading to it and probably is the most difficult lake in this list to reach. The handful of anglers who do find this spot find very good fishing for cutthroat and bull trout. The angler may also find grizzly bears.

Cosley Lake is a fairly large lake about eight miles by trail from Chief Mountain Customs Station. While fishing is only fair for eight- to twelve-inch rainbow, it can be very good for lake trout, the predominant fish in the lake. In 1982, an angler caught one over seventeen pounds from the shore.

Cracker Lake lies at the foot of mighty Mt. Siyeh, six miles by trail from Many Glacier. Cracker has a good number of small bull trout, which are stunted due to a shortage of food.

Cut Bank Creek offers good fishing in heavy brush and timber for eight- to ten-inch brook and rainbow trout.

Elizabeth Lake is a popular backcountry lake nine miles from Chief Mountain Customs Station. The open shoreline makes bank-fishing a pleasure. Sometimes wind-swept, sometimes placid, the lake has excellent fishing for grayling and rainbow from twelve to eighteen inches.

Lake Ellen Wilson provides very good fishing for brook trout up to fifteen inches long. Situated in mountain goat country, the lake is reached only after a nine- or ten-mile hike either from Lake McDonald of the Jackson Glacier Overlook. With either route, the angler faces a vertical gain of about 3,600 feet.

Lake Evangeline is another great spot for fishing away from civilization. Cutthroat twelve to fifteen inches swim in this beautiful cirque lake at the top of the Camas Creek drainage. Special fishing regulations are enforced here.

Fish Lake can be good for cutthroat early in the season, when anglers can reach the deep water beyond the lily pads. This swampy but beautiful little lake is a steep 1.9-mile hike from Lake McDonald.

Fishercap Lake is rather slow fishing for pan-sized brookies in a beautiful area 1.5 miles from Many Glacier.

Francis Lake has good fishing for ten- to eighteen-inch rainbow. Six miles up the trail from the U.S. end of Waterton Lake, this lake also features a dramatic waterfall above its southwestern side.

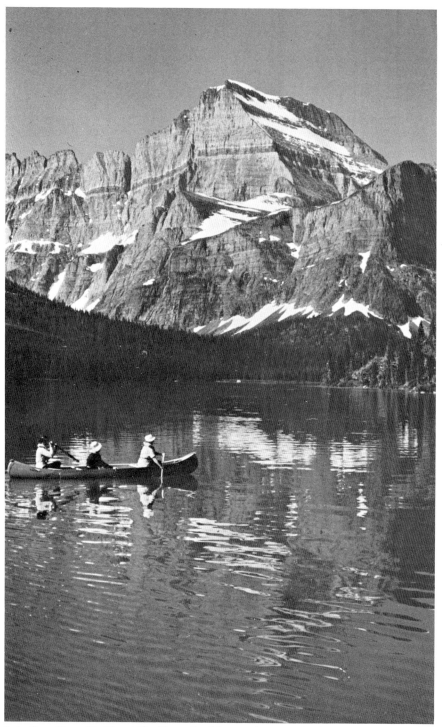

Lake Josephine with Mount Gould as a backdrop. Who cares if the fish are biting? Michael Sample photo.

Glenns Lake is long and narrow with a shallow shoreline. Anglers should look for the deeper spots to fish for fourteen- to eighteen-inch lake trout.

Grace Lake is a relatively easy nine-mile hike from the trailhead past Logging Lake. As it is difficult to cast with a fly rod from shore, anglers might favor spincasting for twelve- to fifteen-inch cutthroat.

Grinnell Lake is an easy one-mile hike from the Lake Josephine boat dock. In addition to incredible beauty, anglers often find nine- to twelve-inch brook trout.

Gunsight Lake is a phenomenally spectacular spot to fish for ten- to fourteen-inch rainbow as well as a few lunkers. Anglers must hike about six miles from the Jackson Glacier Overlook.

Harrison Lake harbors, cutthroat, bull trout, and kokanee. Anglers need to take a lengthy hike from West Glacier to get here, except possibly late in the season when fording the Middle Fork of the Flathead cuts the trip down to four miles.

Hidden Lake is the highest lake in the park that contains fish. In this case, twelve- to sixteen-inch wily cutthroat are the quarry. An up-and-down three-mile hike from Logan Pass, the lake is good for fly fishing and wading.

The Howe Lakes are a short hike from the trailhead along the dirt road from Fish Creek Campground to Polebridge. Best early in the season before the water warms up, both lakes are good for cutthroat trout fishing. The upper lake is the deeper, but smaller, of the two.

Isabel Lake supports some nice nine- to thirteen-inch cutthroat and small bull trout. Depending on which trail the angler chooses, Isabel is twelve to seventeen miles from road access.

Josephine Lake is just over a small rise no more than a mile from the Many Glacier Hotel. Some small brookies and kokanee provide the sport.

Katoya Lake has excellent fishing for nice cutthroat—when grizzly bear activity has not closed the seven-mile trail from Cut Bank Campground.

Kintla Lake is a six-mile-long, narrow lowland lake with cutthroat trout, kokanee, lake trout, and some bull trout. Fishing in this scenic lake is best done from a boat, but the bank angler willing to walk away from the road and campground can find some good fishing. Upper Kintla Lake, 2.5 miles from the east end of the lower lake, holds native bull trout.

Lincoln Lake, an eight-mile hike from Lake McDonald, has good fishing for pan-sized cutthroat and brookies.

Logging Lake is an eight-mile-long, narrow, lake with nine- to twelve-inch cutthroat and some bull trout. The best fishing is reached by walking the shoreline to deeper water. Fly fishing is difficult due to the timbered banks. From the North Fork Road, anglers need to hike 4.5 miles.

McDonald Creek has sparse numbers of small cutthroat, brookies, and bull trout, as well as an occasional kokanee. Above the lake, the stream is beautiful to behold but disappointing to fish.

Lake McDonald is the largest and most used lake in the park. This nine-mile-long lake holds lake trout, kokanee, and cutthroat. Trolling for lake trout averaging fifteen inches probably is the best bet for action, but some shore anglers catch cutts ten to twelve inches long. Boats are available for rent. Fishing here may test the patience; most serious anglers go elsewhere.

Medicine Grizzly Lake, a five-mile hike from Cut Bank Campground, has fair fishing for foot-long rainbow.

Mokowanis Lake has easy fishing for eight- to twelve-inch brookies, but

Early morning on one of the many hidden lakes of Glacier Park. Michael Sample photo.

anglers must hike eight to fifteen miles to reach this attractive lake.

Oldman Lake is home for some large, crafty cutthroat that cruise the shoreline in plain view of sometimes-frustrated anglers. Wet flies may be the ticket. This lake which requires a seven-mile hike from Two Medicine Campground, also harbors some big beavers.

Ole Lake is a small, remote lake with good fishing for mostly pan-sized cutthroat.

Otokomi Lake, six miles from the Rising Sun Campground, has some ten- to fourteen-inch fat cutthroat which are elusive but sometimes fall for wet flies.

Ptarmigan Lake is a small body of water with an open shoreline that gives fly fishermen a good chance for brook and rainbow trout. Anglers in good shape can reach the lake with a stiff five-mile hike from Many Glacier.

Quartz Lake is a very good spot for large cutthroat and even larger bull trout. However, the lake has no trails around the shoreline, and anglers must hike in from Bowman Lake over a ridge.

Red Eagle Lake can be good for large, two- to four-pound rainbow-cutthroat hybrids. In 1955 the new state record cutthroat, a sixteen-pounder, was taken from this lake. An easy eight-mile hike from St. Mary, the lake is better to fish once the water recedes from the brushy banks.

Redrock Lake offers fair fishing for nine- to twelve-inch brookies three miles up the trail from Many Glacier.

Lake Sherburne is actually a reservoir with fluctuating water levels controlled by a dam just outside the east boundary of the park. Sherburne is the only lake in the park with northern pike, feisty fish averaging eighteen inches and ranging up to enormous.

Slide Lake, five miles from Chief Mountain Highway, offers fair fishing for twelve- to sixteen-inch cutthroat.

Snyder Lake is a cold lake with little food for the multitudes of seven- to nine-inch cutthroat that greet anglers who have made the 4.5 mile hike from Lake McDonald.

St. Mary Lake is an extraordinarily beautiful roadside lake renowned for its scenery, not its fishing. Trolling from a boat sometimes rewards anglers with whitefish, rainbow, or brookies.

Swiftcurrent Lake, literally just out the back door of Many Glacier Hotel, has proven good fishing for nine- to eleven-inch brook trout plus some kokanee. Boats can be rented to paddle around this beautiful, ninety-nine-acre gem of a lake.

Trout Lake is another of the specially regulated lakes in the Camas Creek drainage. Unfortunately, the brushy banks make fly fishing difficult, but those who solve this problem find good fishing for pan-sized cutthroat plus some bull trout. Anglers must make a four-mile hike into bear country to reach this lake and should be alert.

Two Medicine Lake, along with its upper and lower sister lakes, offers fair fishing mostly for rainbow and brook trout. The vast majority of the trout in these lakes measure under fifteen inches, but in 1983 an angler caught an eastern brook trout that weighed almost nine pounds even after it had been cleaned. Had the angler left the guts in the fish, it would have easily broken the state record. These lakes make beautiful places to fish and contemplate the mountains on quiet days.

Waterton Lake is a large, scenic, often wind-swept lake spanning the U.S.-Canada border. Best fished by boat, the lake surrenders a few lake trout among the predominant catch of whitefish.

YELLOWSTONE NATIONAL PARK

Although Yellowstone Park owes its world-fame to its spectacular geysers, abundant wildlife, and unique scenery, the park also offers exceptional angling opportunities. Over 160,000 anglers a year take advantage of its high quality fishing. Yellowstone is richly endowed with over a hundred superb trout streams and subalpine lakes.

Despite the tremendous and ever-increasing pressure from anglers, fishing in the park has actually been improving over the past ten years. Regulations aimed at protecting the fishery and the complex food chain of this extraordinary ecosystem were extensively revised in 1970. Today, Yellowstone Park has some of the most restrictive and successful regulations in the country. They include local and seasonal closures to protect spawning fish, the elimination of bait fishing, size and creel limits, catch-and-release areas, and fly fishing only waters.

The results have been more fish, a greater diversity of fishing opportunities, and more anglers taking advantage of these opportunities. The percentage of successful anglers has risen, and in many waters, average fish size is increasing. Park policy has shifted away from consumptive fishing toward a fish-for-fun philosophy that seems to be working. The large variety of regulations required in this management effort make it essential for the angler to read the park's fishing regulations carefully to avoid violations.

Yellowstone Park is divided into six fishing zones, each with unique fishery characteristics and regulations. Opening day varies from May 28 to July 15, depending on the zone. Creel and size limits vary from zone to zone, as do catch-and-release or fly fishing only waters, so check the regulations. No matter where in the park they fish, however, all anglers must obtain a free fishing permit.

Fishing in the park is limited to single-hook, artificial flies and lures. (Treble hooks are considered a single hook under the regulations.) Fish mortality, particularly in the catch-and-release waters, has significantly declined with the elimination of bait fishing.

A wide variety of flies and lures are effective in the park. Standard dry flies used on lakes or smooth-surfaced streams include the Adams, Blue Dun, Ginger Quill, and Light Cahill. Royal Wulffs, Humpies, elk hair caddis, and hoppers bring the best dry fly action in the fast, broken water stretches. Salmon fly patterns are good in season on the Yellowstone River. Wet flies worth trying include Wooly Worms, Muddler Minnows, and a variety of dark-colored streamers. In the park, Hamilton Stores has helpful clerks and supplies of fishing gear. Outside the park, West Yellowstone and Gardiner are amply supplied with fishing shops that can provide up-to-date information for specific waters. They also have guide services for park fishing.

Lures are particularly successful in the park's lakes but can be used effectively in many rivers and streams as well. A selection of red-and-white spoons, Mepps, Panther Martin, and Bolo spinners should provide good action. On

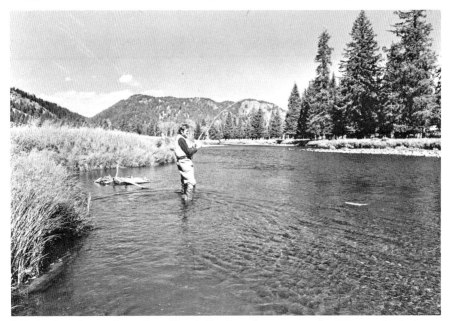

Bringing in a fat cutthroat from Slough Creek, only one example of the excellent stream fishing found in Yellowstone Park. Michael Sample photo.

rivers, a fly and bubble on spinning gear may prove the most successful for the spin fisherman.

The fishing potential in Yellowstone Park is almost limitless. The kind of fishing preferred or the species of fish desired will influence where one chooses to fish. Yellowstone Park fisheries biologist Bob Gresswell believes that "the best fishing in the park is found in catch-and-release areas for cutthroat trout. There are good populations of nice-sized fish in these waters, and the fish are catchable." By comparison, brown and rainbow trout fisheries in the park, such as the Madison River, provide tough fishing for the average fisherman, with a substantially lower average catch rate. Brook trout fishing is fast and hot, but the fish are small. The percentages of fish caught per species reflect these conditions: seventy percent cutthroat, ten percent rainbow, seven percent brown, and seven percent brook trout. An amazing fifty percent of the fish caught in Yellowstone exceed fourteen inches.

Some twenty-four waters receive over ninety-five percent of angler use in Yellowstone Park. These provide the best combination of good fishing and easy access. Most are accessible from park roads and require little or no walking.

Backcountry lakes and streams require permits (readily available at any ranger station) for overnight camping. Remember that Yellowstone is home to black bears and grizzly bears, both of which can be dangerous. The park service has an information pamphlet on how to avoid bear trouble that is definitely worth reading.

Yellowstone's Twenty-four Most Popular Fisheries

Yellowstone Lake and River are cited first in this list because together they account for fifty percent of the park's fishing use. The remainder are presented alphabetically for easy reference.

Yellowstone Lake is the most popular fishery in the park, and with good reason. Whether fishing from shore or by boat, anglers enjoy amazingly consistent results.

The pure native cutthroat fishery in the lake has had its ups and downs over the years. In 1975, the park service established a regulation which allows anglers to keep fish only up to a maximum of thirteen inches. Since the advent of this rule, the fishery has responded magnificently. The average cutthroat now measures 14.6 inches and, for the first time in many years, a few go over twenty inches.

Anglers hoping to enjoy trout for dinner sometimes have a happy problem— all the fish they catch measure over the thirteen-inch limit. Richard Parks, who operates Parks Fly Shop in Gardiner, has a solution—for boating anglers at least. He has observed that the bigger fish tend to hang out closer to shore in the shallow water. To catch smaller fish, he advises, "move away from shore and fish deeper—that's where the little ones are."

Yellowstone Lake opens later than some other waters in the park. From the opening to the end of July, catch rates generally are sensational. Thereafter, Parks observes, the fish spread out more, go deeper, and become harder to find.

A huge body of water with a surface encompassing 88,000 acres surrounded by over a hundred miles of sandy beaches, rocky breaks, and forested shorelines, Yellowstone Lake has a general weather pattern anglers should heed. The early morning hours usually find the lake's surface wonderfully smooth, but by late morning, the breezes have started up at least a light chop. Afternoon often see violent thunderstorms and sudden high winds with large waves that can swamp small craft. Even during the hottest days of summer, these bone-chilling waters pose the immediate threat of hypothermia—survival time is short. Anglers should keep constant watch on the weather and stay within easy reach of shore. And be sure to check boating regulations.

Virtually the whole lake offers excellent fishing. The south and southeast arms have reputations for even better angling, but they are miles from the nearest road and have some restrictions on boat motors. The whole north shore parallels park roads, while hiking trails reach remote sections on the east and south. Public boat launches and marinas at West Thumb and Bridge Bay offer convenient services.

As to what lure or fly to use, Parks says that "almost anything catches fish— the standard brands and patterns all work." Flies work well early in the season when cast to rising fish. Spoons and spinners brings results almost any time. Parks notes that the most popular lure is Jake's Spin-a-Lure, a heavy metal lure about the size of a domino with red spots on its side. Small to medium sizes work best. Lures with more than one cluster of hooks are illegal.

The Yellowstone River ranks as one of the nation's premier trout streams. Thousands of anglers annually wade into the river and think they have discovered Heaven right here on Earth.

The river actually begins in wilderness to the south of the park and flows down to Yellowstone Lake through the Thoroughfare, a wild section of the park far removed from civilization. When it flows into the Southeast Arm of the lake, it is already a river of substantial size. People who value wilderness experiences trek to the Thoroughfare to enjoy these trout-laden waters in the solitude they treasure.

Now much more conveniently available to the angler, the river gently flows back out of Yellowstone Lake through several miles of pines and meadows, past the Sulphur Cauldron, and across the tranquil, wildlife-rich Hayden Valley before cascading violently into the picturesque Grand Canyon of the Yellowstone.

The Hayden Valley portion is closed to all fishing, but anglers can ply the waters at either end provided they release any fish they catch. The upper end, between Fishing Bridge and the Sulphur Cauldron, draws the most anglers and has been called the most intensively fished reach of wild trout population in the United States.

The fishing begins spectacularly on opening day when the resident river cutthroat and some of their lake cousins are just concluding their spawning. Stacked along the banks, behind logs and rocks and across the gravel bars, the thousands of fish are readily visible to even casual observers. Although not in the best condition after their recent strenuous activity, these beautifully colored fish readily take flies and lures in the first days after opening. Landing rates are sometimes fantastic; some anglers consider this cutthroat fishing at its finest.

As the weeks pass, the fishing becomes progressively more difficult. Parks suggests that the lake's cutthroat have moved back to the lake, leaving the resident river fish more room and less urgency about feeding. He also thinks the fish get smarter after being caught several times. "There's a learning curve situation here," Parks says. "They are in much better shape and much more wary by the end of the summer." Parks caught one fish which had plainly been

YELLOWSTONE NATIONAL PARK

to Cooke City

Gardiner

Mammoth Hot Springs

YELLOWSTONE

SLOUGH CREEK

Tower Jct.

GARDNER RIVER

GREBE LAKE

Norris Jct.

Canyon

RIVER

LAMAR RIVER

N

To West Yellowstone

Madison Jct.

GIBBON RIVER

MADISON RIVER

FIREHOLE RIVER

Fishing Bridge

YELLOWSTONE LAKE

To Cody

Old Faithful

SHOSHONE LAKE

West Thumb

LEWIS LAKE

HEART LAKE

YELLOWSTONE RIVER

LEWIS RIVER

FALLS RIVER

SNAKE RIVER

To Grand Teton National Park

- - - - HIGHWAY
- - - - COUNTY OR UNPAVED ROAD
△ OFFICIAL PUBLIC ACCESS
☐ RANGER STATION
✗ BRIDGE
〜〜〜 DIVERSION DAM

one mile

YELLOWSTONE NATIONAL PARK

caught seven times before. This is recycling at its finest.

Except briefly at LeHardy Rapids, the river is one smooth glide from the lake outlet to the bridge just above the Upper Falls. Bank-fishing is very good along this stretch; wading is even better. Floating is prohibited.

Spinners and spoons and such do catch fish here, but most anglers tie on flies, even if they have only a spinning rod and reel. With a bobber and a little lead, spin anglers who have never used a fly before often surprise themselves by catching plenty of fish.

This section of the river has an inconsequential salmon fly hatch about July 15, mostly in the LeHardy Rapids. Plentiful mayflies and some caddis and baetis round out the hatches. Experienced angler Mike Brady watches especially for a big grey mayfly, the grey drake. He also notes that some fine hatches of small mayflies come off the water during and after stormy weather. And for attractor flies, Brady singles out the house and lot fly, sometimes known as the hair wing variant, as a must to keep on hand.

From the Lower Falls down through the Grand Canyon, past Tower Junction, through the Black Canyon, and on to Gardiner, the river continues to offer outstanding fishing. Except at a bridge near Tower Junction, anglers must be willing to hike several miles down to river, then climb steep trails back out. Parks points out that this is not appropriate for cardiac patients.

Still, there are several attractions to the fishing here. Because the river is more remote and anglers must expend considerable effort just to reach it, the crowds do not fish here. Incredible as it may seem to some, an angler could walk an hour to the river, fish all day in one of the finest trout fisheries in the country, and hike out without seeing another single angler.

This section of the river has some of the best fast water fishing in the park. For example, anglers can fish Seven Mile Hole ("seven miles down and a hundred back up," in the words of Maury Leach, author of *The Yellowstone Angler*), or the bottom three miles of the canyon. The remainder of the Grand Canyon is off limits due both to the dangers of climbing in the canyon and to bear closures.

Then, too, this river section has the attraction of a late and often very good salmon fly hatch. In Parks's experience, fishing salmon fly patterns produces excellent results in July and sometimes early August, even after the hatch is over. Thereafter, the fishing "holds up very well through the season," the best bets for success being caddis imitations, attractors, grasshoppers, and little streamers.

From Gardiner to Knowles Falls, the river has a more varied population of game fish. In addition to the predominant cutthroat, anglers can also find a few brookies, good numbers of browns and rainbow, and some rainbow-cutthroat hybrids with interesting color variations. Since the trout are not fished much, they tend to be less selective and sophisticated than most, but Parks observes that, once on the hook, they are scrappy fighters.

The Bechler River, located in Yellowstone's southwest corner, runs its course in an area of beautiful waterfalls and large meadows far from the sight of most of the fishing public. A road well off the usual tourist routes runs from Idaho into the Bechler Ranger Station, with a spur to the Cave Falls picnic area near the mouth of the Bechler. Because mosquitoes by the zillions use the Bechler's soggy meadows for their breeding grounds, most anglers avoid wetting a line in the Bechler until the end of the summer.

Most of the larger trout in the Bechler swim in the lower end of the river,

A big brown making a spawning run up the Gardner River. Michael Sample photo.

from its junction with the Falls River up to Bechler Falls. Most of the rainbow and cutthroat average ten to twelve inches, but a few of the rainbow grow considerably larger. Especially in the meadow sections of the stream, deep pools and undercut banks provide excellent cover. Anglers use a wide range of flies and lures effectively, but trying a grasshopper imitation can be dynamite.

The Falls River runs along the southwest border of the park. The river can be reached by road from Idaho into the Cave Falls picnic area. Fishing is excellent for rainbow and cutthroat averaging ten to eleven inches. Trails provide some access to the upper reaches.

The Firehole River is one of Yellowstone's nationally famous trout streams. It is also the fourth most popular fishery in the park. The river's thirty miles are restricted to fly fishing, with a stretch through the Old Faithful geyser basin and above the water intake closed to fishing. The Firehole is one of the most picturesque rivers in the park as it winds its way through meadows dotted with geysers. Some geysers erupt literally into the Firehole. Bison and elk are commonly seen grazing along the river.

Unless the weather has been unusually cold, anglers should try other waters in July and August. As Parks says, "the fish go on a hopeless hunger strike" during the heat of the summer. As much of the Firehole's water comes from thermal features along its course, summer water temperatures sometimes reach eighty-five degrees, which puts trout into a feeding funk.

Instead, local anglers save the Firehole for early and late in the season. In June, provided the river is not too turbid, modest-sized nymphs and streamers generally work best. Toward the end of June, Parks sometimes has good luck with dry flies—perhaps mayfly imitations, but more likely caddis.

In autumn, most experienced anglers regard the Firehole as a spring creek and fish accordingly. With long, fine leaders and size 18 flies such as Quill Gordons and blue wing olives, anglers stalk the spooky trout, which Parks describes as having "Ph.D.s in fisherman avoidance." These rainbow and browns average about a foot in length, but a few large fish haunt the Firehole. Parks fooled one of these, a 5.75-pound brown, on a Wooly Bugger in 1983. This seems like a phenomenally large fish for a relatively small trout stream, but then the Firehole in the fall has magical qualities.

From Biscuit Basin downstream to the mouth is the most popular fishing stretch and has the best fish habitat. Wading is easy on the Firehole, but watch for occasional deep pockets. Geyser activity keeps the water warm, further enhancing the wading. There is good road access along the entire length of the river.

The Gallatin River has its beginnings in the park, but most of the fishing takes place outside park boundaries. (This book devotes a full chapter to the Gallatin.)

The upper reaches of the Gallatin run through big meadows. Undercut banks and deep holes punctuate the meandering, easily wadable stream. With no trees to hinder backcasts, the upper Gallatin is an excellent place to teach kids how to fly fish. Lots of aggressive pan-sized trout and whitewater fish keep the attention level high.

The Gardner River runs almost its entire course within the park, joining the Yellowstone River just outside the border at the town of Gardiner on the north edge of the park. This is a classic pocket-water stream. The fast current is broken by an abundance of rocks that provide terrific holding water for fish.

Osprey Falls in Sheepeater Canyon divides the river in two. The upper eight miles above the falls has mostly nine- to ten-inch brookies and a few small rainbow. The lower twenty-three miles has brown, rainbow, and brook trout averaging nine to twelve inches. Almost all the larger trout caught in the Gardner come from the lower end of the river, which is warmed by the runoff

When the cutthroat are hungry, fishing Yellowstone Lake can be fabulous. Michael Sample photo.

from Mammoth Hot Springs. Most of the lunkers here have migrated out of the Yellowstone River. The park service protects some of the spring and fall spawning with seasonal closures. But when the season is open, this beautiful, rushing trout stream provides some excellent fishing.

The Gibbon River is another of Yellowstone's famous and scenic fishing streams. Much smaller than the Madison or Yellowstone, the Gibbon provides superb fly fishing. The Gibbon flows for thirty-seven miles from its headwaters at Grebe and Wolf lakes to Madison Junction, where it joins the Firehole to form the Madison River. The river above the exquisite eighty-four-foot Gibbon Falls was originally barren of sport fish, but now supports a good population of brook, brown, and rainbow trout. The meadows around Elk Park, Gibbon Meadows, and Norris Basin feature fine fishing when a hatch is on and the fish are rising.

Below the falls, the river provides fairly good fishing for brown trout and some rainbow and brook trout. There are lunker browns in here, but they're not easy to catch. This water is restricted to fly fishing only. Attractor flies work very well in the broken water. The river provides ideal trout habitat as it meanders through meadows.

Park roads run along most of the Gibbon's length, providing easy access. This is one of Yellowstone's more heavily fished waters, although the success rate is only fair compared to most of the park's fisheries. It just takes a little more skill to outwit the Gibbon River trout.

Grebe Lake, about a 3.5-mile, level hike near Canyon, provides good catch-and-release fishing for beautiful pan-sized and larger grayling. Cutthroat-rainbow hybrids, running from ten inches on up in size, provide another attraction.

Anglers have a very good success rate here and consider Grebe Lake one of the most satisfying fisheries in the park. Remember the possibility of encountering a grizzly here. The big bears occasionally graze on the area's succulent meadows in the early summer.

Heart Lake is a backcountry lake about eight miles in from the trailhead on the south entrance road. Though not a difficult hike, the lake receives only moderate pressure, especially considering its attributes. Spectacular scenery, interesting vegetation, and geyser activity add significantly to the pleasures of fishing this beautiful lake, the fourth largest in the park.

Both the native cutthroat and the introduced lake trout grow to large sizes. The lake trout average eighteen to twenty inches, but sometimes much larger individuals are caught. The cutthroat average sixteen to eighteen inches, but John Varley and Paul Schullery, in their beautiful book, *Freshwater Wilderness*, note that a few monsters in the two- to eight-pound category swim in this lake and suggest that, before the introduction of lake trout, these lunker cutthroat were probably more plentiful.

Heart Lake has special restrictions protecting the cutthroat. Best fishing for lake trout is in the fall, when they are in shallow waters for spawning.

Indian Creek is a small stream flowing northeast for 13.5 miles to join the Gardner River. The stream has very good fishing for seven- to ten-inch brookies. Indian Creek is remarkably popular for its size.

The Lamar River flows for sixty-six miles across the northeast section of the park to its junction with the Yellowstone River. One of the longest rivers in Yellowstone Park, the Lamar also provides some of the best fishing. The Lamar has staged a remarkable come-back since fish population slumped in the 1960s. The lower third of the river, easily accessible, is now catch-and-release only for cutthroat trout.

The Lamar features excellent fishing for cutthroat; rainbow (including a few large rainbow in the lower reaches); and occasional, beautifully colored rainbow-cutthroat hybrids. Anglers heavily pressure the obvious, easily accessible spots, but much of the Lamar sees very few hooks. Angler Bill Schneider notes that even a short, mile-long hike increases the success rate considerably.

Parks regards the Lamar as one of the premier terrestrial waters in the park. From mid-July through August, Parks fishes hopper imitations along the banks and at the riffle-corners. He finds that by early September, the water has dropped, the fish are spooky, and the fishing slumps badly.

The Lamar reacts to rainstorms in just the wrong places with a shot of muddy water that makes the river unfishable.

Lewis Lake, near the south entrance, is the third largest lake in Yellowstone. This popular fishing lake features road access, a boat launching ramp, and a 100-unit campground on its shore.

Originally barren, Lewis Lake now supports a good population of brown trout and lake trout and a rare big brook trout, but these fish are hard to catch. Like Shoshone Lake, Lewis Lake has a reputation for trophy-sized trout. During the summer, boat fishermen have significantly better success than the shore angler. The best times to try for lake trout are just as the ice comes off in June, and in the fall, when they are in shallower water for spawning. At other times, anglers must get their lures very deep.

The Lewis River flows south out of Shoshone Lake through Lewis Lake to its junction with the Snake River just south of the park. Marshy swamplands along the river below Lewis Lake provide excellent habitat for moose. Downstream from Lewis Falls there are turnouts with good views of the steep Lewis Canyon.

The most popular section of river is the catch-and-release water below Lewis Falls. Since the advent of catch-and-release fishing, the landing rate has improved, providing good fishing for ten- to twelve-inch brook trout. Some lunker brown trout in the Lewis River prove very hard to catch. The river through the canyon is mostly inaccessible. Steep walls make walking treacherous and hiking in most areas is prohibited.

The channel between Shoshone and Lewis lakes has become a popular fall fishing spot, despite the requisite five-mile hike and unpredictable weather. A broad, slow-moving stream that can be canoed during the summer, this channel is normally only a moderate fishery. But in the fall, the upper half of the river is a major spawning ground for large brown trout averaging eighteen inches and ranging up to huge. The river is shallow and crystal clear at this time, making fishing difficult but spectating fabulous.

Only fourteen miles of the famed *Madison River* flow in Yellowstone Park. (Montana claims the vast majority of this superlative river, and the nonpark Madison is treated in its own chapter in this book.) Nonetheless, the fourteen miles of river that flow through the park catch more fishing pressure than any other waters in the park except Yellowstone Lake and Yellowstone River. Part of this attention is due to the location of a major campground at Madison Junction, where the union of the Firehole and Gibbon rivers gives the Madison its beginnings. Another reason for this attention is its national reputation in sporting magazines and trout fishing books.

Without doubt, the Madison in the park is a superb trout stream. But anglers

Fishing the Yellowstone River below Fishing Bridge, one of the most heavily fished and most productive fisheries in the world. Michael Sample photo.

new to this section of the Madison should keep in mind two qualifications: First, stating that the river is superb does not mean it is easy to catch fish. In fact, fully half the anglers who try the Madison do not catch any. The river and its wily fish prove stern taskmasters even for expert anglers who long ago graduated from Basic Fishing 101. The entangling weed beds, glassy water, and shaky banks swing the odds in favor of the trout.

Secondly, because roughly a quarter of its water comes from thermal areas along the Gibbon and the Firehole, Madison trout suffer from heat stress in July and August. Parks suspects the fish feed on a midnight to 4:00 a.m. shift, but otherwise the fishing action is usually desultory except during a cold spell.

As with the Firehole, most knowledgeable anglers trek to the Madison either in June, when the water is still cool (and sometimes turbid), or in September and especially October. And like the Firehole, the Madison has a fly-fishing only restriction. Again, most anglers use either small dry flies or modest-sized nymphs and streamers. Mike Brady recommends mostly nymphs in the spring; perhaps pale morning duns from June 15 to July 7, soft hackle flies in September, and Maribou Muddlers and Spuddlers in October. Parks claims that "the faith of the fisherman matters about as much as the pattern." If you're unsure about the difference between gold-ribbed hare's ear nymphs and elk hair caddis, and therefore have little faith, check with the friendly, informative tackle shop keepers in West Yellowstone.

Due to conducive water temperatures, prodigious amounts of food, excellent cover, and protective restrictions, the Madison supports a large number of trout. Varley and Schullery suggest that were it not for the influxes of spawning fish from Hebgen Lake and the resulting multitudes of fish fry, the river might support even more resident trout. Instead, it gives up some of its resources in order to serve as a nursery or rearing area for fish ultimately destined to head downstream to Hebgen Lake.

Still, the fall spawning runs of rainbow and browns add excitement to the already extraordinary experience of fishing the Madison. Anglers return year after year to try their skills again. During the runs, fish in the fifteen- to twenty-inch range become quite common. Nice as these fish are, what really buzzes through some anglers' minds is the knowledge that a true monster trout might be the next to take the hook. Brady cites the example of the night Montana Fish, Wildlife, and Parks Department (FWP) biologists set four gill nets in Hebgen Lake and the next day found a brown of at least ten pounds in each net. Also, he remembers a twenty-pounder caught in June 1982 in Hebgen Lake. While any trout over five pounds is probably a one in 10,000 fish, and while not all Hebgen Lake browns spawn in the Madison, just the possibility of tying into the fish of a lifetime puts zest in one's waders.

Anglers can easily reach most of the Madison from the road that closely parallels the river. Some incredibly mucky bogs guard the river in spots above the seven-mile bridge. The music of bugling elk often accompanies fall fishing here.

Nez Perce Creek flows for about fifteen miles from Mary Lake into the Firehole River. It is bordered by forest and meadows and is a popular area to see bison. The Mary Mountain Trail follows the creek most of the way to Mary Lake.

Nez Perce Creek has ten- to eleven-inch brown and rainbow trout, but the fishing is only fair. The most popular area of river is the lower end, accessible by car.

Obsidian Creek is a small stream bordered by the road between Mammoth and Norris. It flows for nearly sixteen miles, ending in the Gardner River. There is good fishing for pan-sized brook trout that provide great action for kids of all ages.

Pelican Creek extends for fifty-two miles from its mouth on Yellowstone Lake east of Fishing Bridge. Pelican, a broad, slow-moving creek, flows through willowy swamplands at its lower end. This is a likely area to see moose. The road crosses Pelican Creek, but you can reach the fishable portions of the creek only by trail.

Pelican is the second largest tributary to Yellowstone Lake and provides critical spawning grounds for the lake's cutthroat trout. There is also a sizable population of resident cutthroat. Because of spawning, the lower end of the creek is closed to fishing. The remainder is catch-and-release. The season does not open until July 15.

Pelican Creek offers some of the finest fishing in Yellowstone Park. The cutthroat run fourteen to sixteen inches and are very catchable. Anglers give Pelican Creek the best overall rating for quality of fishing. This is also good bear country, so be on guard.

Riddle Lake is located just south of Grant Village. A two-mile hike is necessary to reach the lakeshore, which is bordered by large meadows west and south. Riddle Lake has good fishing for foot-long cutthroat. Check the regulations for special restrictions.

Shoshone Lake is the second largest lake in Yellowstone, covering twelve square miles, and reportedly the largest lake in the U.S. without road access. Restricted to motorless craft, the lake provides excellent canoeing. It is also easily accessible by trail either from the north via the DeLacy Creek Trail (3.1 miles) or from the south at the north end of Lewis Lake. Despite the hike, this is a rather popular fishing spot.

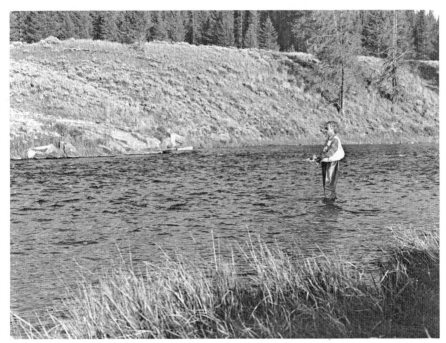

October fishing on the Madison River, one of the more challenging fishing streams in Yellowstone Park. Michael Sample photo.

Originally barren of fish, today Shoshone has a good population of big lake trout, some brown trout, and a few brook trout. These browns are lunkers averaging a tremendous sixteen inches, with brook trout only slightly smaller. Boat fishermen get most of the lake trout, while bank fishermen do better for browns and brookies. The lake trout generally hang out in deep water (requiring special rigs) until October and November, when they move into shoals to spawn.

Slough Creek, in the northeastern corner of the park, is one of the most highly rated fisheries in Yellowstone. Approximately sixteen miles of the stream are within the park, but this stretch is accessible only by trail for all but the lower end, where a campground provides access. Since the introduction of catch-and-release-only regulations in 1973, cutthroat size has increased, and the trout now average a healthy thirteen to fourteen inches, with a respectable number exceeding sixteen inches. Slough Creek also has a small population of rainbow and rainbow-cutthroat hybrids in its lower reaches. Anglers frequently use terrestrial patterns such as Joe's Hopper and attractors such as the Royal Wulff, as well as the usual nymphs, small streamers, and small mayfly and caddis imitations.

Despite its limited access, this is one of the more popular fishing streams in the park. It provides outstanding fishing in a pristine setting. In its lower end, Slough Creek has a rocky bottom and riffly water interspersed with large boulders. Upstream a few miles, it opens into the meadows of Slough Creek Valley, where the water is exceptionally quiet.

The Snake River extends for forty-two miles along the southeastern boundary of the park before leaving Yellowstone at the south entrance. This is a moderate fishery for cutthroat, brown, rainbow, brook, and lake trout.

Much of the Snake River has limited access. There is road access at the south entrance, but the majority of the river requires some hiking. The first ten miles of trail are good, but from there the going gets rough.

The Snake is a deep river with wide gravel streambeds. It runs through scenic canyons intermixed with peaceful meadows.

Soda Butte Creek is bordered by the park road from the northeast entrance near Cooke City. It is a popular stream, providing good fishing for ten- to eleven-inch cutthroat and a few rainbow trout amidst a valley of magnificent scenery.

Sylvan Lake is a popular roadside fishery, complete with picnic tables, located on the road between Fishing Bridge and the park's east entrance.

Anglers do well hooking ten- to twelve-inch cutthroat trout. Due to the heavy pressure this small, twenty-eight-acre lake was receiving, it has been designated catch-and-release fishing only. Sylvan Lake now has one of the highest catch rates in the park.

SELECTED SPORTING GOODS DEALERS AND FISHING GUIDES

For a complete list of fishing guides, contact the Montana Outfitters and Guides Association, Box 9070, Helena, MT 59604, (406)449-3578 or Fishing Outfitters Association of Montana (FOAM), Box 67, Gallatin Gateway, MT 59730, (406)763-4761.

Absarokee
Outdoor Supply

Anaconda
Don's Sport Center
Rainbow Sporting Goods

Baker
Baker Trading Post

Big Sky
East Slope Anglers
Gallatin Riverguides
Lone Mountain Ranch

Big Timber
Bob's Sport Shop

Billings
Big Bear Sport Centers
Gibson's Discount Centers
Scheels Sport Shops
The Classic Angler

Bozeman
The River's Edge
Bob Ward and Sons
The Powder Horn Sportsman's Supply
Montana Troutfitter's Orvis Shop

Butte
Fran Johnson's Sport Shop
Bob Ward and Sons
Tom's Sport Shop
Fish-On Fly and Tackle

Clinton
Rock Creek Fishermans Mercantile

Columbia Falls
All Season Sport & Cycle

Cooke City
Cooke City General Store

Deer Lodge
JB's Sporting Goods

Dillon
Frontier Anglers
Fishing Headquarters
Hitchin Post Sporting Goods
Green Mountain Sports Center

Ennis
Beartooth Flyfishing
Bob's Tackle Box
Headwaters Angling
Madison Sport Shop
Madison River Fishing Company

Eureka
Coast to Coast
Green Mountain Sports Center

Fort Peck
The Sportsman

Fort Smith
Big Horn Angler
Big Horn Trout Shop
Big Horn Troutfitters
Quill Gordon Fly Fishers

Gardiner
Park's Fly Shop
Trailhead Sporting Goods

Glasgow
D & G Sports

Glendive
Coast to Coast

Great Falls
Montana River Outfitters
Fly Fisher's Retreat
Big Bear Sports Center
Scheels Hardware & Sports Shops
Hilbig's High Country Tackle & Bait

Hamilton
Angler's Roost
Riverbend Flyfishing
Fishaus Tackle

Hardin
Wagner's Travel Shoppe

Harlowton
Ray's Sports & Western Wear

Havre
Bing 'n Bob's Sports Shop
Master Sports

Helena
Montana Fly Goods Company
Capital Sports
Coast to Coast
Duffle Bag Discount Center
Base Camp
Bob Ward and Sons
Gibson's Discount Center
Montana Outdoor Sports

Kalispell
Hahn's Sporting Goods
Kalispell Army/Navy Store
Sheppard's Mercantile
Snappy Sport Senter
Western Outdoor Store
Angler's Choice

Laurel
Shell Shack
Terry's Quik Stop

Lewistown
Coast to Coast
Don's Sport Center

Libby
Libby Sports Center
Mac's Market and Sporting
  Goods

Lincoln
Garland's Town & Country

Livingston
Dan Bailey's Fly Shop
George Anderson's Yellowstone
  Angler
Trailhead Sporting Goods
Wilderness Outfitters
Montana's Master Angler
Army/Navy Store

Miles City
Red Rock Sporting Goods
King's Bait & Tackle

Missoula
Miller Barber's Streamside
  Anglers
Sportsman's Surplus/Hi Country
Western Sportsman
Bob Ward and Sons
Army/Navy Economy Store
Grizzly Hackle International
  Fishing Co.
Missoulian Angler
Trailhead

Plentywood
Hi-Line Sports

Polson
Village Sporting Goods
Coast to Coast
Big Foot Discount

Red Lodge
Sir Michael's Sport Shoppe

Ronan
Ronan Sports & Western

Shelby
Coast to Coast

Sidney
D & G Sport Shop
Pamida Discount Center

Sheridan
Ruby River Sports

Stevensville
Hunting Shack, Inc.

Thompson Falls
Lakeside Sporting Goods

Three Forks
Willow Creek Fly Fishing Center

Townsend
Coast to Coast

Trout Creek
Lakeside Sporting Goods

Troy
Miller's Coast to Coast
Troy Auto Parts & Supply

Twin Bridges
Four Rivers Fishing Company

West Yellowstone
Madison River Outfitters
Bud Lilly's Trout Shop
Blue Ribbon Flies
Eagle's Tackle Shop
Jacklin's Outfitters for the World of
    Fly Fishing

Whitefish
Coast to Coast
Sunshine Mountain Company
Lakestream Flyfishing Company

Whitehall
The Alpine Sporting Goods

White Sulphur Springs
Lone Wolf Sporting Goods

Wise River
Complete Fly Fishers

Wolf Creek
Missouri River Trout Shop

Yellowstone National Park
Hamilton Stores

FOR MORE FISHING INFORMATION

Montana Department of Fish, Wildlife and Parks

State Headquarters
1420 East Sixth Avenue
Helena, MT 59620
444-2535

FW&P Regional Headquarters

Region 1 - Kalispell
490 North Meridian Road
Kalispell, MT 59901
752-5501

Region 2 - Missoula
3201 Spurgin Road
Missoula, MT 59801
542-5500

Region 3 - Bozeman
1400 South 19th
Bozeman, MT 59715
994-4042/4043

Region 4 - Great Falls
4600 Giant Springs Road
P.O. Box 6609
Great Falls, MT 59406
454-3441/3442

Region 5 - Billings
2300 Lake Elmo Drive
Billings, MT 59105
252-4654/4655

Region 6 - Glasgow
Rural Route 1-4210
Glasgow, MT 59230
228-9347/9348

Region 7 - Miles City
Rural Route 1, Box 200
Miles City, MT 59301
232-4365/4366

Region 8 - Helena
1404 8th Avenue
Helena, MT 59620
444-4720

National Parks

Glacier National Park
West Glacier, MT 59936
888-5441

Yellowstone National Park
Wyoming, 82190
(307) 344-7381

OUT HERE THERE'S NO ONE TO ASK DIRECTIONS

Let Falcon Be Your Guide

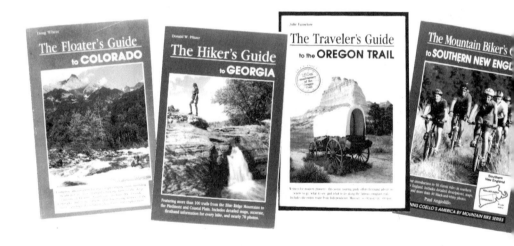

The **FALCON**GUIDES series consists of recreational guidebooks designed to help you safely enjoy the great outdoors. Each 6 x 9" softcover book features up-to-date maps, photos, and detailed information on access, hazards, side trips, special attractions, and more. So whether you're planning you first adventure or have enjoyed the outdoors for years, a **FALCON**GUIDE makes an ideal companion.

For more information about these and other Falcon Press books, please visit your local bookstore, or call or write for a free catalog.

Falcon Press • P.O. Box 1718 • Helena, Montana 59624
1-800-582-2665

FALCON™